MUSIC-IN-ACTION

This volume brings together DeNora's work published between 1986 and 2007. It includes twelve essays, some of which have had a major impact on the field. The chapters trace the development of her work from its early concern with musical meaning, historical ethnography and the 'everyday' perspective, to its current focus on music in action. Topics covered include Adorno on Schoenberg and Stravinsky, a theory of music as a space and place for interpretive work, research methods for historical musicology, and the first key statement of her theory of music as an active ingredient in social life. These building blocks are then employed to investigate music and embodied experience, sexuality and gender differentiation, and music's role as a technology of health. The essays are set in a multi-disciplinary context with an autobiographical introduction.

ASHGATE CONTEMPORARY THINKERS ON CRITICAL MUSICOLOGY

The titles in this series bring together a selection of previously published and some unpublished essays by leading authorities in the field of critical musicology. The essays are chosen from a wide range of publications and so make key works available in a more accessible form. The authors have all made a selection of their own work in one volume with an introduction which discusses the essays chosen and puts them into context. A full bibliography points the reader to other publications which might not be included in the volume for reasons of space. The previously published essays are published using the facsimile method of reproduction to retain their original pagination, so that students and scholars can easily reference the essays in their original form.

Music-in-Action

Selected Essays in Sonic Ecology

TIA DENORA
Exeter University, UK

ASHGATE CONTEMPORARY THINKERS
ON CRITICAL MUSICOLOGY

ASHGATE

Published by
Ashgate Publishing Limited
Wey Court East
Union Road
Farnham
Surrey GU9 7PT
England

Ashgate Publishing Company
Suite 420
101 Cherry Street
Burlington, VT 05401-4405
USA

Ashgate website: www.ashgate.com

ISBN 978-1-4094-1996-9

British Library Cataloguing in Publication Data
DeNora, Tia.
  Music-in-action : selected essays in sonic ecology. –
  (Ashgate contemporary thinkers on critical musicology)
  1. Music–Social aspects. 2. Music–Psychological
  aspects.
  I. Title II. Series
  781.1'1-dc22

Library of Congress Control Number: 2010937263

Printed and bound in Great Britain by
TJ International Ltd, Padstow, Cornwall.

Contents

Acknowledgements

The chapters in this volume are taken from the sources listed below. The editor and publishers wish to thank the authors, original publishers or other copyright holders for permission to use their material as follows:

'Structure, Chaos and Emancipation: Adorno's Philosophy of Modern Music and the Post-war II Avant-garde', in R. Monk (ed.), *Structures of Knowing*, Lanham, MD: University Press of America (1986), pp. 293–320.

'How is Extra-musical Meaning Possible? Music as a Place and Space for "work"', *Sociological Theory*, **4**(1), (1986), pp. 84–94.

'Deconstructing Periodization: Sociological Methods and Historical Ethnography in Late Eighteenth-Century Vienna', *Beethoven Forum*, **4**, (1995), pp. 1–18.

'The Musical Composition of Social Reality? Music, Action and Reflexivity', *Sociological Review*, **43**(2), (1995), pp. 295–315. Copyright © 1995 the Editorial Board of the Sociological Review.

'The Biology Lessons of Opera Buffa: Gender, Nature, and Bourgeois Society on Mozart's Buffa Stage', in Mary Hunter and James Webster (eds), *Opera Buffa in Mozart's Vienna*, Cambridge: Cambridge University Press (1997), pp. 146–64. Copyright © 1997 Cambridge University Press.

'Music and Erotic Agency – Sonic Resources and Social-Sexual Action', *Body & Society*, **3**(2), (1997), pp. 43–65. Copyright © 1997 SAGE Publications.

'The Concerto and Society', in Simon Keefe (ed.), *Cambridge Companion to the Concerto*, Cambridge: Cambridge University Press (2006), pp. 19–31; 263–4.

'Music as Agency in Beethoven's Vienna', in Ron Eyerman (ed.), *New Directions in the Sociology of the Arts*, New York: Paradigm Press, (Part of the Yale Series in Cultural Sociology) (2006), pp. 103–119.

'The Pebble in the Pond: Musicing, Therapy, Community', *Nordic Journal of Music Therapy*, **14**(1), (2006), pp. 57–66.

'Health and Music in Everyday Life', *Psyke & Logos*, **28**, (2007), pp. 271–87.

For *SocArts*, Present, Past, Future:

Sophia Acord, Kari Batt-Rawden, Arild Bergh, Pedro dos Santos Boia,
Elizabeth Dennis, Sigrun Lilja Einarsdottir, Pinar Guran, Trever Hagen,
Mariko Hara, Simon Procter, Craig Robertson, Ian Sutherland,
Susan Trythall

and for Hugh ('Bud') Mehan
who first introduced me to the concept of socially distributed ability

Introduction

Aesthetic Ecology, Distributed Ability

Reflecting on these essays, selected to highlight the main themes in my work over the last twenty-five years, my thoughts turn to the considerable help I have received from others. Those others include my teachers at undergraduate and postgraduate level, my husband Douglas Tudhope, my colleagues and my students. To begin this introduction with a list of acknowledgements is, of course, to thank them. But the point I wish to make here is different and goes beyond gratitude. It leads to what I see as the key theme in the work reproduced in this volume: the dual concepts of distributed ability and aesthetic ecology. These are fundamentally sociological concepts and they are nowhere better illustrated than in musical activity.

By the term aesthetic ecology, I mean a cluster of people and their relations to and with each other, as well as materials and settings, situated vocabularies, symbols, values, patterned ways of doing and – importantly – happenstance. But I also mean the equally important 'inside' of action, its pre-cognitive and non-verbal features such as emotion, impulse and embodiment. These things are the conditions of action and they are collectively negotiated as part of what action is. Through these conditions, the identities and abilities we come to associate with actors, collective and individual, are made apparent.

Of course, music is just one of part of aesthetic ecology and I am often asked what is 'special' about music. For example, why should we study it any more than, say, woodworking? The answer I normally give comes in four parts. First, due to mechanical reproduction and now digitization, music is ubiquitous. Second, and around the world, music accompanies ceremony, ritual, commemoration and work where it is associated with forms of entrainment, both individual and collective. Third, and related to its ubiquity, music is – at least in modern Western cultures – a medium of identity formation, closely associated with emotional experience. And finally, music is an important cultural modality for being together in time. The question, then, is how to explore music as a condition of action and experience, a question that includes music as it is made (composed, performed) as well as received.

The first two essays in this volume, both published in 1986, together provide the germ of what has since become, for me, an attempt to address that question. Both pieces took inspiration from the unlikely combination of Theodor Adorno and John Cage. And both highlight music as a medium for making social life. The differences between these two essays, however, serve to highlight one of the ways that my work has diverged from musicology, including 'radical', 'critical' 'new' or 'cultural' musicology. In fact, whether there is such a thing as 'musicology' in the singular is questionable. So perhaps what I really mean to say is that my work is turned away from structuralist impulses (whether in musicology or sociology) and toward investigations of culture 'in action', by which I mean the study of how identities, knowledge forms and acts are put together, are changed over time and flow from place to place. To develop this point I will dwell upon these first two essays, both published in 1986.

'Structure, Chaos and Emancipation' (Chapter 1) began its gestation while I was in the final year of my undergraduate degree at West Chester State College. I had entered university as a music major and had discovered sociology in my second year, after some inspiring teaching that included a segment on Freud's *Civilization and Its Discontents*. The professor, Jon Cowen, was a former student of Philip Rieff. I did not know then that Rieff's critique of the psychoanalytic world-view would eventually become as important as it is in my most current work today, but more on that below.

I went along to the first supervisory meeting for my senior thesis. My adviser, Harvey Greisman, critical theorist and clinical sociologist, handed me his copy of the 1972 Seabury edition of Adorno's *Philosophy of Modern Music*. He suggested that, if I wanted to write about the sociology of music, and if I was interested in the music of John Cage, I could do no better than begin with Adorno's work. This was at a time when, apart from Martin Jay (1973), Rose Rosengarde Subotnik (1976; 1978) and Susan Buck Morss (1977), and Harvey's own work (Greisman,1976), there were few scholars at work on music and critical theory.

I took away Harvey's copy of Adorno, and began to ponder Adorno's seemingly impenetrable but (I thought) beautiful prose. As time wore on, some of what Adorno was articulating began to sink in, albeit slowly and in a fragmentary way, perhaps not so altogether out of keeping with the spirit of his text.

Then a catalytic moment occurred. I had fallen in love with the county town of West Chester. Originally settled by Quakers, birthplace of Samuel Barber, the town where Lincoln's publicity campaign for the presidency was launched, West Chester is also not too far away from Gettysburg and the echo of Lincoln's famous words – 'of the People, by the People, for the People'. Graced with eighteenth-century row houses and renowned for its ancient trees (the streets are named after the trees that were planted along them) West Chester was a place of magic for me.

It was early morning, and I was walking to the bus stop, headed to Philadelphia where I worked as an intern for a CBS-TV affiliate. As I rounded the corner of Walnut and Cedar, a pigeon fell from the sky, landing at my feet with a thud. I remember my surprise on lifting it up how heavy it was (I thought someone should move it off the pavement). I suppose I also felt a little shocked by the event. It was raining but the sun was out and the pavements, made from bricks smoothed by two centuries of footfall, glowed red.

As I continued my journey it was with heightened perception of the beauty and spirit of the place. It was an emotional experience but it gave rise to a thought, namely, that I would always remember this as *the moment* when I recognized an affinity between Adorno's *Philosophy* and ideas I had previously admired in the philosophy of John Cage. For me that meant, as I understood it then, an emphasis on the particular, the material, and on the partial or non-identity of things, their 'this-ness' or *haecceity*, as the philosophers call it. When I got home that evening I began to write up my notes on what I then understood to be important connections between Adorno and Cage and on music as a way of knowing, a resource for the structuring of knowing. I have never forgotten that moment and I am continuing to write that text today.

As I reread 'Structure, Chaos and Emancipation' now, I see it as articulating a set of endings and beginnings in what I have since come to call Music Sociology (as distinct from Sociology 'of' Music; see DeNora, 2003). The endings are, perhaps, obvious and they are certainly ironic: I see now that the form of scholarship I was then attempting was one I have since abandoned. It consisted of pointing out identifications, a kind of 'this means that, that goes with this' form of analysis in which, guided by Adorno's own procedure, composers (or works) are identified as progressive, restorative, good, or bad. And so, in retrospect, I see both endeavours, Adorno's and my own, as useful only to the reputations of composers and to being a participant in the exercise of musical identity work, and one that positions the scholar as knower-in-chief. Just as all babies are said to be beautiful to their mothers, so too music's aesthetic qualities and its potential for action in the world will vary according to local conditions of production and reception. The scholar, in her air-conditioned library and sitting behind a desk, might simply be too far removed there to notice what is important on the ground.

As I quickly learned (and roughly around the time that this essay was published) there are other ways to theorize music as a form of knowing that do not involve reading music as a text. It is here that I see the essay on Adorno as offering some 'beginnings' for the music sociology I practise today. One of those beginnings was, as I have already suggested, the notion that music, non-representative, often abstract and wordless, is nonetheless a mode of knowing (the book in which this piece was published was entitled, *Structures of Knowing*). To be sure, Adorno made this point himself in relation to Schoenberg. In embracing, 'all the darkness and guilt of the world' (1973, p. 133), Schoenberg's music Adorno considered, offered a corrective against reification. According to Adorno, Schoenberg's musical complexity *empowered* its listeners to consider those things that pre-given forms of thought elided: in and through its handling of musical material it invited the listener to be an active sense-maker. Under cover of this 'darkness', in other words, where conventional boundaries and dividing lines were blurred, lay the potential for alternative and contradictory knowledge-making. As I understood Adorno, he said that ambiguity provided a resource for innovative and contradictory structures of knowing and thus for critique. I continued to work on this essay after arriving at UCSD where I took inspiration from Charles Nathanson and his encouragement to pursue a programme of study in which the artwork 'acts'. Chapter 2 in this volume, 'Music as a Place and Space for "Work"', takes up that theme, courtesy of Bud Mehan's seminar in Ethnomethodology as well as Aaron Cicourel's work (1973) and seminar in Cognitive Sociology where I wrote a short paper on Jürgen Streeck's critique of Searle's speech act theory .

This second essay develops the notion of music as cognitive workspace explicitly and in ways that highlight my ongoing interest in the music/philosophy of John Cage. It was in this piece that I first began to be interested in how 'what' music comes to mean, and what it does, is not 'in' the music but is in the relation between musical texts and their appropriations, mediated by the ways that texts are framed through resort to familiar conventions, through what people say about them, through how they are used and through where they come to be sited. This is by no means to say that music does not condition its own reception and that music scholarship need only study what people say about music. But it does mean that the analysis of texts is never sufficient and that the study of how people engage with music is a vital component of music study.

If meaning is not 'in' the music but rather distributed in the environments where musical response occurs, then music offers a resource for meaning-making, it is implicated in what comes to happen in relation to it. This understanding of musical meaning neither collapses music into sociology nor sociology into musicology. Instead it describes a perspective devoted to how actors may find, in musical structures, various 'things' (meanings, values, imageries). The ways that we then come to project – or 'hang words on to tones', as I put it in a paraphrase of Wittgenstein – renders music habitable as a space and place for 'work'. (The word 'work' here is understood in the ethnomethodological sense as the procedures by which we make our world into the world we take to be given, natural, normal, beautiful, good and true.) Conceived in this way, musical response is inevitably also ethical action since it always involves and invokes a politics of representation.

The question then is how musical materials provide conditions for this process, and, inspired by Adorno's thoughts, in this 1986 piece I began to sketch a programme of study for how musical meanings are made manifest. That programme would consist, I suggested, of a focus on family resemblances between musics, as perceived by analysts but also by musical actors, listeners, for example, the social relations of meaning production and the framing devices by which music is drawn into concourse with extra-musical communicative media, such as talk about music, programme notes, criticism, music education, and the material environment. The point overall was to respecify the study of culture, to shift the focus from a concern with culture's 'contents' (what is there to know) in favour of a focus on how what comes to count as 'our' or 'their' culture is articulated and stabilized. Culture and cultural production is, I concluded, nothing less than the production of a habitat; and thus, I think it is fair to say, it was in this relatively early piece that my later concern with aesthetic ecology was first implied. It was also in this article that I first used the concept of music's appropriation.

In the mid-1980s, UCSD came to be recognized as one of the top departments in the country for cultural sociology. We were taught that subject by Bennett Berger who continually exhorted us to locate culture in terms of its 'who, when, where, what and how'. At the same time, I discovered a kindred spirit in the music department, Jann Pasler, through her seminars on sociology of music and reputation. I have Jann to thank for introducing me to a concern with the interconnections between networks, worlds, reputations and works, and for introducing me to her vision of empirical musicology that empowered musicology to address topics otherwise at the time beyond its remit – power, statecraft, identity and stratification (Pasler, 2007; 2009). It was in the context of the second seminar I took with her (on reputation) that I began to develop the research into *Beethoven and the Construction of Genius*. That it happened to click with Bud Mehan's work at the time, on 'learning disability' as an identity that emerges from within interactional settings and cultural meaning systems (Mehan et al., 1984) was more than fortuitous: it resulted in a joint publication on identity construction (Mehan and DeNora, 1995).

With these resources, it was a short step from ethnomethodology of music into historical methodology and my initial thesis work on Beethoven (DeNora, 1995). The next piece reprinted here, 'Deconstructing Periodization' (Chapter 3), highlights this progression.

This was the essay in which I first suggested that we study biography as a topic, a narrative achievement and as negotiated – ethnobiography in short. This would consist of a focus on the local production of identity situated in place and time. That project gives music history a different emphasis, of course. It asks, for example (pace Bennett Berger), what is it that we 'do' with Beethoven and the writing of his life, and how that doing is not so different from what Beethoven and his contemporaries did themselves. The challenge, then, is to learn how to listen and watch historical actors ethnographically, to look for their meaning-making practices, their projects in their worlds. While such a task is destined for imperfection, the attempt to probe other times in terms of the disjunctions between those worlds and our own is, I still believe, nobler than making the assumption that such a task is impossible or unnecessary. How to listen with the ears of Beethoven's contemporaries, then, and how not to be too hasty in judging them as, from our own value-laden viewpoints, as 'right' or 'wrong'. There is more to listening, in other words, than in knowing how to reproduce the given wisdom about what is good, better, best' (what is 'good' is usually contested and it may or may not match what we value today) and there is more to the casting of a life-narrative than literary tropes. Practices and materials are also part of the story since they mediate and nurture representations and, perhaps more importantly, provide resources for action.

'The Musical Composition of Social Reality' (Chapter 4) takes this last point as its springboard. This is the essay that helped me to develop the orientation put to work in *Music in Everyday Life* (2000) and helped me later to distinguish between the sociology 'of' music and the more symmetrical project of music sociology (DeNora, 2003). I suggested in this 1995 piece that, within the sociology of music, music's social content – music's meaning, but, more importantly, its dynamic powers in social life – had been sidelined in favour of its social shaping. The concern with 'content' was prompted by discussions with my colleague at Exeter, Robert Witkin (Witkin, 1994; 1998). By contrast, 'The Musical Composition …' posed music as an 'active ingredient' of social life. It argued that the 'career' of a musical work is by no means 'over' once it is created, nor even after performers have performed and critics criticized. Rather, I suggested, we would do well to focus attention on the points where music and actors meet and how, in that meeting, our sense of time, our orientation as agents and our subsequent acts may be understood to be 'musically composed' as music becomes a ground for action and its composition. How music comes to provide such a ground, however, is by no means pre-ordained by music. Rather, the directions of influence between music and action are so tightly interwoven that textual analysis is insufficient for understanding how music provides a work space for social life. For that, a focus on music in action is required.

In the early 1990s, I had been conducting a research project for the Economic and Social Research Council on feminist perspectives, body politics, knowledge production and lay expertise in alternative contraception (DeNora, 1996). It was certainly a topic far removed from Beethoven's Vienna. Conceptually, however, the earlier work on Beethoven and the Science and Technology Studies focus on alternative methods of knowledge production were not dissimilar. Both were about knowledge-based controversies, and both highlighted the various 'roads not taken', as facts and values are institutionalized and harden up as 'givens' within particular contexts (and into a history of 'winners'). In other words, Beethoven's genius and the effectiveness of cervical mucus contraception were both institutionally produced realities and both depended upon ways of seeing, instruments and relations of production, and climates of reception. In the one case (Beethoven), context allowed for development, appreciation and, over time, an increasingly closer fit between categories of perception, methods of musical production and renown. In the other case, in the face of new and challenging technologies in reproductive health, the flow of resources required to nurture and develop mucus-based knowledge was diverted such that the method came to be cut off from the ecological conditions that might otherwise have nourished it.

This phase of my research career led me toward an interest in the history of science, to a focus on the sociology of embodiment, and to a sharper interest in music as an active ingredient in the making, remaking and challenging of gender roles. Out of this interest came the next two pieces of writing: 'The Biology Lessons of Opera Buffa' (1997; here Chapter 5), written originally for a Cornell conference on opera buffa in Mozart's Vienna organized by Mary Hunter and James Webster in 1994; and 'Music and Erotic Agency' (1997; here Chapter 6). The former concluded that opera provided a 'workspace' for the imaginative elaboration of gender difference in ways that partook of connections to other cultural realms (music never in isolation), in particular botany, and Mozart's connection to the van Jaquin family in 1780s Vienna. Music and science were, I suggested, mutually reinforcing such that the image of woman fleshed out in opera buffa was one of subjugation to biology and to the then emerging bourgeois notion of marriage and the private sphere. One might reasonably ask how this essay further elaborated the 'in action' focus articulated in Chapter 4. It probably did not push that project forward, apart from helping to highlight that musical production is by no means autonomous but rather takes shape – in the case of opera – in relation to visual, literary and sonic mediation of ideas, images and texts that develop concurrently. By contrast, 'Music and Erotic Agency' considered music and the body not in terms of bodily representations but in terms of the far more interesting question of how the body itself – the material body – can be understood to be 'musically composed'. In some ways this focus presaged the aerobics work later developed in *Music in Everyday Life*. Looking back at the piece now, I think the emphasis on embodied sociology, and on being willing to consider the relationship between culture, nature and agency in ways that are neither 'too tight' nor 'too loose' (Chapter 6, p. 96) provided the crux of this work, helping to put the body in a cultural-material context (ecology) from which it emerges, bringing bodily 'realities' into focus in particular ways. Culture-nature is produced in part through *learning* how to be the bodies we think we already had.

A concern with the body, and thus with materiality, implied, in turn, a concern with material practice in music and so, via Nicholas Cook's work on performativity (2003; 2007), I found a renewed interest in performance. In the next two essays ('The Concerto and Society' and 'Music as Agency in Beethoven's Vienna') I sought to develop what Jann Pasler calls an, 'everyday life of the past'. Such a perspective is much in keeping with my earlier work on Beethoven, and with a methodology focused on reception and on what people 'do' with music, as opposed to what we, as music analysts, might 'do' with music (ergo, there is more to music studies than reading music as text). As Pasler puts it, this focus offers a way of decentering history by giving voice to a wider range of cultural participants (2007, p. 20). Going back to the place and period I knew best was a way to gather my interests in embodied, material practice, gender and music in action and these two commissioned essays – one for Simon Keefe's edited collection on the concerto (here Chapter 7) and the other a keynote for a conference on arts sociology at the Center for Cultural Sociology at Yale (here Chapter 8) highlight some of the variations on the theme of material (and therefore often tacit) agency. This theme is developed initially in dialogue with Susan McClary's reading of Bach's Brandenburg 5 (McClary, 1987) and moves on through time to consider gender segregation at the piano. The Yale essay takes the focus on material practice one step further by following the ways that embodied, technological and sonic practices in turn come to be connected (by historically located actors themselves) to a network of many other things, among them philosophical notions (such as the sublime), so as to offer a complex of possible attitudes, roles and action trajectories. In this essay, the concept of musical ecology, historically conceived, was broached.

In *Music in Everyday Life* I had begun to explore music therapy, as a way in to understanding what can – with deliberation – be done with music and how music (under the right circumstances) can be transformative, whether in large ways or in small. In October 2004, I was invited to Oslo University for a national symposium on music, emotion and action, organized by Professor Even Ruud. This was to be the third so far in my career of 'watershed moments' (or the fourth if I count meeting my husband in 1980), primarily because it brought me into much greater contact with music therapists, and at a key moment in the history of that field. There I met not only Even Ruud, Brynjulf Stige and Randi Rolsjvord (all major figures in the field internationally), but also Gary Ansdell and Simon Procter of Nordoff Robbins. After the conference, Brynjulf asked me if I would write a review of Gary and Mercèdes Pavlicevic's recently published *Community Music Therapy* (Ansdell and Pavelicevic, 1994). When the word count swelled, Brynjulf graciously offered to let me develop it into a review essay, in the form that appears here as Chapter 9 ('The Pebble in the Pond'). Specifically, he asked me to preface the piece with a brief statement of my sociological orientation. Round about p.61 (p. 151 below) I think my enthusiasm for the then-emerging notion of Community Music Therapy and its link to my own focus on lay expertise and on identity as environmentally afforded will be clear. For me, the connections from music studies back to a sociology of action were then perhaps nowhere better articulated than in this new form of 'health musicking' where one could not only see culture 'getting in to action' but where it was also possible to watch culture being manipulated and deployed in ways that facilitated the emergence of health identities. Collaborating with members of SocArts who were also working on music and health (Batt-Rawden, Trythall and DeNora, 2007) pushed me further down this road. Increasingly, I saw the study of music therapy as the perfect venue for linking a perspective of music as a 'workspace' with a focus on how, through its uses, music could be seen to transform (holistically understood) bodies, minds, social relations, and identities.

Reading and writing about Community Music Therapy – which Ansdell and Pavlicevic termed 'the pebble in the pond' – did indeed create ripples. It led to a much closer research association with the Nordoff Robbins Centre for Music Therapy in Hampstead and, since 2006, to the (pseudonymous) BRIGHT Community Music Therapy Project with Gary Ansdell. For BRIGHT (the 'Borough (Centre for) Rehabilitation, Interaction and Group Activity, Hospitality and Training'), a community centre for people in various stages of recovery from acute mental health conditions, we have collected longitudinal data (video, participant observation, interviews) on music's connection to mental health. Among other things, the project has helped to highlight how, in and through music, clients and others help each other to flourish, and to participate musically. In this sense, our work at BRIGHT has examined the construction of a musically-led community, via a cultural (and musical) ecology. This focus on health as connected to social and aesthetic ecology has underscored the communal bases of identities and statuses such as 'mental illness'. It has also reinforced the critique of individualistic perspectives on illness and therapy described by Rieff in the 1960s (see Rieff, 1961).

The lay expertise involved in knowing how to appropriate music in everyday life situations for health promotion is a key theme in our work at BRIGHT (and I have learned considerably from watching and talking with Gary about his virtuosic, but unobtrusive, craft as a music therapist). As a complement to this, the penultimate essay collected here, 'Health and Music in Everyday Life' (Chapter 10) provided an opportunity to think through some of the conceptual issues being explored in community music therapy, perhaps most importantly the ecological basis of health – or indeed, all identities – via the dual notions of affordance and appropriation (notions that I first developed via perceptual psychology in *Music and Everyday Life*). This I did through reference to the work of Kari Batt-Rawden's action research on music as a technology of health, but the themes are resonant with what I have learned by working with other members of the SocArts team, (Acord and DeNora, 2008; Bergh and DeNora, 2009; Bergh, Bergh and DeNora, forthcoming; Hagen and DeNora, forthcoming; Sutherland with DeNora, forthcoming; Hara and DeNora, forthcoming).

And so we come to the final essay, 'Evidence and Effectiveness' (Chapter 11). This is the point at which my interests in Science and Technology Studies and Music Therapy come together. The paper was originally presented to a symposium on Evidence-Based Practice and Music Therapy at Nordoff-Robbins, where it was meant to provoke discussion about appropriate 'measurement' techniques for music therapy. Thinking about music-led music therapy, I suggested, helps to highlight the local craft practices, and lay forms of expertise involved in musical 'healing' and in ways that perhaps better serve to illuminate how music helps, what sort of good it is, and what it is good for. And that focus, fully music-centred but also sociological, highlights the question of culture as it gets into action and action as about movement and relation within a collective and material world. In short, to music is to act through the medium of music. And so we go, *da capo* (back to where we began, with Adorno and music as a structure of knowing) but also forward to *al coda* in the brief *Postlude* ('Two or more forms of music'). In the final, short piece reproduced here as Chapter 12, I return to John Cage and his notion of 'silence' to consider music as a 'silent practice' of human organization. By posing the body as, itself, a musical instrument, I suggest, we not only expand the category of music, but prepare the ground for thinking about the musicality of our physical, animal being, as it takes shape in reference to soundscape and in ways that are capable of eliding simplistic or reductionist conceptions of either music or our bodies. This understanding of music's 'silence' takes the social study of music ecology literally under the skin. It also resonates with current work in medical and neurological fields, particularly around such topics as biofeedback, mind–body interaction and the placebo effect. Perhaps most importantly, an inclusive (empirically founded rather than artistic) sense of music reconnects the term 'aesthetic' to a focus on the senses and sensory practice. In so doing, it underlines the study of organized sounding as one of the newest and most intriguing branches of the life sciences.

References

Acord, S.K. and DeNora, T. (2008), 'Culture and the arts: From art worlds to arts-in-action', *The Annals of the American Academy of Political and Social Science*, **619**, pp. 223–37.

Adorno, Theodor W. (1973), *Philosophy of Modern Music*, translated by Anne G. Mitchell and Wesley V. Blomster, New York: The Seabury Press.

Batt-Rawden, K., Trythall, S. and DeNora, T. (2007), 'Health Musicking as Cultural Inclusion', in J. Edwards (ed.), *Music: Promoting Health and Creating Community in Healthcare*, Cambridge Scholars Press, pp. 64–82.

Bergh, A. and DeNora, T. (2009), 'From Wind-up to iPod: Techno-cultures of Listening', in N. Cook, E. Clarke, D. Leech-Wilkinson and J. Rink (eds), *The Cambridge Companion to Recorded Music*, Cambridge: Cambridge University Press, pp. 102–19.

Bergh, A., Bergh, M. and DeNora, T. (forthcoming), 'Forever and Ever: Mobile Musicking in the Lives of Young Teens', in S. Gopinath and J. Stanyek (eds), *Oxford Handbook of Mobile Music*, Oxford: Oxford University Press.

Buck Morss, S. (1977), *The Origin of Negative Dialectics: Theodor W. Adorno, Walter Benjamin, and the Frankfurt Institute*, New York: Macmillan.

Cicourel, A.V. (1973), *Cognitive Sociology: Language and Meaning in Social Interaction*, London: Penguin.

Cook, N. (2003), 'Music as Performance', in M. Clayton, T. Herbert, and R. Middleton (eds), *The Cultural Study of Music: A Critical Introduction*, London: Routledge, pp. 204–14

Cook, N. (2007), *Music, Performance, Meaning: Selected Essays*, Aldershot: Ashgate.

DeNora, T. (1995), *Beethoven and the Construction of Genius: aesthetic politics in Vienna, 1792–1803*. Berkeley, Los Angeles and London: University of California Press.

DeNora, T. (1996), 'From Physiology to Feminism: Reconfiguring Body, Gender and Expertise in Natural Fertility Control', *International Sociology* (winner of Worldwise Competition for Young Sociologists, 1994), **11**, pp. 359–83.

DeNora, T. (2000), *Music in Everyday Life,* Cambridge: Cambridge University Press.

DeNora, T. (2003), *After Adorno: Rethinking Music Sociology*, Cambridge: Cambridge University Press.

Greisman, H.C. (1976), 'Disenchantment of the World', *British Journal of Sociology*, **27**, pp. 497–506.

Hagen, T. and DeNora, T. (forthcoming), 'Music for the Room: Unofficial Music Distribution and Listening Practices in Hungary and Czechoslovakia under Socialism', in T. Pinch and K. Bijsterveld (eds), *The Oxford Handbook of Sound Studies*, Oxford: Oxford University Press.

Hara, M. and DeNora, T. (forthcoming), 'Leaving Something to the Imagination: Seeing Place and Nations through a Musical Lens', in C. Gorbman, J. Richardson and C. Vernallis (eds), *The Oxford Handbook of New Audiovisual Aesthetics*, Oxford: Oxford University Press.

Jay, M. (1973), *The Dialectical Imagination: A History of the Frankfurt School and the Institute of Social Research 1923–1950*, Boston: Little Brown and Company, Canada.

McClary, S. (1987), 'The Blasphemy of Talking Politics during Bach Year', in R. Leppert and S. McClary (eds), *Music and Society: The Politics of Composition, Performance and Reception*. Cambridge: Cambridge University Press, pp. 13–62.

Mehan, H., Hertwick, A. and Meihls, L. (1984), Handicapping the Handicapped: Decision-making in Students' Educational Careers, Stanford, CA: Stanford University Press.

Mehan, H. and DeNora, T. (1995) 'Genius: A Social Construction', in T. Kitsuse and T. Sarbin (eds), *Constructing the Social*, London: Sage, pp. 157–73.

Pasler, J. (2007), *Writing Through Music: Essays on Music, Culture, Politics*, New York: Oxford University Press.

Pasler, J. (2009), *Composing the Citizen: Music as Public Utility in Third Republic France*, Berkeley, Los Angeles and London: University of California Press.

Pavlicevic, M. and G. Ansdell (1994), *Community Music Therapy*, London: Jessica Kingsley.

Rieff, P. (1961), *Freud: The Mind of the Moralist*, New York: Viking Press; London: V. Gollancz, 1959; rev. ed., New York: Anchor Books.

Streeck, J. (1980), 'Speech Acts in Interaction: A Critique of Searle', *Discourse Processes*, **3**, pp. 133–53.

Subotnik, R.R. (1976), 'Adorno's Diagnosis of Beethoven's Late Style: Early Symptom of a Fatal Condition', *Journal of the American Musicological Society*, **29**, pp. 242–75.

Subotnik, R.R. (1978), 'The Historical Structure: Adorno's "French" Model for the Criticism of Nineteenth-Century Music", *19th Century Music*, **2**, pp. 36–60.

Sutherland, I. with DeNora, T. (forthcoming), *Music Sociology: An Introduction*, Cambridge: Polity Press.

Witkin, R. (1994), *Art and Social Structure*, Cambridge: Polity.

Witkin, R. (1998), *Adorno on Music*, London: Sage.

Bibliography

Books

Beethoven and the Construction of Genius: Musical Politics in Vienna 1792–1803. Berkeley, Los Angeles and London: University of California Press, 1995. Translated as: *Beethoven et la construction du genie* (with preface by H.C. Robbins Landon). Trans. Marc Vignal. Paris: Fayard, 1998.

Music in Everyday Life. Cambridge: Cambridge University Press, 2000.

After Adorno: Rethinking Music Sociology. Cambridge: Cambridge University Press, 2003.

Journal Articles

'How is Extra-musical Meaning Possible? Music as a Place and Space for "Work".' *Sociological Theory* 4:1, pp. 84–94, 1986.

'Musical Patronage and Social Change in Beethoven's Vienna.' *American Journal of Sociology* 97:2, pp. 310–46, 1991.

'Fast, Faster, Fastest: The Social Construction of Racing Outcomes in Swimming. Comment on Chambliss.' *Sociological Theory* 10:1, pp. 99–102, 1992.

'Beethoven, the Viennese Canon and the Sociology of Identity.' *Beethoven Forum* 2, pp. 29–54, 1993.

'Beethoven et l'invention du genie' (trans. F. Marin and M.-C. Pottier). *Actes de la recherche en sciences sociales* 100, pp. 36–45, 1995.

'The Musical Composition of Social Reality? Music, Action and Reflexivity.' *Sociological Review* 43:2, pp. 295–315, 1995.

'Deconstructing Periodization: Sociological Methods and Historical Ethnography in 18th Century Vienna.' *Beethoven Forum* 4, pp. 1–18, 1995.

'Musique et l'action erotique' (trans A. Hennion). *Sociology de l'art* 9, pp. 121–34, 1996.

'From physiology to feminism: Reconfiguring Body, Gender and Expertise.' *International Sociology* 11:3, pp. 359–83, 1996.

'Music and Erotic Agency – Sonic Resources and Social-Sexual Action.' *Body&Society* 3:2, pp. 44–65, 1997.

'Music as a Technology of the Self.' *Poetics: Journal of Empirical Research on Literature, the Media and the Arts* 26, pp. 31–56, 1999.

T. DeNora and S. Belcher. '"When you're trying something on you imagine yourself in a place where they are playing this kind of music": Musically Sponsored Agency in the British Clothing Retail Sector.' *Sociological Review* 1, pp. 80–102, 2000.

'Corpo e genere al piano. Repertorio, technologia e comportamento nella Vienna di Beethoven' ('Body and Gender at the Piano: Repertory, Technology and Comportment in

Beethoven's Vienna') (trans. M. Santoro). *Rassegna italiana di sociologia*, 2, special issue on 'La nuova sociologia della musica', pp. 165–88, 2000.

'Quand la musique de found entre en action' (trans. J.Jeudy). *Terraine* (Mission du Patrimonie du ministere de la Culture, Paris), special issue on 'Music and the Emotions' (O. Roueff, ed.), pp. 75–86, 2001.

'Music into Action: Performing Gender on the Viennese Concert Stage, 1790–1810.' *Poetics: Journal of Empirical Research on Literature, the Media and the Arts*, special issue on 'New Directions in Sociology of Music' (T. Dowd, guest ed.), 30:2, pp. 19–33, 2002.

'The Role of Music in the Daily Lives of Women – The Case of Intimate Culture.' *Feminism and Psychology*, special issue on music and gender (S. O'Neill, guest ed.), 12:2, pp. 176–81, May 2002.

'The Everyday as Extraordinary: Response from Tia DeNora' (response to review symposium on *Music in Everyday Life*). *Action, Criticism & Theory for Music Education* (e-journal), 1:2, pp. 2–8, 2002. http://www.maydaygroup.org http://mas.siue.edu/ACT/index.html

'Music Sociology: Getting the Music into the Action.' *British Journal of Music Education*, 20:2, pp. 165–77, 2003

'Editorial.' *Eighteenth Century Music* 3:1, pp. 3–6, 2006.

'Historical Perspectives in Music Sociology.' *Poetics: Journal of Empirical Research on Literature, the Media, Arts*, special issue on 'The Sociology of Music' (R. Peterson and T. Dowd, eds), 32, pp. 211–21, 2004.

'The Pebble in the Pond.' *Nordic Journal of Music Therapy* 14:1, pp. 57–66, 2006.

'Evidence and Effectivenss in Music Therapy.' *British Journal of Music Therapy* 20:2, pp. 81–99, 2007.

K. Batt-Rawden, E. Ruud and T. DeNora. 'Music Listening and Empowerment in Health Promotion; A Study of the Role and Significance of Music in Everyday Life of the Long-term ill.' *Nordic Journal of Music Therapy* 14, pp. 120–36, 2005.

K. Batt-Rawden and T. DeNora. 'Music and Informal Learning in Everyday Life.' *Music Education Research* 7:3, pp. 289–304, 2005.

'Health Musicking in Everyday Life.' *Psyke & Logos* 28:1, pp. 271–87, 2007.

S. Acord and T. DeNora. 'Culture and the Arts: From Art Worlds to Arts-in-Action.' *Annals of the American Academy of Political and Social Science*, pp. 223–37, 2008.

Book Chapters

'Structure, Chaos and Emancipation: Adorno's Philosophy of Modern Music and the post-World War II Avant Garde.' Pp. 293–320 in R. Monk (ed.), *Structures of Knowing*. Lanham, MD: University Press of America, 1986.

'The Social Basis of Beethoven's Style.' Pp. 9–30 in J.H. Balfe (ed.), *Paying the Piper: Causes and Consequences of Art Patronage*. Urbana and Chicago: University of Illinois Press, 1993.

T. DeNora and H. Mehan. 'Genius: A Social Construction, the Case of Beethoven's Initial Success'. pp. 157–73 in T. Sarbin and J. Kitsuse (eds), *Constructing the Social*. London and Los Angeles: Sage Publications, 1993.

'The Beethoven-Wolffl Piano Duel'. Pp. 259–82 in D. Wyn Jones (ed.), *Music in Austria 1750–1800*. Cambridge: Cambridge University Press, 1996.

'The Biology Lessons of Opera Buffa.' Pp. 146–164 in M. Hunter and J. Webster (eds), *Opera Buffa in Mozart's Vienna*. Cambridge: Cambridge University Press, 1997.

'Aesthetic Agency and Musical Practice: New Directions in the Sociology of Music and Subjectivity.' Pp. 161–80 in P. Juslin and J. Sloboda (eds), *Music and Emotion*. Oxford: Oxford University Press, 2001.

'Musical Practice and Social Structure: The Sociology of Music and its Toolkit.' Pp. 35–56 in E. Clark and N. Cook (eds), *Empirical Musicology*. Oxford: Oxford University Press, 2004.

'Music, Meaning and Everyday Life.' Pp, 147–60 in N. Hanrahan and M. Jacobs (eds), *The Blackwell Companion to the Sociology of Culture*. Oxford: Blackwells, 2004.

'Embodiment and Opportunity: Performing Gender in Beethoven's Vienna.' Pp. 186–97 in W. Weber (ed.), *The Musician as Entrepreneur and Opportunist, 1600–1900*. Blooomington and Indianapolis: Indiana University Press, 2004.

'Patronage.' pp. 390–92 in C. Eisen and S. Keefe (eds), *The Cambridge Mozart Encyclopedia*. Cambridge: Cambridge University Press, 2005.

'The Concerto and Society.' Pp. 19–33 in Simon Keefe (ed.), *The Cambridge Companion to the Concerto*. Cambridge: Cambridge University Press, 2005.

'Music as Agency in Beethoven's Vienna.' Pp. 103–21 in R. Eyerman (ed.), *New Directions in the Sociology of the Arts* (part of the Yale Series in Cultural Sociology). New York: Paradigm Press, 2006.

'Music and Self' (reprint/abridged version of Chapter 3 in *Music and Everyday Life*). Pp. 141–7 in Andrew Bennett (ed.), *The Popular Music Reader*. London: Routledge, 2005.

'Music and Emotion in Real Time.' Pp. 19–34 in K. O'Hara and B. Brown (eds), *Consuming Music Together: Social and Collaborative Aspects of Music Consumption Technologies* (Computer Supported Cooperative Work). New York: Springer Verlag, 2006.

K. Batt-Rawden, S. Trythall and T. DeNora. 'Health Musicking as Cultural Inclusion.' Pp. 64–82 in J. Edwards (ed), *Music: Promoting Health and Creating Community in Healthcare*. Cambridge: Cambridge Scholars Press, 2008.

A. Bergh and T. DeNora. 'From Wind-up to iPod: Techno-cultures of Listening.' Pp. 102–15 in E. Clarke, N. Cook, D. Leech-Wilkinson and J. Rink (eds), *The Cambridge Companion to Recorded Music*. Cambridge: Cambridge University Press, 2009.

'Emotion as social emergence: perspectives from music sociology.' Pp. 159–86 in P. Juslin and J. Sloboda (eds), *Handbook of Music and Emotion*. Oxford: Oxford University Press, 2010.

Guest Edited Journal

Special issue on 'Configuring the Classics' (with R. Witkin), *Poetics: Journal of Empirical Research on Literature, the Media and the Arts*, July 2001.

Handbook Chapters, Encyclopaedia and Dictionary Entries

'Love and Courtship.' Pp. 265–7 in J. Shepherd and D. Horn (eds), *Continuum Encyclopedia of Popular Music of the World*. London: Continuum, 2003.

'Music as Expressive Form.' Pp. 10255–9 in *International Encyclopedia of the Social Sciences*. vol 15, Oxford: Elsevier, 2001.

'Aesthetics', 'The Arts', 'H.S.Becker', 'Cultural Deprivation' and 'Visual Culture' (500–1000 word entries). In B.S. Turner (ed.), *The Cambridge Dictionary of Sociology*. Cambridge: Cambridge University Press, 2006.

'Music Consumption.' In G. Ritzer (ed.), *The Blackwell Encyclopedia of Sociology*. Oxford: Blackwells, 2007.

'Enculturation.' In H. Bruhn, R. Kopiez and A. Lehmann (eds), *Musikpsychologie – das neue Handbuch*. Reinbek/Hamburg: Rowohlt, 2008.

'Culture and Music.' Pp. 145–62 in T. Bennett and J. Frow (eds), *The Sage Handbook of Cultural Analysis*. London: Sage, 2008.

'Interlude: Two or more forms of music.' Pp. 799–803 in L. Bresler (ed.), *International Handbook of Research in Arts Education*, Vol. 1. New York: Springer Verlag, 2007.

Popular Articles, Newsletters, Working Papers (selection)

'Music in the Service of the State: Charlemagne's Imposition of "Gregorian" Chant as a Mechanism for Political Consolidation.' *UCSD Working papers in Sociology* 1:1, pp. 1–10, 1990.

R. Witkin and T. DeNora. 'Aesthetic Materials and Aesthetic Agency.' *Culture: The Newsletter of the Culture Section of the American Sociological Association*, pp. 1–5, 1997.

S. Belcher and T. DeNora. 'Music is Part of the Equipment that Makes Your Body Hard!' *eXercise* (Publication of the National Governing Body for Exercise & Fitness in England) p. 5.

T. DeNora and A.L. Tota. 'Proposal for a European Sociological Association Research Network on the Sociology of the Arts.' *Sociology of the Arts* (Newsletter of Research Committee #37, International Sociological Association) pp. 22–4, 1999.

'Cultural Sociology as Cultural Action: Like a Frog Plunging into Water.' *Newsletter of the European Sociological Association Network on Culture*, pp. 36–9, August 2009.

Forthcoming Publications and Work in Progress:

'Practical Consciousness and Social Relation in *MusEcological* Perspective.' In D. Clarke and E. Clarke (eds), *Music and Consciousness*. Oxford: Oxford University Press, in press.

'Music Space as Healing Space: Community Music Therapy and the Negotiation of Identity in a Mental Health Centre.' In G. Born and T. Rice (eds), *The Privatization and Publicization of Musical Space*. Cambridge: Cambridge University Press, forthcoming.

T. Hagen with T. DeNora. 'Music for the Room: Unofficial Music Distribution and Listening Practices in Hungary and Czechoslovakia.' In K. Bijsterveld and T. Pinch (eds), *Oxford Sound Studies Handbook*. Oxford: Oxford University Press, forthcoming.

M. Hara and T. DeNora. 'Leaving Something to the Imagination: "Seeing" New Places Through a Musical Lens.' In J. Richardson and C. Gorbman (eds), *Oxford Handbook of New Audiovisual Aesthetics*. Oxford: Oxford University Press, forthcoming.

G. Ansdell and T. DeNora. 'Musical Flourishing: Community Music Therapy, Controversy and the Cultivation of Well-being.' In R. MacDonald (ed.), *Oxford Handbook of Music and Health*. Oxford: Oxford University Press, forthcoming.

I. Sutherland with T. DeNora. 'Musical Creativity as Social Agency: Paul Hindemith.' In D. Hargreaves, D. Miell and R. MacDonald (eds), *Musical Imaginations*. Oxford: Oxford University Press, forthcoming.

'Musicians Make Markets: The Aesthetic Regulation of Music Distribution in Beethoven's Vienna.' *European Societies*, Forthcoming.

CHAPTER 1

Structure, Chaos and Emancipation: Adorno's Philosophy of Modern Music and the Post-war Avante-garde

The development of contemporary sociology of music is due largely to the efforts of Theodore W. Adorno (1930–1969). One of the first to explore in earnest the elusive question of music's link to social structure, Adorno forged an inter-disciplinary approach for which he was uniquely qualified, having been trained extensively in musical composition,[1] philosophy and the social sciences. His characteristic focus upon the musical material itself (as opposed to other, ancillary aspects of music making) and the ways in which that material may embody ideological content has led to increasing recognition of his work by scholars within both musicology and sociology (see, for example, Subotnik, 1979 and Ballentine, 1984). Yet, in spite of the attention it has received, Adorno's work continues to stand apart from the discipline of sociology of music as a whole.

What distinguishes Adorno's approach from most subsequent studies of music and its extra-musical meanings is that Adorno never considered the sociology of music to be an end in itself. Rather, his music study is inextricably tied to the critical stance and Freudo-Marxian methodology which he shared with fellow members of the Frankfurt School. In order to fully comprehend Adorno's sociology of music, therefore, it is necessary to see how his "micro" analyses or 'case-studies' of particular musical works are lodged within his larger, typically Frankfurt analysis of socio-economic and political conditions. Specifically, one needs to understand how Adorno formulated the inter-relationship between culture and the patterns of authoritarian domination symptomatic of what he later came to conceive of as the "Administered World." The first purpose of this essay therefore is to review Adorno's sociology of music as it is grounded in his larger, Frankfurt School approach. I shall do this by concentrating upon one of his major works, the *Philosophy of Modern Music* (1973), as it focuses upon Stravinsky and Schoenberg as representatives of the contradictory extremes evident in twentieth century music. I will then apply the perspective developed by Adorno in this work to two more recent composers, Pierre Boulez and John Cage. This task will in turn lead to a critique of Adorno's original formulation.

---

1 Adorno studied composition in Vienna with Alban Berg from 1925–1926 (see Buck-Morss, 1977).

Art and the Administered World

Similar to Max Weber's concept of the "Iron Cage" (Greisman, 1976), the Administered World refers to a post-capitalist, mass society whose bureaucratic management is geared to benefit an increasingly centralized economic substructure and its controlling minority. Although the aims of this administration are in opposition to the best interests of most individuals, its objectives are not achieved by overt domination. Instead, individuals are seen as participating in their own oppression by willingly entering into a process which Adorno calls "Total Sociation." This process is characterized by a mind-set or belief in what Adorno occasionally refers to as the "ontological ideology" (see for example, 1981:62), by which he means a tendency to hypostatize social reality in such a way that social relations or types of experience are conceived as "second nature" (Buck-Morss, 1977:12). In other words, they are made to seem natural or given when in fact they are not, a process which tends to suppress the socially constituted quality of, for example, political and economic institutions. It is this complacency, bred by a belief in the immutability of social reality, which annuls critical consciousness and results in the "total sociation" of individual mind (see Jay, 1984:139). In "free" Western countries, Adorno argued, culture and the culture industry serve as the nexus between individual "free will" and the socio-economic "determinism." Hence, the study of culture became an essential task for Critical Theory.[2]

It is in this context then, that Adorno focused on music. Of the seventy-odd works he produced on the subject, the *Philosophy of Modern Music* (1973), written between 1940 and 1948 and intended as an extended appendix to Adorno's and Horkheimer's collaborative work, *The Dialectic of Enlightenment* (1972), stands out as one of the most significant. It is also, in spite of the difficulty of its prose, one of the best introductions to Adorno's overall thought about the contradictory functions of art in modern society.

In the opening pages of the *Philosophy* Adorno defines the "true," humanitarian function of art: "Art is able to aid enlightenment only by relating the clarity of the world consciously to its own darkness" (1973:15). By illuminating the individual's condition *vis à vis* society and thereby functioning as a form of knowledge art could act as a catalyst for social change. But, according to Adorno, artistic revelation was not necessarily destined to be 'bad news.' In epochs where the individual and the social are judiciously merged, art, by virtue of finding no dark or unclear areas, would function as affirmation and in fact become obsolete: "Only in a society which had achieved satisfaction would the death of art be possible" (1973:15). In twentieth century administered society, though, the need for art was vital and its message was to be unrelentingly pessimistic.

However, art could serve to impede as well as implement knowledge. By catering to the socially determined predispositions of art "consumers" and affirming states of consciousness or perceptions about society which were inaccurate, art had become the instrument *par excellence* of administration, resulting in the progressive extirpation of the art-consumer's critical awareness of his place in society. Complex forms, ambiguity and subtlety of expression were abandoned for "the prevailing neon-light style of the times." (1973:15). As the social

---

2   At its inception, the Frankfurt School was concerned with studying the socio-economic sphere. But by the early 1930's, largely due to the influence of Adorno and Horkheimer, its focus shifted to the cultural superstructure (Jay, 1973).

predicament of individuals worsened, Adorno believed, administered art grew in inverse proportion to it, ultimately to the point where it would eclipse humanitarian art.

To continue to fulfil its true function art had to distinguish itself from mainstream artistic tendencies: "In our totally organized bourgeois society which has forcibly been made over into a totality, the spiritual potential of another society could lie only in that which bears no resemblance to the prevailing society." (1973:25). Artists attempting to fulfil art's true function had no choice but to contradict mainstream culture through an emancipated art, one liberated from conventional aesthetics and associations, i.e. an avante-garde.

Music and Administration

By the turn of the twentieth century the musical syntax, predicated on the system of functional tonality[3] which had served as the basis of composition for over two hundred years seemed, to many composers, as if it had worn itself out. Musical meaning, as it relied on deviation from listener expectation, had necessitated a constant expansion of the tonal language which by the end of the nineteenth century had resulted in unwieldy works, stretching tonality to its audible limit. Within the tonal framework it seemed that there was nothing new to say; the language had reached the point of diminishing returns. Consequently, twentieth century composers concerned with advancing the expressive possibilities of music were faced with the problem of generating new forms and expressive frameworks.

By the 1920's, two composers emerged as leaders in the avant-garde search for new expressive frameworks, Schoenberg (1874–1951) and Stravinsky (1882–1971). In the *Philosophy* Adorno examines the work of these two composers in depth, juxtaposing them as representative of the extremes evident in twentieth century musical composition. For Adorno, Schoenberg and Stravinsky not only illustrated diametrically opposed approaches to the problem of musical meaning. They were also representative of the opposite directions art followed in the age of administration. To Schoenberg, who abandoned tonality, Adorno bestowed the distinction "radical," linking him to humanitarian art. Stravinsky, who did not relinquish tonality was, for Adorno, a reactionary composer whose music embodied repressive tendencies in society.

According to Adorno, Stravinsky attempted to solve the problem of musical meaning by ignoring it: "He is drawn in that direction where music – in its retarded state, far behind the fully developed bourgeois subject – functions as an element lacking intention, arousing only bodily animation instead of offering meaning" (1973:140).

Adorno traces Stravinsky's progressive liquidation of the subjective, individual element in art from "Le Sacre" (1912) to his neo-classical phase i.e. the 1930s: "The works between 'Le Sacre' and the turn to neo-classicism imitate the gesture of regression, as it belongs to the dissolution of individual identity. Through this attitude these works would appear to achieve collective authenticity. . . The search for musical equivalents of the 'collective

---

3   The American composer Eric Salzman defines functional tonality as, "a representation of a basic scale formation within which certain hierarchies prevail – expressed as points of stability and instability....every musical event has a function or a functional role which relates it to what has come before and what will happen next" (Salzman, 1974:4).

unconcious' prepares the transition to the installation of a regressive collective as a positive accomplishment" (1973:162).

Eventually, even the idea of the subject's sacrifice is made tacit: with neo-classicism Stravinsky's music becomes domesticated; the shock value, present in "Le Sacre" is now entirely forgotten as the accessibility of his compositions increases, presenting fewer and fewer enigmatic aspects. The content or meaning of the music becomes manifest and obvious from the start – music becomes a pseudomorphism of painting which, "at its innermost core, it is the abdication of music" (1973:162), because, "All painting – even abstract – has its pathos in that which is; all music purports a becoming" (1973:162).

Stravinsky's music attempts to evade the process of "becoming" by substituting a pre-formed subject matter which replaces expressivity with a form of popular appeal that masquerades as subjective expression, deluding the listener, who believes that the 'essence of things' is being revealed: "Their judiciousness is a phantasm, resulting from the vague familiarity of the materials presented and the reminiscent exultant pomp of it all, the cloak of forced affirmation" (1973:208). Stravinsky's entire output constitutes a grand gesture of aesthetic sacrifice which Adorno believes parallels the sacrifice of each individual to the mechanics of Administration: the latent structure of music (musical essence or meaning) is forfeited in order to preserve music's surface intelligibility (or manifest structure) which Stravinsky accomplishes by holding on to compositional devices vested with obsolete meanings. Thus, neo-classicism served to perpetuate invalid emotions and myths which obviated the true relationship between the individual and the social, affirming the sense of collectivity by projecting a mask of objective authority. The subliminal message of neo-classicism was mindless conformity; as such it became part of the Total Sociation process.

By liberating dissonance on the other hand, Schoenberg's music disposed of the "crutches" of listening, the 'stock phrases', conventions and clichés which were part of the tonal language. By minimizing predictability and familiarity in his work, Schoenberg made increased demands on the listener who was required to more actively interpret the music: "Passions are no longer simulated but rather genuine emotion of the unconscious – of shock, of trauma – are registered without disguise through the medium of music. These emotions attack the taboos of form because these taboos subject such emotions to their own censure, rationalizing them and transforming them into images" (1973:39). Since his music conveyed meaning without resorting to musical devices which defined musical situations by invoking pre-formed images, Schoenberg purged music of the tendency toward depiction which had developed since Monteverdi[4] and returned music to its purer, more abstract state of "becoming." By virtue of its pure form, Schoenberg's music refused to affirm the listener's pre-existing states of consciousness. For this, Adorno felt, reason retained the potential to transcend given social conditions as well as awaken critical consciousness.

---

4   Monteverdi was the first exponent of the baroque practice of "doctrine of the affections" employing musical devices to illustrate and convey the meaning of words or passages in the text. The affections were "conveyed by a means of systematic regulated vocabulary, a common repertory of musical figures or devices" (Grout, 1973:299).

Neutralizaton and Absorption

By the late 1920's, the radical potential of Schoenberg's music, said Adorno, had retreated. Specifically, Adorno argued that Shoenberg's introduction of the twelve tone method of composition as a way of ordering dissonance democratized sound combinations. Until that point in music history, dissonance differed qualitatively from consonance – it was invested with connotations. When Schoenberg's compositions unfolded in unrestrained dissonance (as they did in the years between 1903 and about 1914 when he began to develop the twelve tone method) they were imbued with meaning, expressing for Adorno, "all the darkness and guilt of the world" (1973:133). Thus, Schoenberg's music, prior to the implementation of the twelve tone method, possessed an expressive content which the listener, forced to more actively interpret the music, could discern: its dissonances reminded the listener of the contradiction between individual and society, illustrating it with the contradiction between melodic development (the musical subject) and formal organization (objective form). With twelve tone music, however, dissonance was reduced to a quantitative category, emptied of its connotations and used interchangeably with consonant intervals to create musical form. Schoenberg, the "one time pariah" as Adorno called him (1967:149), had made a sacrifice no less significant than Stravinsky's by allowing subjective material to be dominated by objective form.

Similarly, any sort of "agit-prop" or realist music was destined to fail. For Adorno, political-realist music offered even less in the way of radical potential than Schoenberg's. Its "radical" message was so obvious, that its threatening or subversive content could be easily severed from its non-threatening musical means, leaving behind an innocuous form. Moreover, because it did not present puzzling or challenging forms it therefore perpetuated a passive listening attitude. Adorno called such music *gegangelte Musik*, or "being led by the nose music" (Jay, 1973:196). It is particularly important here to understand why Adorno felt as he did about agit-prop since his position against it may be used as a foil for uncovering an additional aspect of his position *vis à vis* Schoenberg and Stravinsky. In turn, this aspect, or tacit premise of Adorno's theory sheds additional light on Adorno's characteristically "elitist" opinions of popular music and jazz.[5]

This additional premise concerns the ways in which music's formal properties, or the com-positing of musical material, imply specific types of social relations between the musician and his/her listener. In the case of Stravinsky, agit-prop and popular music (and positivistic social science as well)[6], Adorno perceived the relation as authoritarian because the listener is merely spoken to or 'swayed' by the musical rhetoric or sensual appeal of easily recognizable, "pre-figured" meaning. Schoenberg's music, on the other hand, exemplified

---

5   Adorno was notoriously ignorant of jazz. His "On Jazz" was written on the strength of what he had learned about jazz from talking with Mátyás Seiber. At that point it is doubtful whether Adorno had ever actually listened to any (Jay, 1973:186).

6   Ironically, Adorno has often been accused of elitism and "aestheticism." Actually, as Buck-Morss observes: "In comparison, the positivist, 'scientific' notion of social engineering, which held that an elite group first acquired knowledge and then attempted through manipulation of the others to recreate the world in accord with that knowledge, was far more guilty of 'aestheticism' in the negative sense connected with political totalitarianism...." (1977: 124).

a reinstitution of the listener as a partner to the composer, as a composer in his/her own right. Rather than attempting to maintain the illusion that the listener "received" the music's meaning or message, Schoenberg presented the listener with musical figures or "ciphers" with which the listener collaboratively interacted to com-pose the meaning of the piece. In this more egalitarian relation, the two "com-posers" meet at the "riddle figure" of the musical object. Essentially, this is the musical acknowledgement of the dissolution of the subject-object dichotomy and a recognition that what is recognized as the musical "object" is the product of collaboration or praxis.[7]

It is in this context that Adorno's disdain for what Christopher Ballentine has called "thesis art" (1985:120) becomes understandable. For any art form devoted to the conveyance of an integral idea or impression was a way of speaking to as opposed to with the listener and thus reduces him/her to the status of *mere* listener. It was also a form of listener management, an attempt to engineer the listener's response by resorting to recognizable stock devices. Hence, Appollinaire's early twentieth century poetic mandate, "O mouths, man is looking for a new language/no grammarian can legislate" (Ballantine, 1985:120) recognized the need for a naturally evolved language. Similarly, if music were to be authentic, according to Adorno, it would need to emancipate itself from authoritarian modes of presentation as well as new attempts to fabricate a new musical language such as the twelve tone system.

If the possibility seemed slight that radical music would continue to fulfil its function before the 1940's, music in the post-war period seemed to Adorno to have forsaken its radical potential altogether. Neo-classicism was beginning to prove a style which offered diminishing returns (Stravinsky himself abandoned it and embraced the twelve tone method after Schoenberg's death in 1951) and the post-war generation of avant-garde composers began to pursue non-tonal lines, initially derived from Schoenberg. These efforts were led by Pierre Boulez (b. 1925) who propounded Serialism, an approach which took Schoenberg's twelve tone principle to its logical extreme by rationalizing all parameters of sound, bringing them under systematic control by calculating pre-determined series of rhythmic and dynamic values, pitches and musical punctuation (attacks and releases) which were then employed as musical material for composition. Boulez began to create, via serialism, a modern equivalent to the functional tonal framework and attempted to synthesize a new language for music. Meanwhile an opposite trend was emerging. John Cage (b. 1912) began writing music using elements of chance and, in an attempt to call attention to the idea that music is not by nature bound to the twelve pitched tones which it had traditionally employed, proposed that all noise possessed musical potential.

For Adorno, neither approach embodied the radical element present in Schoenberg. In the 1956 essay "Modern Music is Growing Old" Adorno described the serialists' compositions as "abstract in a negative sense, that is to say empty and care-free"… compositions in which "nothing happens at all" (108). The fundamental problem with the Boulez approach to serialism was that music carried on as if it possessed expressive content – maintaining a hierarchical composer-listener relationship and closed self-contained forms – when it was in fact, devoid of subjectivity. This type of music, Adorno said, was suffering from

---

7   In this regard Adorno's theory has much in common with recent developments in construction theory. Both theories have roots in early Marx (see Mehan, 1983:90).

senility but carried on, oblivious to its own state, as if it were mentally fit. As for the Cagian development of chance-determined music and the use of environmental sound as the material of composition, Adorno simply dismissed it outright calling it regression to the pre-musical.

Adorno: Dead-End Philosophy of Music?

Following Adorno's labyrinthine analysis through to its conclusion results, it seems, in a dialectical dead-end: in an age when the need for revolutionary art forms was imminent, music relinquished its radical quality to the development of its own rational lines and the pursuit of a new musical language whereby the subject (or content) would again be fused with objective form. Yet, as Adorno argued, this state of reconciliation had not existed since the middle period of Beethoven (Subotnik, 1978), and would remain an impossibility as long as discrepancies between individual and society prevailed. One begins to suspect, along with Adorno's critics, that Adorno seems committed less to instigating social change than to cultivating a position of "last connoisseur" in an era of art's increasing popularization and vulgarization (Blomster, 1977; Greisman, 1976). Feher's description of Adorno's criticism of twentieth century music as reminiscent of "the comfortable and aesthetically deliberate posture of he man glancing into the depths from the glass veranda of the Grand Hotel Abyss" (1975:109) seems partly accurate.

Yet, to abandon Adorno's work because it failed to find any immediate positive prospect for social change is to miss his point entirely. Whether or not one accepts all of Adorno's pronouncements on composers, techniques of composition and the state of modern music, what cannot be denied is that Adorno deeply enriched the study of music by bringing to it both a critical attitude and a method of relating music to social life. These can and should be used in new contexts, particularly his dual concepts of radical and reactionary art forms. Rather than accepting Adorno's prognosis for modern music with passive resignation, Adorno's method should be applied to the music of the post-World War II era in order to see if perhaps Adorno over-looked a way out of the musical *cul de sac*.

As Heinz Klaus-Metzger observes (1960), Adorno's conception of art is predicated on the notion of subjective expression, which is the basis for nineteenth century romanticism. For Adorno, the only music to be taken seriously was music in the bourgeois tradition of which romanticism was a part.[8] One must not forget that Adorno was himself a composer (he studied with Alban Berg in 1925) and perhaps, this link played a part in his ideas on later developments. It seems reasonable to believe that Adorno, as Klaus-Metzger suggests, was attempting to evaluate post-war music according to criteria which Adorno developed for music's pre-war phase. It seems reasonable, therefore, to take another look at post-World War II music, specifically the music of Boulez and Cage, in order to see whether either fulfil the true function of art as Adorno saw it. Indeed, developments in more recent music are still based on innovations made by Cage and Boulez in the late 1950's and early 1960's, with many contemporary composers following either experimental lines (Cage) or the avant-garde

---

8　Adorno believed this period in music began around the time of Monteverdi, in the early seventeenth century. Similarly, Georg Lukacs, father of representative Marxist aesthetics believed Shakespeare to be the start of the bourgeois era in literature (see Feher, 1975:109).

(Boulez). Therefore, Cage and Boulez remain the representative composers of the extremes inherent in contemporary music. By examining the work of these two composers according to the framework developed by Adorno in the *Philosophy* a critique of that work will emerge which, it is hoped, will shed light on Adorno's original categorization of Schoenberg and Stravinsky.

Boulez: Restoration

> Nor is it of any real assistance to him that he further appropriates so to speak, with his soul and substance a view of the world that belongs to the past, in other words tries to root himself in one of such and, let us say, turns Roman Catholic, as not a few have done in recent times for Art's sake, in order to give their soul some secure foundation, and so enable the definite lines of their artistic product to become themselves something which shall appear to have an independently valid growth."
> – Hegel (quoted by Adorno as an epigraph to his essay on Schoenberg in the Philosophy).
>
> In Bach's time there was an accepted language, an accepted convention. It is not at all the same today. There is no longer a complete frame of expression.... That is what is needed again." – Boulez (Peyser, 1976:157)

What Boulez set out to do in the late 1940's was to "strip" music of its accumulated dirt and give it the structure it had lacked since the Renaissance" (Peyser, 1976:63). By the phrase "accumulated dirt" Boulez meant the associations which tonality had collected since the time of Monteverdi, associations which Adorno said were employed by Stravinsky and his followers to give music the appearance of authenticity.[9] Like Adorno, Boulez believes that music which relies on the tonal language, vested with obsolete connotation, breeds passive listening. Boulez compares the process to Pavlovian conditioning; music merely evokes responses, i.e., memories and associations. If Boulez and Adorno share a disdain for the familiar in music, they differ with respect to what they hold to be the aims of composition.[10] At the heart of Boulez's efforts is a desire for reinstituting a sense of totality to art, a totality which, according to Adorno, is not possible in the twentieth century and which if attempted,

---

9   The twentieth century "conquered for musical symbolism the entire range of inner life" (Adorno, 1973:139, fn).

10 In conversation with Célestin Deliège (1976:115), Boulez describes the way in which he believes such clichés ought to be avoided: "...in the eighteenth century...there was a set course to guide the aesthetic language one produced. In our own time – as a consequence of Romanticism – there is no set course of any description; there is merely elaboration of and for the moment, because the memory is put out of action by material that is usually too rich or too complex.... So the memory only comes into play for extremely banal criteria and clichés...." Boulez, like Adorno, wants to do away with the Romantic, totalitarian imposition of personality onto musical composition and no doubt would agree with Adorno's formulation in Aesthetic Theory (1984:241) that: "A work of art becomes objective when it's completely artifactual, completely man-made, that its, when all its moments are mediated by a subject. What holds true in epistemology, namely that the input of subjectivity and that of reification complement each other, is doubly true in aesthetics." It is interesting to note that Adorno was one of the few music critics respected by Boulez. In fact, Boulez was to have provided an introduction to the English version of the Philosophy but, although publication of the book was delayed for two years waiting for him to do so, he never did. (personal communication from W. V. Blomster, 1980).

results in a false reconciliation of structure and content. Boulez's efforts from the late 1940's to the present may be viewed as a prolonged attempt at forcing such a reconciliation. With Boulez, the problem of musical meaning, crucial to Adorno, is dismissed (rather than merely ignored as in Stravinsky) for Boulez was critical of Stravinsky's stop-gap attempts at counterfeit meaning. But Boulez's allegiance to the syntactical approach to composition (preserving the idea of musical language) led him to commit the same mistake as Stavinsky: devising an arbitrary system of composition in order to achieve a complete framework of expression. Although Boulez's serialist method did rescue music by proposing a new way of organizing the raw material of composition, the logical organization is hermetically sealed; to the listener Boulez's music is not perceived as a form of language.

Boulez points to Joyce (particularly Joyce's novel Finnegans Wake) as a critical symbol: "the specificity of technique for each chapter, the fact that technique and story were one. The technique reflected exactly what Joyce meant ...." (Peyser, 1976:80). Boulez's early works, written in the late 1940's and early 1950's, were twelve tone compositions similar to Schoenberg's in their expressive quality. But with the dual-piano composition "Structures" in 1952, Boulez defined his commitment to total serialism. Every aspect of the piece is controlled; no pitch recurs with the same duration, intensity or attack. The result is a sparse, pointillistic-sounding work, in which Boulez extends the application of serialism to all parameters of sound, taking up Messian's (Boulez's teacher at the Paris Conservatory) idea of employing pre-determined modes of rhythmic, dynamic and pitch movement in order to structure the musical composition.

Boulez planned "Structures" to be an "Art of the Fugue" for the serial language (Peyser, 1976:69). It was to consist of three books which would definitively map out the new grammar. But even at the time of composition Boulez realized that the new language posed limitations and inscribed on the first page of the manuscript, "A la limite du fertile pays." Boulez's attempt at 'synthesizing' a grammar for music was no more of a success than Stravinsky's earlier attempts at ignoring the problem of musical meaning. Adorno's statement about Stravinsky seems equally applicable to Boulez: "The second language of music is synthetic and primitive; it bears the markings of technology. Stravinsky's attempt to achieve such a language recalls that of Joyce: nowhere does he come closer to his basic desire to construct what Benjamin called the primitive history of the modern" (Adorno, 1973:183).

But Boulez was not so naïve as Stravinsky, as Adorno notes in a later essay on Schoenberg: "the efforts of Boulez and the younger twelve tone composers in all countries to achieve total abstraction are by no means 'youthful blundering' but rather the continuation and development of one (italics mine) of Schoenberg's intentions" (Adorno, 1967:170), i.e., Schoenberg's preoccupation with the problem of how to organize sound which eventually led him to develop the twelve tone method.

With his next major piece, "Marteau sans Maitre" Boulez broke away from rigid serialism. Based on poetry by Rene Char, this piece shows a relenting in Boulez's stringent adherence to the serialist method which produced "Structures," a piece which he later described as "not total but totalitarian" (Peyser, 1976:37). An effort to create the effect of permeability between the three musical cycles which shape the work, the style of "Marteau" is less sparse, more resonant than "Structures," a turn, as Paul Griffiths has described it, from Weberian symmetry to Debussian allusiveness (1981:89). Boulez described this work as the "first step towards the effective breaking of traditional musical continuity" (Peyser, 1976:101). By the mid-1950's Boulez had become the undisputed leader of the avant-garde, his serial grammar was accepted by other composers and in "Marteau" he was able to relax, even to the point of using musical techniques borrowed from the past (for example, the song-speech used by Schoenberg in "Pierrot Lunaire," 1913). Of all Boulez's works, perhaps "Marteau" comes closest to Adorno's idea of "radical music": the message of the text is gloomy – civilization is dying and the individual can do nothing to stop it. The music evolves, says Boulez, "Like a timetable of trains that never move" (Peyser, 1976:103). In "Marteau" Boulez attempted to find a way out of the stultifying complexity he had created with the serialist grammar. In Darmstadt, the center of avant-garde activity in 1955, Boulez was dismayed that composers made the newly embraced serialist panoply into a fetish.

But "Marteau" was both the first and last piece in which Boulez attempted to create a conventionally meaningful work within the confines of the serialist grammar. By the late 1950's, Boulez's authority as the leader of the avant-garde had begun to wane. Threatened by the chance-composition procedures initially developed by John Cage in the mid-1950's and later embraced by Stockhausen, Boulez's now famous pupil at Darmstadt, Boulez began to move in a new direction.

Chance, as propounded by Cage, was anathema to all that Boulez represented. In an article published in 1957 Boulez attacked the Cagian brand of chance, stating that it "masks a basic weakness in compositional technique.....the resort to a more subtle poison that destroys every last embroyo of craftsmanship" (Boulez, 1964). In virtually the same breath, Boulez went on to propose his own version of chance composition, one which would be combined with controlled composition. Boulez called his version "alea." His "Third Piano Sonata," "Constellation Mirror," and "Pli Selon Pli" were the first compositions in which Boulez utilized his new technique. The element of chance in these compositions lies in performer choice; Boulez presents various options to the performer who may decide which sections he wishes to play and in which order. But the underlying principle remains one of control; although Boulez desired to break out of the closed form with aleatoric techniques his compositions never really achieve this aim because they do not share the responsibility of composition with the performer. Instead they allow the performer token freedom in deciding which section to play first.

Ironically, like Stravinsky (and the later Schoenberg) Boulez abandons Adorno's true goal of music (knowledge) in order to rescue musical language. Moreover, it would seem that Adorno's description of Stravinsky is applicable to Boulez: "the immediately musical validity is, as a consequence, almost impotent: the structure is externally superimposed by the composer's will" (1973:167) (or in Boulez's case by the pre-determined order of the series). The listener, in fact, can not aurally distinguish totally organized music from music which is randomly ordered and is forced into a passive listening attitude. The listener is not required to make sense of the sound but is required to listen to it in the conventional way. With Boulez, one could argue, music "becomes the victim of rational domination of nature" (1973:192) just as Stravinsky's music had. And, in more recent years as director of the Institut de recherché et coordination acoustique/musique (IRCAM), Boulez's goal has remained more or less the same: "Our grand design today, therefore, is to prepare the way… through an increasingly pertinent dialogue, to reach a common language which would take

account of the imperatives of musical invention and the *priorities of technology* (emphasis mine)" (IRCAM, 1983:6).[11]

From Adorno's perspective, what Boulez fails to realize is that social conditions today differ from "Bach's time" (Peyser, 1976:157). As Adorno recognized in his discussion of late Beethoven (1976 and Subotnik, 1978), there can be no authentic unity of form and content in music when a corresponding social unity does not exist. A "complete frame of expression" as Boulez puts it, cannot be built from scratch by any one composer and if it is, its presentation of an indecipherable organization of sound may lead, as Adorno pointed out, to oblivion rather than critical awareness.

Cage: Progress?

"Pure insight, however, is in the first instance without any content; it is rather the sheer disappearance of content; but by its negative attitude towards what it excludes it will make itself real and give itself a content" – Hegel (quoted as the epigraph to Adorno's essay on Stravinsky in the *Philosophy*)

"Sounds, when allowed to be themselves, do not require that those who hear them do so unfeelingly. The opposite is meant by response ability" – Cage (1961:10).

In 1952 (the same year Boulez wrote Structures I), Cage wrote 4'33" ("Four minutes and Thirty Three seconds"), a piece which most clearly embodies his ideas about the place of art in the twentieth century. It remains today the most notorious composition in the entire repertoire of Western music. Initially "composed" for piano solo, the piece consists of three movements during which the soloist sits motionless at the piano, producing no sound whatsoever. The music of the piece consists of inadvertent noises produced by the audience and concert hall itself (such as coughs, creaking ceilings or chairs, shuffling noises). Originally, according to Cage, 4'33" was a gesture designed to make a clean break with the musical past but the piece speaks of much more than a polemical message about methods of composition. Implicit in 4'33" is the idea that the social structures and assumptions inherent in traditional art forms should be given up: the idea of the artist as creative genius who "speaks" to the layman, the idea that music must proceed in accordance with a commonly accepted musical language, that it must unfold in an orderly sequence according to its internal rules of construction or even that it needs to be organized at all and that music must consist of no other sounds but the twelve, equal tempered tones.

4'33" was originally attacked as nihilistic, nothing more than a prank played at the listener's expense and it remains generally misunderstood today. Actually, 4'33" does not make as drastic a break with tradition as it initially seems to do. What Cage did was to thoroughly divest music of syntactical meaning, a process intimated by Schoenberg and

---

11 For a discussion of Boulez's "centralized" empire, IRCAM, his close ties to the French Government and IRCAM's focus on computer research, see Robert Carl (1984), "The Distant Shore as Seen From Two Sides." Between 1981 and 1983 according to Carl, Boulez narrowed the focus of IRCAM research from all aspects of contemporary composition to musical applications of the computer.

carried on by Webern, Schoenberg's pupil.[12] In his compositions Cage carries to extreme what Schoenberg only hinted at fifty years earlier: preconceptions in and about art are upset; familiarity is completely dispelled, forcing the listener into active participation with the music in an attempt to find in it something meaningful. "Most people," Cage says, "mistakenly think that when they hear a piece of music that they're not doing anything but that something's being done to them. Now this is not true and we must arrange our music, we must arrange our art, everything, I believe, so that people realize that they themselves are doing it and not that something is being done to them" (Nyman, 1974:21).

But Schoenberg is not Cage's only stylistic antecedent. Indirectly, Cage is also an outgrowth of Stravinsky, though not the side of Stravinsky which Adorno so disdained. On the one hand Stravinsky wanted to reinvest art with the appearance of authenticity, which is the aspect of Stravinsky's output on which Adorno focusses. On the other Stravinsky possessed an aversion to system and to subjective expression which led him to create art to the second degree, or art about art, which Adorno perceived as the relinquishment of individual will and awareness about society. Due to Stravinsky's lack of concern for subjective expression he did not need to evolve a consistent, systematic idiom. Rather, he played with many styles, often adopting them in hermit-crab fashion.[13] Although Stravinsky moved to neo-classicism in order to achieve the appearance of integrity he was not interested in tonality as a language but in its binding ability; what he required was a means of linking together, in building-block or collage fashion, many disassociated ideas which he built up in layers. Stravinsky's compositions hold up musical objects to the listener who finds them meaningful in much the same way that objects are included in collage-art; subjectivity and personal opinion are held back at a distance.[14]

In anticipating the demise of the Romantic heritage of art as expression, Stravinsky, more accurately than Schoenberg, anticipated developments of the post-war avant-garde. But Stravinsky was unable to take the next step, to act upon his idea. Instead, he remained "in the haven of safety" and heralded "the pre-formed, which (he has) been able to comprehend and realize as the new" (Adorno, 1973:36). This quality, though, for Adorno, made Stravinsky a reactionary composer. Interestingly, Adorno is not critical of Stravinsky's dislike of syntax: "The modern aspect in Stravinsky is that which he himself can no longer bear: his aversion, actually, to the total syntax of music. All of his followers *with the possible exception of Edgar Varese* (italics mine) are completely void of the sensitivity" (1973:153).

---

12   "Webern shook the foundation of sound as discourse in favor of sound as sound itself. But in Webern the supremacy of pitched relations remains. And so he was really tied to an earlier time" (see Peyser, 1976:58).

13   After Schoenberg's death, Stravinsky adopted the twelve tone method. Stravinsky would appropriate a style (primitivism, neo-classicism) and use it until it was exploited or outgrown, discard it and embrace a new one. Leibowitz, the French-Polish twelve tone composer and teacher of Boulez, referred to Stravinsky as "the Telemann of the Twentieth century" (Peyser, 1976:33).

14   Salzman (1974:29), describes "Le Sacre" as "a piece of high artifice in the best sense," a piece about primitivism in which "disassociated ideas appear as artifacts set into block structures built up in layers." Later, by turning to neo-classicism Stravinsky continued to stand at a distance from personal expression, creating art about art or parodying art in a manner similar to Picasso.

It is through Varese (1883–1954), who called twelve tone serialism "musical hardening of the arteries" (Mellers, 1967:131) that the link between Cage and Stravinsky becomes apparent. Varese brought the aversion to syntax to its next phase by suggesting that if music was not to abide by the *tonal ordo*, then it need not consist of the twelve pitched tones. Instead, Varese redefined music loosely as organized sound and proceeded to introduce to music new, non-pitched noises, both naturally and electronically produced. For Cage, Varese is the true father of modern music (Cage, 1961:84). Combining the Stravinsky-Varese attitude toward syntax and the Schoenbergan impulse to re-activize the listener with a dadist wish to destroy the aura of the art work which he inherited from Satie, Cage came up with his own, utterly new but traditionally derived approach to music.

Early in his compositional career Cage was influenced by Ananda Coomaraswamy and he began to review art as imitative of nature: "that is very different from believing that one must have something to say – feelings and ideas that should be given form and content. In traditional music everything depends on your having something to say and on saying it in a perfectly fused way, with form and content balancing one another. It seemed to me that there was no sense in doing that unless you were being understood. Yet no one was being understood at the time…. So I moved away from the concept of understanding to the concept of direct experience" (Peyser, 1976:59).

The history of Cage's development falls into three stages: non-random compositions which make use of chance procedures. Over the years Cage has employed five different types of chance procedures in his work (Cope, 1975): The first makes use of graphic or indeterminate notations, as in "Variation I" and "Fontana Mix" which graphically plot areas of a location in which sounds will occur. "Variations I" for instance, requires that a transparent "score" be placed over a map of the performance area." Dots on the score determine which areas of the location will be fitted with microphones and recorded in order to employ naturally occurring sounds in the taped composition. The second type of chance procedure employed by Cage is composer-used indeterminacy, music written out in traditional notation but composed according to a method which insures complete indeterminacy. Cage used this technique in "Music of Changes" (1952). To determine each musical event Cage tossed a coin thus insuring a completely random composition. The third type of chance procedure is simply performer indeterminacy (improvisation)[15] and the fourth is the aleatoric method (the Boulez version of chance) where composer determined events are randomly ordered. The fifth type of chance technique, which Cage employed in 4'33", merely outlines the parameter which will envelope musical material.

What Cage has done, then, is to invent a procedure of musical composition whereby the composer has little or no subjective input or control, where there is no idiom. Of it he says, "In this new music nothing takes place but sounds: those that are notated and those that are not. Those that are not notated appear in written music as silences opening the doors of music to the sounds that happen to be in the environment" (1961:7). Expression and the maintenance of musical forms and techniques which imply communication (musical language, closed forms) are abandoned; listening occurs entirely outside a pre-established

---

15   On the freedom Cage's music grants the performer see, for example, Pauline Oliveros' notes on performing Cage's work "Atlas Eclipticalis" (UCSD, 1980).

frame of reference. The "artist," rather than creating something removed from everyday life, merely creates situations in which listeners can focus on the sounds around them. The listener becomes, in effect, the artist; he is forced to organize the sounds on his own. Cage describes this process as dissolving art into the flow of everyday life, investing all of the sounds of events of common experience with artistic potential. In a nutshell, the Cagian aesthetic says that art is where you put the frame.

"Purposeful Purposelessness"

Returning to Adorno's most fundamental delineation of radical music – frustrating the listener's preconceptions, music as 'becoming' rather than 'being', meaning latent rather than manifest and most importantly, active rather than passive listening – Cage's music does seem to meet Adorno's criteria by attempting to serve the true function of art. The crux of Schoenberg's radical nature was, for Adorno, his re-activization of the listener: "the actual revolutionary moment for (Schoenberg) is the change in function of musical expression" (1973:39). Music no longer depicts emotions which the listener 'observes' from a distance but requires the listener to experience emotion in its more ambiguous form, as it is experienced in real life. In a later essay on Schoenberg Adorno further develops this idea:

> Schoenberg's music demands from the very beginning active and concentrated participation, the most acute attention to simultaneous multiplicity, the renunciation of the customary crutches of a listening which always knows what to expect… it requires the listener to spontaneously compose its inner movement and demands of him not mere contemplation but praxis (1967:149).

The listener, placed in a situation where nothing may be taken for granted, must attempt, with little help from Schoenberg, to derive, rather than receive second hand, meaning from the work, to compose its "inner movement;" in other words, to take on the role of composer.

Ultimately, Schoenberg's reinvolvement of the listener constitutes a rebellion against the traditional, hierarchical structure of artistic communication, which it accomplishes by narrowing the distance between composer (communicator) and listener (receiver). The listener and composer become collaborators, working to uncover musical meanings which are more subtle and complex than the familiar language could convey. In Cage's music the rebellion against the structure of listening comes full circle; the listener is not required to be the composer's partner but the composer himself, to redirect his attention to sounds which occur around him. Thus Cage differs from Schoenberg in abandoning altogether the goal of expression. Rather, Cage says his only purpose is to remove purpose (1961:12), a statement which leads to the most radical aspect of his work.

In renouncing purpose and creating music completely devoid of composer intention, Cage recognizes the fact that closed, expressive art presents an illusory image of the world. Implicit in any work of art which endeavors expression is a form of hegemony, a view of things which arises from the artist's own perceptions but which is put forward as a genuine or absolute portrayal:

> Does not a mountain unintentionally evoke in us a sense of wonder? Otters along a stream a sense
> of mirth? Night in the woods a sense of fear?....These responses to nature are mine and will not
> necessarily correspond with another's. Emotion takes place in the person who has it. And sounds,
> when allowed to be themselves, do not require that those who hear them do so unfeelingly. The
> opposite is what is meant by response ability (1961:10).

Art's illusory nature does not stem merely from the fact that the artist's interpretation of the
world is portrayed as the interpretation; it is related to the nature of expression itself. Meaning
emerges in art when the artist selectively emphasizes certain aspects of life at the exclusion of
others, distorting life in order to focus on particular aspects and, hopefully, reveal something
about them. But in the process of examining specific aspects of life art runs the risk of too
narrowly defining them. Adorno discusses this problem in the *Philosophy:*

> The dissolution of the illusory features in the work of art is demonstrated by its very consistency. But
> the process of dissolution ordained by the meaning of the totality – makes the totality meaningless.
> The integral work of art is that work which is absolutely paradoxical (1973:70).

Stravinsky recognized this problem and decided against attempting to create integral,
expressive works, and compromised by composing music about music, removed from
personal statement. But these compositions resulted in music which was doubly illusory since
they put forward a false, second hand view of the world as the genuine article. Schoenberg,
on the other hand, attempted to deepen the view of the world which art presented by refusing
to smooth the surface of his compositions in order to give the appearance of authenticity. He
attempted to show, among other things, that unambiguously stated meanings perpetuated
false, one dimensional images of the world. However Schoenberg adhered to the tradition of
the integral work of art – he continued to create expressive music.

By creating music which is totally open and which allows any sound to constitute music,
Cage has created a new aesthetic based on what Leonard Meyer has called radical empiricism
(1967); each musical experience requires the individual listener to form his own conclusions
about what the sounds mean, as opposed to being 'informed' through music, a process which
perpetuates the passive listening attitude best suited to Administration. Cage describes his
aim as "purposeful purposelessness," the point of which is the "demilitarization of language:
a serious musical concern" (Gena, 1982:44). Cage's music is the first to move away from the
post-Renaissance idea that man is the measure of all things, fit to thoroughly and judiciously
administer his way of life (Meyer, 1967). Instead, it implies a denial of the traditional idea
of linear progress, of the belief in unconditional truths and of the wealth of accumulated
symbology in art which reinforces the belief that the categories of emotional experience
and the definition of aesthetic qualities are permanently fixed. In *Negative Dialectics*
Adorno argued that "thought honors itself by defending that which is damned as nihilism"
(1973b:381). It is therefore ironic that he was unable to see Cage's principle of chance and
"purposeful purposefulness" as a possible exception to the "aging " of modern music.[16] For it

16 In his recent book on Adorno (1984:154), Martin Jay speculates that Cage's "Beckett-like"
silences may have been a possible exception to what Adorno perceived as the lack of any authentically
"progressive" music after World War II. In part, this speculation is based upon Adorno's remarks on

seems that by proposing an art which is open-ended, Cage directly contradicts the type of art most consonant with Total Sociation and puts into practice Adorno's principle that "any order which is self-proclaimed is nothing but a disguise for chaos" (1973:xii).

REFERENCES

Adorno, T. W.
1984 Aesthetic Theory. London: Routledge & Kegan Paul.
1981 In Search of Wagner. New York: Schocken.
1980 "Music and the New Music." Telos 43:124–138.
1973 Philosophy of Modern Music. New York: Schocken.
1973b Negative Dialectics. New York: Seabury.

Adorno, T. W., and M. Horkheimer
1972 Dialectic of Enlightenment. New York: Seabury.

Adorno, T. W.
1967 Prisms. London: Neville Spearman.
1956 "Modern Music is Growing Old." The Score.

Ballantine, C.
1984 Music and its Social Meanings. New York: Gordon and Breach.

Blomster, W. V.
1977 "Adorno and his Critics: Adorno's Musico-Sociological Thought in the Decade Following His Death." Musicology at the University of Colorado: 200–217.

Boulez, P.
1975 Conversations with Célestin Deliège. London: Eulenburg Books.
1964 "Alea." Perspectives of New Music 1:11:42–53.

Buck-Morss, S.
1977 The Origin of Negative Dialectics. New York: The Free Press.

Cage, J.
1961 Silence. Connecticut: Wesleyan University Press.

Carl, R.
1984 "The Distant Shore as Seen From the Other Side." College Music Symposium 24:1:148–157.

Cage in "Music and the New Music," a talk given by Adorno for North German Television in May 1960: "....only by no longer being 'lovely' does it offer any presentment of beauty. The expression of threat in this music is unmistakable wherever it further casts off its immanent lawfulness as an illusion, delivering itself rather up to chance. The Piano Concerto by John Cage consequent and meaningful only in its taboo regarding any idea of coherence of musical meaningful only in its taboo regarding any idea of coherence of musical meaning, offers an extreme example of the musical catastrophe" (1980:130, pointed out to me by Jay, personal communication 1986).

It is possible that Adorno may have been moving toward an appreciation of Cage but the case remains unclear. It seems most likely that his position regarding Cage was one of ambivalence.

Cope, D.
1975 New Directions in Music. Dubuque, Iowa: WMC Brown Co.

Feher, F. 1975 "Negative Philosophy of Music – Positive Results." New German Critique 1:4.

Greisman, H. C. 1976 "Disenchantment of the World; Romanticism, aesthetics and Sociological Theory." British Journal of Sociology 27:4:425–507.

Gena, P. (ed.)
1982 A John Cage Reader in Celebration of his 70th Birthday. New York: C F Peters.

Griffiths, P.
1981 Modern Music: The avant garde since 1945. London: JM Dent.
1978 Boulez. London: JM Dent.

Grout, D. J.
A History of Western Music. New York: Norton.

IRCAM
1983 Public Relations Pamphlet. Paris: IRCAM.

Jay, M.
1984 Adorno. Cambridge: Harvard University Press.
1984b Adorno in America. New German Critique 31:157–182.

Jay, M.
1973 The Dialectical Imagination. Boston: Little, Brown and Co.

Klaus-Metzger, H.
1960 "Just Who Is Growing Old?" Die Reihi 4:63–80.

Mehan, H.
1983 "Social Constructionism in Psychology and Sociology." Sociologie et Societes XIV:2:77–96.

Mellers, W.
1967 Caliban Reborn; Renewal in Twentieth Century Music. New York: Harper and Row.

Meyer, L.
1967 Music, the Arts and Ideas. Chicago: University of Chicago Press.

Nyman, M.
1974 Experimental Music, Cage and Beyond. London

Peyser, J.
1976 Boulez. New York: Schirmer.

Salzman, E.
1974 Introduction to Twentieth Century Music. Englewood Cliffs, New Jersey: Prentice Hall.

Subotnik, R.
1983 "The Role of Ideology in the Study of Western Music." The Journal of Musicology II:1:1–12.
1976 "Adorno's Diagnosis of Beethoven's Late Style: Early Symptoms of a Fatal Condition." Journal of the American Musicological Society 242–275.

UCSD
1980 Notations: John Cage; musical messages. La Jolla, California: UCSD Music Department.

Wolin, R.
1979 "The de-aestheticization of art: On Adorno's Aesthetische Theorie." Telos 41:105–127.

CHAPTER 2

HOW IS EXTRA-MUSICAL MEANING POSSIBLE? MUSIC AS A PLACE AND SPACE FOR "WORK" *

The Problem:

It is a pervasive idea in Western culture that music is in some way capable of symbolizing emotions, images or ideas. Equally pervasive however, within the fields of philosophy, musicology, social psychology and linguistics, is the view that, in spite of increasing attention devoted to the topic, attempts to explain empirically music's communicative ability have met with relatively little success. Thus, from the outset, the issue of musical meaning is characterized by paradox: at the level of the listening experience music seems infinitely and definitely expressive while, at the level of taxanomic analysis, the same music seems perpetually capable of eluding attempts to pin it to semantic corollaries. There is, in other words, a tension between the apparent validity (at the level of listening) and the apparent invalidity (at the level of empirical analysis) of music's symbolic capacity.

This "gap," as John Rahn (1972 p. 255) has put it, "between structure and feeling," is not necessarily problematic for the study of musical meaning. It can, as I shall argue below, be seen instead as a resource, making the study of musical meaning all the richer. Yet the conventional ways in which the paradoxical aspect of musical meaning has been attended to, have consisted, for the most part, of attempts to collapse the issue into one or the other of two equally unsatisfactory extremes. On the one hand the formalist position describes music as essentially abstract and expressionless whereas on the other, the expressionist position likens music to language in that its compositional elements may be said to possess extra-musical referents of one kind or another. As the sociologist of music Ivo Supičić has argued:

> The scientific flaw of all formalist and expressionist concepts lies in their readiness to generalize, to put forward one principle and aspect and exclude all others, or at least to play down the value of other principles and aspects (pp. 198–199).

The major consequence then, of framing the study of musical meaning in terms of formalism and expressionism is that the initial richness of the issue is lost.

The general intent of this essay is therefore to arrive, via a re-evaluation of some of the basic premises of each side, at a "resolution" of the formalist and expressionist positions. I shall argue that the factors which impede such a resolution are related to the way in which the initial question has conventionally been formulated (i.e. "does music have extra-musical significance and can it therefore be conceived of as a language?") and that this formulation is a product of a fundamental misconception of language predicated upon a referential theory of meaning. Taken together, these two factors have constrained the debate over musical meaning by focusing inquiry upon the *music itself as the locus of meaning*. My fundamental task is to reformulate the initial question of whether music is or is like language by redirecting it at the source of tension itself, that is, to the issue of how it is possible that music is experienced as inherently meaningful when there may be no one-to-one correspondence of meanings to musical elements.

To this end, what follows is organized in three parts: (1) an over-view of the formalist-expressionist debate with an emphasis on previous expressionist explanations of musical meaning, (2) a critique of the fundamental conception of language shared by both expressionists and formalists and (3) a proposal of an alternate approach to the question of musical meaning which builds upon recent work in the area of sociolinguistics, cognitive sociology, ethnomethodology and especially, social construction theory as it locates social and cognitive structures in the interaction between people (Mehan 1983). The purpose of this alternative approach to the topic of musical meaning is to redirect the force of the initial descriptive (and implicitly linguistic, musicological or psychological) question of *what* music means to an explicitly sociological question of *how* musical meaning is possible. Finally, in fulfilling these three aims I hope to show, first of all, that the study of musical meaning has implications for the study of connotative meaning and interpretation more generally and, second, that these implications are in turn consequential for the way in which the relation between social actors (as individuals and as collectivities) and culture is conceived of and therefore, for the ways in which sociological studies of culture ought to proceed.

* I would like to thank Bennett Berger, Hugh Mehan and Charles Nathanson for their encouragement and helpful comments. An earlier version of this paper was written for Hugh Mehan's seminar in ethnomethodology at the University of California, San Diego.

The Expressionist-Formalist Debate:

To speak of expressionism as a unified theoretical "block" is, of course, misleading for there is certainly as much difference of opinion *within* the expressionist position as there is between it and the formalist view. In the first place, expressionists can be classified according to methodological approach (see, for example, Lippman 1981): *semiotic* (Nattiez; Ruwet; Dunsby; Coker; Cooke); *hermeneutic* (Plavsa; Duisberg; Harris and Sandresky; Kretchmar); *phenomenological* (Schutz; Clifton; Blacking). However these classifications are problematic in that they are to some extent arbitrary, not always mutually exclusive and not, in every case, self-proclaimed. The "loose" (and not self-acknowledged) semiotics of, for example, Ferguson or Coker bears little resemblence to the more rigorous version practiced by Ruwet or Nattiez and, for that matter, Ferguson's approach is quite different from Coker's in the first place. For these reasons, a survey of expressionism using as its dividing principle methodological approach is, ultimately, of little use.

More productive would be a classification which contrasts expressionist theorists according to intellectual influences. In this way, distinctions between, for example, the semiotics of Coker on the one hand (as it is steeped in the tradition of Charles Morris and George Herbert Mead) and Nattiez on the other (as it is derived from the work of Nicolas Ruwet and Zellig Harris) can be preserved. One can understand, given these differences, why it is not surprising that Coker is explicitly concerned with extra-musical or, as he calls it, extra-generic meaning and Nattiez tends to focus upon what he terms the "neutral level" or purely musico-logical level of a piece (what Coker terms "congeneric meaning") and the way in which this level is related to music's formal intelligibility.

It should be clear then, that any study of "expressionism" as a body of thought would need to emphasize the ways in which expressionism can *not* be thought of as a unified approach. For the purposes of this paper however, I shall do exactly the opposite. In this section, I wish to examine, first of all the way in which the work of all expressionist theorists is unified by a common theoretical assumption that the locus of extra-musical meaning is in the musical object itself, and secondly, I shall explore the ways in which different expressionist theorists come to "operationalize" this assumption according to their particular methods and intellectual influences.

Essentially, the aim of expressionist theorists concerned with the issue of extra-musical meaning is to establish the "objective" nature of musical meaning. They are not particularly interested in "subjective" responses for their own sake. Rather, they look for *reliable* connotations, by which it seems fair to say they mean isomorphic links between musical symbols and extra-musical referents, notations and connotations. Given then, these operant terms, "symbol" and "referent" as terminological "constants," one can classify expressionist theories (and formalist theories as well) along two "axes": first, the way in which the symbolic unit is defined (whether it it a note of the scale, an interval, a phrase, the entire piece) and second, that unit's degree of specificity (whether it refers to a particular object, image or idea—such as the "cuckoo" in Beethoven's Pastoral symphony—or whether it alludes in a more general way to a less precise object of reference—for example, the more general sense of "the countryside" to which Beethoven's symphony allegedly refers).

In *The Language of Music*, for instance, Deryck Cooke argues:

> In some way or other, we feel (music) conveys to us the subjective experience of composers. But in what way? . . . how can it be done in music which can only represent a few physical objects, vaguely suggest a few others, and make no explicit description of anything at all? To try and find the answer to this question we must turn to a consideration of the analogy between music and literature and an investigation of the problem of music as language (p. 10) . . . The task facing us is to discover how music functions as a language, to establish the terms of its vocabulary and to explain how these terms may legitimately be said to express the emotions they appear to (p. 34).

Cooke then proceeds to define music's (and it is important to note, *tonal* music's) expressive framework as it is constituted through intervals. A minor second, for example expresses "spiritless anguish" (p. 90) while a major second is equated with "pleasurable longing," a minor third, "stoic acceptance" and so on through to the octave, "neutral; finality" (p.89). Using this "dictionary," Cooke's method of analysis consists of toting-up intervals in order to arrive at a composite picture of the emotional content of any given piece. Although he admits that his linguistic correlates are far from precise ". . . I am only too well aware that by using the simple everyday words for human emotion to make my classification of the terms of musical language, I have only scratched the surface of a problem of will-nigh infinite depth . . ." (p. 272), Cooke concluded that it is or will one day be possible to arrive at a complete lexicon of musical significance:

> A pyschologist of deep insight and great understanding will be called for; perhaps psychology will have to link hands again with philosophy and metaphysics before the language of music yields up its innermost secrets . . . (pp. 273–274).

Although Cooke's approach is not nor has ever been received by music scholars with particularly high regard, it is worth noting because it is one of the few attempts to account for fairly specific emotional reference at the "micro" musical-structural level of intervalic relations.

Taking a slightly larger unit of analysis, the phrase, Donald Ferguson (1960) puts forward the Aristotelian argument that, "melodies which are mere sounds resemble dispositions" (p. 123). The crux of his argument is that, "Emotion (is) . . . conveyed by the musical substance" (p. 79), or in other words, the musical structure "communicates" non-musical content. Music is able to function communicatively, Ferguson argues (along the same lines as Meyer, 1954 260 and Coker, 1972 34) because purely physical aspects of musical processes are analogous to types of experience. On the basis of this idea of contiguous meaning, Ferguson rekindles the Mendelssohnian argument that music is actually *more* expressive than words precisely because it is able to offer sonic parallels of types of unmediated experience (for example, music does not *signify* the feeling of sudden-ness, quiet, confusion, etc., by *telling* the listener about an instance of any of these feelings; rather it *recreates* the feeling through the medium of sound). Tones, Ferguson suggests, are "a truer profundity than is possible with the machinery of nouns and verbs" (p. 123).

With a one and a half bar fragment from Wagner's *Ring* . . ., Ferguson attempts to demonstrate that the type of tonal relations found in it posses "verbal counterparts", by which he means, "one or more affective words, such as ecstasy, anticipation, warmth, poignance . . . If we attempt to fuse all these factors together in a single impression of feeling character it will not be difficult to identify the experience with which this music must be associated. This is patently a type of love music" (p. 95). And, in spite of the fact that one could come to the same conclusion based upon the libretto Ferguson argues that the same conclusions could be arrived at even if one had absolutely no idea of what the particular fragment was meant to accomplish (a point which he develops in an analysis of one of the fugues from the *Well Tempered Clavier*).

As a final example it is worth looking at the recent work of Catherine Harris and Clemens Sandresky (1985) who use as their unit of analysis the entire piece. This work consists of an unusual "synthesis" of Schenker's structural approach, Meyer's use of information theory, the Meadian theory of gestures and significant symbols and the formalist idea of music as "unconsummated symbol" (Langer 1953, p. 30) or "myth" (Levi-Strauss; one reason perhaps, why they focus upon the piece as a whole). Specifically what Harris and Sandresky are concerned with is showing the correspondence between, on the one

hand, harmonic and melodic structural relationships and, on the other, social typifications of collective meanings. Through a series of examples, they draw parallels between musical structure and extra-musical phenomena in order to explain why certain musical works connote some things and not others. Along the lines of Ferguson, they put forth a theory of meaning by contiguity. Where they differ from Ferguson (and for that matter from Cooke as well,) is that they make explicit the idea of cultural mediation of musical meanings or, in their words, of typifications and it is this which gives their approach slightly more of a sociological tilt. They argue, in other words, that the musical tone as such does not necessarily have any definite *a priori* meaning but, given contiguous constraints and set in a cultural context (by which they mean, or seem to mean, a pre-existing set of shared meanings, cognitive, moral and aesthetic) it comes to seem, for all practical purposes as if its meaning is intrinsic. For instance:

Music plays a remarkable role in communicating a notion of the 'character' or style of emotional expression of a particular people, nationalities and historical periods. It has symbolized collective feelings of grief and joy, excitement and despair . . . The list could go on. Some examples are in order (p. 296).

and to take of their many examples:

The exuberance of our national anthem, *The Star Spangled Banner*, gives form to one aspect of patriotic feeling; the quieter radiance of *America*, another. When sung with conviction, *who among us can resist* a feeling of pride and community? (p. 296, emphasis mine).

With this example, Harris and Sandresky seem to have made a progressive move away from the implicitly psychological thrust of Cooke and Ferguson only to re-establish *a priori* meaning by relocating it at the level of culture or, in other words, by relocating the objectivity of musical reference in the cultural mediation of the tone itself (as if culture closes off what would otherwise be, to use a term from Berger and Luckman, a "world open" relationship between social actors and their social environment, by making that environment seem "given," "natural" or "world closed"). What this determinist (and essentially Durkheimian) conception of culture tends to obliterate however, is the *contested* aspect of culture, implying instead a naive, anthropological picture of culture as a "ground" in which social actors or more accurately, enactors (in this case music listeners) are embedded (and also implying a naive approach to the study of culture, a form of "meaning reading," what Berger (1981) refers to as "culturology" and Bittner, in a similar vein, as "naive realism" (1973). This is a point I shall discuss in more detail below).

MUSIC FOR "WORK"   87

It seems reasonable, for example, that for many listeners, *The Star Spangled Banner* may not connote a "feeling of pride and community." Think, for instance of the Jimi Hendrix version of this piece. Or, even allowing for the qualification, "sung with conviction," would *any* version of the *Star Spangled Banner* evoke or connote national pride and community spirit among *all*, or even *most*, Jimi Hendrix devotees? Unless the answer to this question can be an unequivocal "yes," we must reconsider the fruitfulness of attempting to enunciate lexicons (whether universally valid or culturally circumscribed) of extramusical meaning as it is found *in the music itself*. It is about here then, that one can begin to see why the formalist position is often perceived as the more "intelligent" side of the musical meaning debate, aloof as it is from this morass of expressivist issues.

In a review article of semiotic approaches to music, Patricia Tunstall observed that the usefulness of semiotic inquiry as it has been developed in other fields is called into question in music because of the problems involved in elucidating the semantic connotations of music:

> Music seems to involve primarily syntactical, not semantic relationships; it does not exhibit a systematic one-to-one correspondence of each specific musical element with a specific nonmusical meaning. According to Saussure's definition, then, music must be considered not a system of signs but a system of signifiers without signifieds. Therefore musical analysis can make only limited use of the particular virtues of the semiological approach . . . Its element are not signs, but the relations between them are coherent and meaningful. It is these relations themselves, the formal operations performed upon sonorous elements, that are the essence of musical structure. Perhaps, then, that structure is a uniquely lucid and unmediated reflection of the formal operations of cognition (1979, p. 62).

What is important to note here is that Tunstall, like the expressionists she criticizes, directs her attention to the musical object itself, and, by virtue of the fact that she concurs with Saussure's definition of music as a system of signifiers without signifieds, she reaches a dead-end with respect to music's semantic content. As an alternate route, she suggests that musicologists pursue a kind of syntactical structuralism, which is what she means when she argues that music study ought to focus upon the "formal operations themselves" (a conclusion which, as Jonathan Dunsby has pointed out in his 1983 review of music semiotics, Nattiez and Ruwet had already reached).

This conclusion is not a particularly new one; the Vienniese music critic, Edward Hanslick, argued along similar lines in his book *The Beautiful in Music* (1885). Hanslick's approach is worth noting since he remains one of the few writers to appreciate the paradoxical aspect of musical meaning, namely that music may be perceived as expressive, yet simultaneously elude analytic attempts to pin it to semantic corrolaries. Hanslick challenged the appropriateness of applying the metaphor of language to music by objecting to the idea that there exists any one-to-one correspondence between the musical symbol and a specific, external referent:

> The fundamental difference consists in this: while sound in speech is but a sign, that is, a means for the purpose of expressing something which is quite distinct from its medium, sound in music is the end, that is, the ultimate and absolute object in view. The instrinsic beauty of the musical in the latter case and the exclusive dominion of thought over sound as a mere medium of expression in the former are so utterly distinct as to render the union of these two elements a logical impossibility (1957, p. 67).

and for this reason, he thought it philistine to attempt to pin music to *an* interpretation since this ultimately destroyed the musical beauty which was not so much a product of intrinsically meaningful symbols mechanically strung together but due to the fact that music was a kind of polymorphous, sonorous logic in a pre- or unconscious, tactile sense (this is more or less the same argument Mendelssohn made). Hanslick did not want to reduce what he called the "beauty" of a piece of music to verbal concepts. He was objecting to the idea that music expresses things *to* a listener, which he believed was a quality of language but not of music. Music, he argued, had, over the course of the nineteenth century, been subsumed under an essentially inappropriate model of verbal language based upon a correspondence theory of meaning.

We have now come full circle back to the initial paradox. Music cannot satisfactorily be analyzed as a language because it lacks sufficient examples of what David Osmond-Smith (1971) has called "double articulation" (i.e. music is best conceived of as a system of signifiers without signifieds). Nevertheless, it is frequently experienced as if it were a type of language, capable of extra-musical reference. As Jacques Barzun has described it:

> The issue then, boils down to: sounds with or without connotation, those voting aye to "Without!" being divided into pure sensualists and pure Platonists; those voting aye to "With!" being still at a loss to account for music's connotative powers beyond the few effects based on association—church bells or military trumpets (1980 10).

What this problem suggests then, is that the real

question of interest is not so much psychological, musicological or linguistic as *sociological*, not so much *what* any given music means as *how* it is possible that music can be experienced as inherently meaningful when, in fact, there may be no one-to-one correspondence of meaning to musical elements.

What remains is to attempt to answer this question and in so doing, attempt to resolve the formalist objection of extra-musical meaning and the expressionist sense of it. In order to do this, however, it is necessary to back up a bit and examine the model of language implicit in both formalist and expressionist theories, for it is this model, I wish to argue, which is responsible for many of the problems identified by each position with regard to the other.

Problems with the formalist and expressionist conception of language:

First and foremost, all the writers so far reviewed shared the tacit and unchallenged premise that verbal language is characterized in practice by an "ideal speech situation," as it has been described by Habermas (1976) and Grice (1975), in which what is said is equal to what is meant is equal to what is understood. Leonard Meyer (whose ideas about the nature of musical meaning are particularly hard to classify) for example, argues that the listener, "must respond to the work of art as the artist intended . . ." (1956, p. 41). Dusan Plavša (1981, p. 67) hypothesizes that, if the programs to Sibelius' *Swan of Tuonela*, Strauss' *Till Eulenspiegel* and Smetana's *Sarka* were exchanged, listeners hearing these pieces for the first time would still be able to find that the programs would evoke associations, "which simply cannot be related to the music one hears," the point being that music is representative because the "wrong" tones, like the "wrong" words, will not convey the initial intent of their author. In other words, formalists and expressivists alike tend to assume that language is characterized solely by a referential theory of meaning in which form (the symbol or utterance) and function (the "received" meaning of that utterance) are inextricably linked. Yet this is hardly the way that actual day to day speech situations proceed, as Wittgenstein (1953), Austin (1962) and more recently, speech act theorists (Labov and Fanshel 1977, Searle 1967 and particularly Streeck 1980 in his critique of speech act theory) have recognized in their respective discussions of "language games," "performatives" and "speech acts."

The performative utterance *looks* like a statement and grammatically, it would be classified according to its literal meaning, however it is recognized by the hearer as something quite different. Its illocutionary and perlocutionary forces, in other words, are not identical. What this means is that a statement or utterance may function in a way that has little to do with its actual form. (For example, the statement, "It's hot in here," may be understood as a request that a window be opened.) In this regard, Wittgenstein made an analogy to chess: speakers use words like chess pieces in a simultaneous multiplicity of language games (of which there may be an infinite variety). It is important to note here that, as Jurgen Streeck has argued in his critique and extension of speech act theory, the meaning or function of speech acts relies upon the hearer as well as the speaker, being assigned to some extent in retrospect according to the type of response it provokes. Thus, the statement, "It's hot in here" would only be understood as a request to open the window *if* the hearer actually acknowledges it as a request. Otherwise, it will (ostensibly anyway) be defined as a statement of fact (Though there may, on the part of speaker and/or hearer be a tacit recognition that the initial function of the statement was one of request).

The point then, is that speech is not nearly as referential in practice as it is conceived of in idealized terms. Therefore, rather than comparing music to formal speech and grammatical rules it may be more productive to compare it to speech in practical contexts, to study meaning in *use*, in which case *both* music and speech may exhibit the problem of being perceived as connotative in cases where there is no explicit link between form and function.

In fact, it may be that the conception of music as referential language is *doubly* confused because it is founded upon an initial misconception of language and verbal meaning itself, one which implies an over-determined (and sociologically under-determined), idealized view of composer-listener interaction which over emphasizes composer intentionality on the one hand, and undervalues listener participation on the other. At this point, it is worth examining in greater depth some of the assumptions upon which these misconceptions of meaning and language are based and the implications for the study of meaning in general and musical meaning in particular which they carry.

First of all, most conventional approaches to the problem of meaning take, implicitly or explicitly, what some scholars have called a "theoretical short-cut" (Bittner: 1965; Dore and McDermott 1982) based upon a metaphor of meaning *transmission* or meaning *exchange*, as if bits or pieces of meaning may be arranged in mosaic-like pictures according to the rules or regularities of what may be "done" with any given bit or of how it can be treated (see also, Mehan 1983, for a discussion of this transmission model). What makes the metaphor of transmission a "theoretical shortcut" is that it assumes encoded meanings are meaningfully received because meaning receivers (or "hearers") come equipped (or are equipped by their culture; in other words, "socialized") with a kind of decoding device or lexico-grammar (Dore and McDermott 374 and Bittner 246).

Whenever a theorist states that, for some specified universe a particular utterance, object, act has a corresponding set of functions which, in turn, correspond to a finite set of interpretations on the part of the hearer, s/he may be said to be taking this short-cut which, simply put is the belief in the absolute referentiality of meaning and a denial of meaning through use (and as such the theoretical short-cut may be seen as a form of stimulus-response theory). This is not, however, to deny that objects, utterances or acts may possess seemingly greater and lesser degrees or referentiality, or in other words, that they will provide their interpretors with varying degrees of interpretative constraint and that, in some cases, that constraint will be so great that, for all practical purposes, the problems implicit in taking the theoretical short-cut will be "merely theoretical." In many cases however, the implications of assuming that "shared meaning" facilitated by culturally coded significances is a general feature of all "communication" are far from trivial. For one, it implies that the meaning "transmitter" or speaker (or composer) must have access to or have internalized the lexico-grammar in order to "transmit" meaning. For another, it implies that what is "transmitted" corresponds to (a) specific meaning(s) (which implies means-end intentionality on the part of the transmitter) and further, that the meaning receiver is essentially passive in that s/he has no impact upon the meaning of the object, utterance, act but rather that s/he merely receives it in its complete form. One should now be able to see how, given these assumptions about meaning and language, there could be only one implied methodological task for the study of any type of meaningful activity: to provide a thorough enunciation of that activity's lexicon of culturally coded significances.

My point in this section has been to argue against determinist explanations of meaning (whether universalist—in which the meaning of the utterance cuts across cultural or sub-cultural boundaries—or particularist—in which the meaning of the utterance is determined by the cultural, sub-cultural or even psychological context of which it is a part and in which it may be said to be "hermetically sealed") though this is in no way to deny that there are, within certain contexts as these are conceived by actors, probabilistic distributions of the ways in which utterances, acts and objects are interpreted. Rather, I wish to call attention to the fact that there is a fine line between speaking of objects, utterances or acts as if they possess intrinsic and immutable meaning (as if form and function are linked) and to speak of these as socially constructed through use according to various constraints. The former view (as I shall argue below) presents an implicit picture of culture as uncontested whereas the latter does not. To put it in other words, my point has been to move away from idealized conceptions of speech and meaning "transmission", as they characteristically assume (and as Streeck has enumerated): 1) that the meaning of an utterance is constituted by the speaker (or "author") of the utterance (and not at all by the hearer or interpreter) 2) that meaning is therefore a function of the sentence uttered and therefore that function is linked to and dependent on the form of the words uttered and 3) that, at least at a deep structural or cultural level there is a rule which can account for the way in which the utterence was used. These assumptions imply a dyadic relation between object and interpretation (or between object and subject) grounded in a logical view of language which has come under increasing criticism in recent years, in that it depicts actors as enactors or "cultural dopes" who are frozen in to their cultures without the possibility of reflexive behavior (or insincerity, alienation etc.), a depiction Streeck describes as treating "context as given" (p. 144).

Both musical meaning and verbal meaning (at least in the case of implicit verbal meanings) may be best considered as what D'Andrade (in reference to other types of meanings) has called "count as" phenomena, by which he means that their meaning does not correspond to a concrete or "brute factual" category which exists objectively *outside* of the interaction in which it is constructed (as it does, for instance, in the case of nouns such as "tree," "hand," or "stone"). Instead, its meaning is assigned through an enacted process. So, for example, a musical utterance takes on meaning because an individual or group adheres to a constitutive rule which constructs a sort of aura of significance around that utterance. This in turn enables it to be "counted as" an example of that category of meaning, and the maintainance of that significance is dependent upon actors who continue to perceive and act toward the phenomenon as "counting as" what it "counts as" (or it will fail to count and, perhaps, count as something else). Thus, as with all "institutionalized facts" the "instance" perceived under the proper felicity conditions" (D'Andrade refers here to Austin's work on speech acts) counts as an exemplary instance of an "objective" category. What the meaning of "count as" phenomena depends upon is not transmission/reception of pre-coded information (which would appear and reappear *to* the receiver) but upon the active social and social-psychological intersubjective processing of that information which *transforms* (and therefore "produces") it (and I use the term transform here to include cases where repetition or re-cognition occurs).

In down-playing the active role of the listener then, expressionists concerned with making taxonomic distributions of musical meaning attempt to treat music as a species of language, when it actually may be more appropriate to treat language "as a species of music," a point brought up by the English poet and essayist Sidney Lanier in the seventeenth century (see Hollander 1973, p. 11). Bearing also in mind the implications of Wittgenstein's suggestion that language may be something on which to "hang tones" or, in other words that words may be moulded in such a way as to have a multiplicity of forces (1953), one might be tempted to add, "and tones are something upon which to hang words." The implication is that the imputed illocutionary force of tones may rely, in part, upon the perceived context supplied by the words imputed to these tones by composers, performers, listeners and critics. Thus what taxonomic approaches fail to realize is that musical meaning may be achieved or realized through the compositional "work" of the very listeners who may act "as if" they are merely "receiving" that meaning. And because of this failure, any lexicon which an expressionist approach may propose would be little more than an artifact of the methodology used to "discover" or "reveal" that meaning in the first place. In other words, music scholars posses the same "tools" or "folk methods" of sense-making as music listeners and perhaps the greatest of these tools is the assumption (and its retinue of implied sub-assumptions) that the locus of meaning is *in the music* when it seems more likely that it is not "received" but is *achieved*, the product of interactive work.

The perspective of "Interpretive Studies"; Social Construction and its Constraints:

Given then, that there *appears* to be, or actors act *as if* there exists an objective system of overlapping meaning—a core culture or collective conscience or culturally-coded lexicon—which is shared to some degree by all members of the cultural setting and which is defined by that setting, the Interpretative Studies question asks *how* does objectivity get socially constructed. With respect to music, the question is therefore: how do listeners come to recognize a piece as embodying some qualities but not others or, more generally, how is it that an audience comes to define any piece of music as meaningful in the first place?

To answer this question requires a focus upon cohort production, the idea that the social world or *Lebenswelt* (or "Nature") is produced through the scenic practices, interpretive procedures, members' methods or "work"; how through interaction (collaboration, conflict, collusion) actors come to construct an aura of naturalness about the object, utterance, act, "as if" the properties perceived *in* that object are actually and intrinsically *of* it. Thus, Interpretive Studies looks at the transformative

practices which construct the illusion of idealized meaning transmission and inherent meaning.

What these practices consist of is a process of "filling in" of objects (including others' identities, one's own identity, one's "subjectivity") *at the level of interaction*. The task of Interpretive Studies then, is to tell the "local history" of how the phenomenon was "realized," and that history would consist of a chronicle of all aspects of meaning "production": the (to use a Marxian analogy) *mode* of that production as it is characterized by its *forces, relations* and *available technology* or in other words, all of the seemingly "objective" constraints upon the process of naming or meaning production.

With regard to the "tools" of sense-making, then, it is important to recognize at the outset that we, as social actors, approach objects with what may perhaps be best described as a "systematic bias" in favour of meaning; we are perhaps, as Merleau-Ponty has put it, "condemned to meaning." For this reason, we need to have some understanding of the types of interpretive procedures (Cicourel 1974) which operate beneath the level of normative constraint. Social action may, to varying extents be seen as a process of *ad hocing* whereby actors attempt to align their informal procedures with formally defined rules and meaning categories (a process similar to Berger's notion of "ideological work" (1981) and C. Wright Mills' idea of "situated vocabularies of motive," (1940)).

First of all, we assume that there is, between actors, a "reciprocity of perspectives" through which each is able to overcome his/her individual biases due to physical or mental position in order to establish with others the objective features of phenomena. We assume that, if a reversal of perspective were possible, we would each see the world through the eyes of the other (a proposition which is of course merely hypothetical). Secondly, we assume, according to a kind of "law of good continuation" that the phenomena we encounter will possess an internal logic and completion which we will be able to perceive. And third, we interpret "historicismically," letting unclear information pass and later, returning to interpret it according to the "new" light shed upon it from our present perspective. (So, for instance, if we perceive something in an object which strongly contradicts our interpretation of the object up-until-then, we may re-interpret all of what we had encountered of it previously in order to bring it into line with the new "fact.")

Perhaps the main reason we have so little trouble making sense out of just about anything, as Garfinkel's "therapy experiment" demonstrates (Garfinkel 1962), is that we go to "work" at meaning construction given the "materials at hand," i.e. the perceived context of which the phenomenon is also a part and with which it

MUSIC FOR "WORK"   91

reflexively reacts (see Dore and McDermott on context, not as a surround or ground, but as interactively and reflexively related to the object which it "frames"). Thus, one can say that what is produced is constrained by the forces and relations of that production or, by the way phenomena are perceived to be framed and how they in turn frame each other. Thus meaning categories emerge or are constructed according to their perceived contextual constraints, i.e. according to how, where, when and why they are framed and who is involved in framing them (the relations of meaning production).

Framing then, becomes a crucial constitutive tool of meaning construction since it helps to inspire the belief necessary to "drive" the machinery of what has been called in different contexts, "oracular reasoning" (see Evans-Pritchard 1937 and Mehan forthcoming). Mehan describes this process as the way in which an initial emotional, aesthetic or religious commitment to a basic premise or "incorrigible proposition" is further buttressed by "secondary elaborations of belief" which both rationalize the validity of the initial premise and fend off contradictory evidence. In this way then, the phenemenon is "fleshed out" (or transubstantiated"—remembering that this concept was initially used to describe a religious context) as a meaningful or coherent whole. The first step then, to finding meaning in an object is *believing* that the object in question is inherently meaningful and that it deserves to be taken seriously, that it is significant. The primary object of study then, when focusing on musical meaning is to examine the way in which belief is inspired so that the listener listens "in good faith" and thus, cooperates in fleshing out the sketchiness of the music so that it appears to mean something (or so that it *will* mean something or, that it *is* meaning something but that the listener is unable to recognize the meaning at that moment).

Leonard Meyer's discussion of the "preparatory set" (1954, p. 75) refers to essentially this same idea. Regarding the importance to the object's meaning of the perceived frame, he argues that it is the belief that we are about to have an aesthetic experience that is responsible for the fact that we do, subsequently, have such an experience; tone or sounds *as such* do not produce an emotional response. For example, hearing someone practice scales on the piano may "evoke" or "transmit" nothing, yet hearing these same scale patterns played by the same pianist who is now on stage, acting as a soloist may "evoke" quite a lot: "Once the aesthetic attitude had been brought into play, very few actions actually appear to be meaningless" (p. 35).

Thus, one could say that the way in which music is framed provides what Gumperz has called "contextualization cues" (Gumperz 1977) and Erickson, "implicit signals" (Erickson 1982)

which help prepare the listener or "warm up" the machinery of oracular reasoning so that s/he will look and listen for, or "work" toward realizing the meaning of the piece. The preparatory set then, is part of what is required to inspire belief or trust necessary for the collaborative, cooperative relationship between listener and composer which gets the "work" of constituting meaning done in music. Essentially, these cues consist of various conventions or ritual practices that, through experience, come to carry certain con-notations which, one could say, serve as "tools" for the work of sense making and meaning construction. (It is worth noting here that this perspective can explain how instances of self-borrowing among composers can work successfully: for if Plavša's (1981) hypothesis were generally true—that programs of programmatic pieces could not successfully be exchanged—how then, could we explain, for instance, that a piece such as the well-known barcarolle from Offenbach's *Tales of Hoffman* was originally conceived as the Goblin's song *Die Rheinnixen* (Barzun 1980, p. 17), and see ibid for additional examples of self-borrowing).)

In the case of "war horse" pieces (pieces in the repertoire which are programmed year after year and with which even "naive" or musically uneducated listeners are familiar—pieces like the first movement of Beethoven's fifth symphony, Tchaikovsky's 1812 Overture, Ravel's Bolero, Debussy's Afternoon of a Faun) where the listener has easy and frequent access to what the idealized mode of response consists of (i.e., the preparatory set is comparatively larger than for a "first-time-through" world premiere) and therefore some of his/her work has already been done by others. (S/he has perhaps read about the work, heard others discuss it, listened to it with others and already been through the interactive process of constructing its meaning. S/he is offered, prior to listening, a sketch or cognitive map of how to get the work done.) Thus, one could say that listening to "1812" is like assembling something from a "kit": one goes to work with one's pre-fabricated parts and a set of (indexical) instructions telling one what to do. (This is not to say that one will always succeed in one's assembly work or that, given the "kit" one may not discard the instructions, dismantle the parts and proceed from scratch in order to produce a different "object," a process not unlike that which Willis (1977) has described as "penetration.")

In the case of new or unfamiliar music, the belief inspired by the preparatory set or the contextualization cues is crucial. These cues are also more likely to consist of extra-musical devices such as program notes, the identity of the performers (i.e. New York Philharmonic, San Diego Symphony, or a local, amateur organization?), the fullness of the hall, the hall itself, the price of the ticket, the seating arrangements, the gestures of the performers (and perhaps particularly of the conductor—see Adorno (1975, p. 105) on the subject of conductors: "The conductor acts as though he were taming the orchestra but his real target is the audience . . .") One could generate a long list of possible examples of these contextualization cues but in order to describe the tools or available technology, forces and relations of any given listening situation one would have to turn to an ethnographic account of the "setting" or "work place" in which the music's meaning is produced, as aspects of that setting function in the preparatory set of perceived constraints upon the process of meaning construction.

In general, however, the types of things one would look for would consist of: (1) aspects of *the music itself*-to what other pieces, composers, etc. does it bear family resemblance? is it familiar or unfamiliar? in what ways might it resemble sentic, physical or onomotopoeic processes through *rhythm*, *melodic relations* (upward or downward trend, wide gaps or step-wise motion, etc.), *harmonic relations* (open or closed, "consonant" or "dissonant," chordal or polyphonic) (2) the *listener's relation to other listeners* (who they are, how many there are, their perceived or imagined statuses, actions, utterances and attempts at defining the musical meaning) (3) *the listener's relation to the composer* (whether s/he is alive or dead; his/her biography and degree of fame and supporters; how prolific s/he is) (4) *the listener's relation to the conductor and to the musicians* (5) *the listener's relation to (and the composer's relation to) critics* (6) *the music's relation to program notes and other scholarly materials* (7) *props and physical aspects of the setting* (such as seating, clothing, decoration).

Thus a sociology of musical meaning is also a sociology of styles or modes of work done by the listener and as such it should ask questions about how much work the music requires of the listener. For instance, does s/he find many contextualization cues, as occurs in highly ritualized situations (in which cases s/he need only re-affirm a conventional interpretation of the piece). Or, does s/he find so few contextualization cues that s/he must "on the spot" as it were, manage his/her own production by not constructing the interpretation but the cues of context as well? In this regard, it seems reasonable to say that in settings which are not highly contextualized (where perceived cues are scarce) the actor may be offered more latitude or scope for the work of interpreting the object or, in other words acts to a greater degree as a "com-poser." In a sense then, this question is one of interpretive "worker control" over the production of musical meaning. It seems fair to say then, that the more cues provided (or the meaning "managed") the less equivocal the meaning will seem and the less the range of things which can be imputed or "hung on" to it. Thus the more the music will seem untouchable, sacred or "given."

Further, one could compare the cues presented by the speaker/artist/transmitter, the "vertical" axis, with the cues or resources for meaning "recognition" provided by the hearer(s)/audience/receivers, the "horizontal axis." It seems reasonable to suppose that the greater the ratio of cues provided by the speaker and his/her colleagues to cues provided by the hearer and his/her colleagues, the more the hearer will feel "constrained" to "find" the right or "true" or "real" meaning of the object, by which I mean that s/he will attempt to discover what the speaker *meant* by his/her utterance/act. Thus, it seems sensible to say that the more the contextualization cues of the setting, object or situation are made by the speaker, the more the hearer will feel compelled to conform to what s/he perceives is the right interpretation of the "object" and thus, the more the actual process of meaning construction or "work" will be obfuscated or concealed, or, in other words, the more the actual "labour" of meaning construction will seem "invisible." Thus, a crucial aspect of any preparatory set is its characteristic division of labour, whether and to what degree there is "worker control" over the tools and resources of meaning construction.

Implications for the way in which Culture is conceived:

In summary, the meaning of objects, utterances and acts is neither inherent nor invariant but socially constitued. With regard to social or conceptual meanings (that is, "count as" phenomena), this implies a dissolution of the subject/object dichotomy as it is generally implicit in conventional theories of meaning "transmission" and "reception." In other words, the perceiving subject constitutes, given perceived constraints, the "object" through interpretation, and further, the meaning of this response or interpretation is in turn constituted by the response *to* the response, and so on. What this in turn implies is that the "field" of meaning generated by speaker/hearers' utterances/objects/acts and responses ought not be conceived of as a bounded linear or additive progression (as if actors move along a column or tube of meaning) but as a multi-dimensional space. This space may be retrospectively reduced to a linear account for the purposes of use, as, for example, an account of what happened or a history.

Thus it is not only music which is characterized by the "problem" of a lack of double articulation (i.e. no one-to-one correspondence of form and function). The same is true for utterances, objects and acts whenever they are perceived as being invested with aesthetic, ideological or ethical con-notations, and this has serious implications for the way in which culture is conceived. For if music may, to some extent be conceived of as a sonic version of a rorschach ink blot, upon which various "words may be hung," then to argue that ". . . poetry (one could substitute music) makes nothing happen (as Clifford Geertz, quoting Auden, does, 1973, p. 443) is to put forward, at least implicitly, a view of culture as distinct from or disinterested in what Geertz seems to see as the "vulgar" aspects of interests. These interests inhabit the realm of social structure as defined by access to various resources, symbolic and material.

Rather, we should see (as Bourdieu has argued, 1983, p. 92 and throughout) that culture represents a struggle over the definition of social reality and therefore, the issue of the meaning of objects is also an issue of who defines or appropriates them, where, when, how and for what purpose. A group's or nation's culture, in other words, should not be conceived of as a set of "cultural goods," but rather as set of tools, conditions, alibis, etc., whose meaning is reflexively related to the ways in which it is appropriated. Given this perspective, one can see why, for instance, thinkers from Plato and Aristotle through Tolstoy (and continuing today) saw music as a "dangerous art" (Cooke 1960, p. 272) which required legislation, not for the reasons Cooke argues:

". . . whatever else the mysterious art known as music eventually be found to express, it is primarily and basically a language of emotions, through which we directly experience the fundamental urges that move mankind, without the need of falsifying ideas and images — words and pictures" (p. 272).

but because it provides a forum, *par excellence*, for the "work" of appropriation, that is, a place and space for "work."

We should therefore be interested in the social structure which characterizes this appropriation (its "relations of production" between composers as a group; listeners and composers; composers and critics and listeners; and listeners themselves), which we may be able to describe by distinguishing greater and lesser degrees of author-ity on the part of the composer and his/her colleagues on the one hand and response-ability on the part of the listener and his/her colleagues on the other. We should be willing to consider that these social structural "relations of meaning production/construction" may provide "subliminal" or pedagogic messages which relate to taken-for-granted assumptions about meaning, musical and other: where it *is* and how it is (or should be) conveyed. The subject/object dichotomy for example, and the referential theory of meaning which it implies may be seen as a type of ideology which creates a systematic bias in favour of power, symbolic and material, as the oft-quoted passage from Lewis Carroll's *Through The Looking Glass* (where Humpty

Dumpty explains his theory of language, the "use"-based theory, to Alice, an adherent of the referential theory,) aptly illustrates:

"when *I* use a word, "Humpty Dumpty said, in rather a scornful tone, "it means just what I choose it to mean — neither more or less."
"The question is," said Alice, "whether you *can* make words mean so many different things."
"The question is," said Humpty Dumpty, "which is to be master — that's all."

If, as Humpty Dumpty seems to suggest, the question is "who is to be master?" then perhaps the way to gain mastery in "work" situations is to have control over the rhetorical means of making one's interpretations of objects, utterances or acts seem "as if" they are "objective" ("good," "beauitful" or "true"). This would also be the means of "persuading" the hearer to act toward these things "as if" they are inextricably linked to and signify specific things in an absolute, non-negotiable sense, as if their meaning is determined by some higher authority than mere interpretative "work." (In this regard see Bourdieu, 1983 and Mehan's modified version of W.I. Thomas' theorem: "All people define situations as real; but when powerful people define situations as real, then they are real in their consequences" (Mehan, forthcoming).) It is here, then, that one begins to see why music aesthetics has been and is a "political" issue, political in all the senses of that word.

REFERENCES

Aiken, H.D. 1950. "The Aesthetic Relevance of Belief." *Journal of Aesthetics and Art Criticism.* 9:48–51.

Austin, J. 1961. "Performative Utterances." Pp. 220–239 in J.Austin, *Philosophical Papers.* Oxford: Clarendon.

Barzun, J. 1980. "The Meaning of Meaning in Music: Berlioz Once More." *The Musical Quarterly.* 66:1–20.

Berger, B. 1981. *The Survival of a Counter Culture, Ideological Work and Everyday Life Among Rural Communards.* Berkeley: University of California Press.

Berger, P. and T. Luckman. 1968. *The Social Construction of Reality.* Garden City, NY: Doubleday.

Bittner, E. 1965. "The Concept of Organization." *Social Research.* 32:239–255.

——. 1973. "Objectivity and Realism in Sociology." Pp. 109–128 in *Phenomenological Sociology,* edited by G. Psathas. New York: Wiley.

Blacking, J. 1973. *How Musical is Man?.* Seattle: University of Washington Press.

——. 1976. "Review Essay." *Ethnomusicology.* 20:599–601.

Bourdieu, P. 1984. **Distinction:** *A Social Critique of the Judgement of Taste.* Cambridge: Harvard University Press.

Cicourel, A. 1974. **Cognitive Sociology.** New York: Free Press.

_____. 1980. "Three Models of Discourse Analysis." *Discourse Processes*. 3:101–131.

Clifton, T. 1973. "Music and the a priori." *Journal of Music Theory*. 17:66–85.

Coker, W. 1972. *Music and Meaning*. New York: Free Press.

Cooke, D. 1960. *The Language of Music*. New York: Oxford.

D'Andrade, R. 1984. "Cultural Meaning Systems." Pp. 88–119 in *Cultural Theory: Essays on Mind, Self, and Emotion*, edited by Richard W. Shweder and Robert A. Levine. New York: Cambridge.

Dore, J. and R. P. McDermott. 1982. "Linguistic Indeterminancy and Social Context in Utterance Interpretation." *Language*. 58:373–398.

Duisberg, R. 1984. "On the Role of Affect in Artificial Intelligence and Music." *Perspectives of New Music*. 23:6–32.

Dunsby, J. 1982. "A Hitch Hiker's Guide to Semiotic Music Analysis." *Music Analysis*. 1:235–241.

_____. 1983. "Music and Semiotics: The Nattiez Phase." *The Musical Quarterly*. 69:27–43.

Erikson, F. 1982. "Classroom Discourse as Improvisation: Relations between Academic Task Structure and Social Participation." in *Communicating in the Classroom*, edited by Louise Cherry Wilkinson. New York: Academic Press.

_____. "Anecdote, Rhapsody and Rhetoric: Coherence Strategies in a Discussion Among Black American Adolescents." Forthcoming in *Coherence in Spoken and Written Discourse*, edited by Deborah Teirnan. Norwood, NJ: Ablex Press.

Ferguson, D. 1960. *Music as Metaphor*. Minneapolis: University of Minnesota Press.

Garfinkel, H. 1962. "Common Sense Knowledge of Social Structure: The Documentary Method of Interpretation." Pp. 689–713 in *Theories of the Mind*, edited by J. Scher, New York: Free Press.

Grice, H. Paul. 1975. "Logic and Conversation." Pp. 41–58 in *Syntax and Semantics*, vol. 13, edited by Peter Cole and Jerry L. Morgan. New York: Academic Press.

Gumperz, J. 1977. "Sociocultural Knowledge in Conversational Inference." In *Linguistics and Anthropology*, edited by M. Saville-Troike. Washington, D.C.: Georgetown University Press.

Habermas, J. 1976. *Communication and the Evolution of Society*. Boston: Beacon Press.

Hanslick, E. (1885) 1957. *The Beautiful in Music*. New York: Liberal Arts Press.

Harris, C. and C. Sandresky. 1985. "Love and Death in Classical Music: Methodological Problems in Analyzing Human Meanings in Music." *Symbolic Interaction* 8:291–310.

Hollander, J. 1973. *The Untuning of the Sky*. New York; Norton.

Knief, T. 1974. "Some Non-Communicative Aspects in

Music." *International Review of the Aesthetics and Sociology of Music*. 5:51–59.

Labov, W. and D. Fanshel. 1977. *Therapeutic Discourse: Psychotherapy as Conversation*. New York: Academic Press.

Laing, R.D. 1967. *The Politics of Experience*. New York: Pantheon.

Langer, S. 1951. *Philosophy in a New Key*. New York: New American Library.

_____. 1953. *Feeling and Form*. New York: Scribner.

Lippman, E. 1981. "The Dilemma of Musical Meaning." *International Review of the Aesthetics and the Sociology of Music*. 12:181–189.

Mead, G.H. 1934. *Mind, Self, and Society*. Chicago: University *of Chicago Press*.

Mehan, H. 1983. "Social Constructivism in Psychology and Sociology." *Sociologie et Societes*. 14:77–96.

_____. Forthcoming. "Oracular Reasoning in a Psychiatric Exam: The Resolution of Conflict in Language." In *Conflict Talk: Sociolinguistic Investigations of Arguments in Conversation*, edited by A. Grimshaw. Norwood, NJ: Ablex.

Meyer, L. 1954. *Emotion and Meaning in Music*. Chicago: University of Chicago Press.

Nattiez, J-J. 1973. "Linguistics: A New Approach for Music Analysis?" *International Review of the Aesthetics and the Sociology of Music*. 12:181–189.

_____. 1982. "Varese's Density 21.5: A Study in Semiological Analysis." *Music Analysis* 1:243–289.

Osmond-Smith, D. 1971. "Music as Communication: Semiology or Morphology? *International Review of the Aesthetics and the Sociology of Music*. 2:108–110.

Plavsa, D. 1981. "Intentionality in Music," *International Review of the Aesthetics and the Sociology of Music*. 12:65–74.

Rahn, J. 1972. "Review of Coker's Music and Meaning." *Perspectives of New Music*. 11:255–257.

Rosengard Subotnik, R. 1978. "The Cultural Message of Musical Semiology: Some Thoughts on Music, Language and Criticism since the Enlightenment." *Critical Inquiry*. 4:741–768.

Searle, J. 1967. *Speech Acts*. London: Cambridge University Press.

Stopford, J. 1984. "Structuralism, Semiotics and Musicology." *British Journal of Aesthetics*. 24:129–137.

Streeck, J. "Speech Acts in Interaction: A Critique of Searle." *Discourse Processes*. 4:133–153.

Supicic, I. 1971. "Expression and Meaning in Music." *International Review of the Aesthetics and the Sociology of Music*. 2:193–211.

Turnstall, P. 1979. "Structuralism and Musicology: An Overview." *Current Musicology* 27:51–64.

Willis, D. 1977. *Learning to Labour: How Working Class Kids Get Woking Class Jobs*. New York: Columbia University Press.

Wittgenstein, L. 1953. *Philosophical Investigations*. New York: MacMillan.

CHAPTER 3

Deconstructing Periodization: Sociological Methods and

Historical Ethnography in Late Eighteenth-Century Vienna

I n 1962 the sociologist Harold Garfinkel conducted a notorious (and, in retrospect, unethical) experiment in order to study the informal and often tacit practices characteristic of lay and scientific forms of reasoning.[1] Ten volunteer subjects (undergraduates at the University of California, Los Angeles) were told they would be participating in an attempt to assess alternative techniques for student counseling. Each student took part in a session in which she or he was told to describe a personal problem or dilemma to a purported "counselor," who would then respond only to yes/no questions. Located in a separate room and connected by microphone, the counselor could not be seen by the student. After asking each question and receiving an answer, the student was then asked to unplug the connecting microphone and to comment on the exchange. After this, the student was then free to plug the microphone back in and ask another question, in which case the cycle began again. Students were told they could ask any number of questions but that most people tended to ask about ten.

Unknown to the students, the counselor's sequence of answers had been evenly divided between "yes" and "no" and randomly ordered in advance. After the session finished, each student was asked to summarize his or her impressions of the process, and this was followed by an interview. Perhaps not surprisingly, the students had little difficulty in making sense of the answers they received. Not only did they report that they could see "what the adviser had in mind," many commented

1. Harold Garfinkel, "Common Sense Knowledge of Social Structures: The Documentary Method of Interpretation," in his *Studies in Ethnomethodology* (Cambridge: Polity, 1984), pp.76–103.

on the good quality of the advice they were offered. They actively referred to the presence of what they perceived as an underlying *pattern* to the exchanges, and, over the course of the series, they proved extremely adept and creative at accounting for the continued presence of a logical thread to the proceedings.

Garfinkel's titular phrase "documentary method" referred to the two-way, retrospective and prospective process of bringing together individual occurrences (data) and the underlying patterns to which these data are said to conform. The documentary method is the activity of relating pattern and appearance, or "container" and "contents": theories and facts, categories and instances. Garfinkel's experiment illustrated how theories and categories are capacious—they can be modified to accommodate seemingly discrepant instances. It also illustrated how the ways in which investigations proceed (and the ways data are collected, coded, and classified) are shaped by the interpretive predispositions of theories and categories, by the preassumptions and expectations about where order will lie, and by the habits of perception brought to bear on phenomena. Thus, for example, if one accepts the underlying theoretical assumption of "this is a counseling session," advice may be presented in an unusual, idiosyncratic, and seemingly contradictory manner, but it is digested as advice nonetheless.

Garfinkel's early studies, along with the works of philosophers who inspired him, have since become a source of inspiration to the social studies of science, as this subfield has burgeoned over the past fifteen years.[2] The ambition of science studies is by no means to debunk science, although the field is often misread in this way.[3] On the contrary, the new sociology of science attempts to document the *inevitably* social and constructed character of *all* knowledge and to study, as a distinct topic, the procedures, practices, and politics by which knowledge is manufactured. Within this view, knowledge "discovery" is simultaneously knowledge construction, and all knowledge—even those forms that come to be associated with efficacious applications (such as medical remedies)—can be understood as involving selective representations of reality. Thus, it is *through* the process of selection, not in spite of it, that the work of science gets done.

In other words, scientific practice is discursive. Through a variety of historically specific lenses (commitments to underlying patterns and classification), scientific activity constructs its object, as opposed to merely reporting on it. This is true

2. See, e.g., *Science Observed: Perspectives on the Social Study of Science,* ed. Karin Knorr-Cetina and Michael Mulkay (London: Sage, 1983); Bruno Latour, *Science in Action: How to Follow Scientists and Engineers through Society* (Cambridge, Mass.: Harvard UP, 1987).

3. See Barry Barnes, "Thomas Kuhn and the Sociology of Knowledge," in *Common Knowledge (2)* (forthcoming).

3 TIA DENORA

whether that object is a quark, a biological process, the coherence of a string of answers, or, as I shall discuss, the history of a life. The lessons about knowledge production drawn from sociology's focus on practical reasoning can be applied profitably to the topic of Beethoven's life and works.

Specifically, I shall offer an intentionally polemical attempt to rethink or deconstruct the notion of periodization as applied to Beethoven, to look critically at periodization as a way of accounting for Beethoven's artistic development. Assuming that periodization is a retrospectively imposed narrative or way of organizing and describing Beethoven's life and works, I shall consider the effects this narrative has had on the study of Beethoven's career and social identity during his first ten years in Vienna and then from this vantage point explore some of the ways in which the periodization paradigm may have a debilitating influence on how Beethoven's early life and career has been portrayed.

According to Garfinkel, "The documentary method is used whenever the investigator constructs a life history. . . . The task of historicizing [a] person's biography consists of using the documentary method to select and order past occurrences so as to furnish the present state of affairs its relevant past and prospects."[4] Garfinkel wants to reconsider biography as an analytical topic rather than as a resource for more general explanatory narratives. To approach biography as a resource is to put one's investigative energies into the search for the essential, most "accurate" or "true" version of a life. By contrast, treating biography as topic is to approach biography as a representation of reality and as a narrative achievement. And insofar as biography is achieved, it is also negotiated and subject to contention. As Gordon Bowker recently observed, biography as topic is not only "a version of the past capable of being cynically distorted, but [also] subject to forgetfulness, selective rewriting and radical reassessment, a narrative under constant revision."[5] The representation of a life is a micropolitical arena—and the study of biography as a topic is the study of the struggle over *what is to count* as the accepted, and at times officially sanctioned, version.

The details of a given life exceed any narrative or interpretive framework that purports to account for them. For any life, therefore, there are a multiplicity of accounts that could be offered. Yet, in practice these alternative or oppositional readings may often appear untenable. Is this because there are some versions of a life

4. Garfinkel, "Common Sense Knowledge," p.95.
5. Gordon Bowker, "The Age of Biography is upon Us," *Times Higher Education Supplement,* 8 January 1993, p.19.

that are "wrong?" Not necessarily. Any particular narrative will bring some details
to the fore while, inevitably, diverting attention from others.[6] It will divide up a
lived totality into events, phases, stages, advances, errors, and so on. When a
particular biographical discourse is authorized, and a life is cast within specific
configurations of such things as motivation, culpability, credibility, and agency,
alternative attempts to account for the reality of this life will often appear tenuous,
fictitious, or inaccurate representations of "what happened." It is crucial to recognize the constitutive role that interpretive frameworks play in identity construction
because in schools,[7] courts of law,[8] and other institutions explicitly concerned with
the production and assessment of identity these consequences can be serious.

The sociologist Norman Denzin has suggested that lives are produced through
words, through the narrative shapes into which events are cast. According to
Denzin, biography as topic should be approached with the analytical techniques
associated with literary theory. Biography should be studied for its conventional
structures, figures, metaphors, and registers. Periods, turning points, stages, phases,
crises, advances, setbacks, tragedy, comedy, and farce are all to be considered as
examples of the convenient molds for shaping a life. Denzin's concern with *literary*
devices leaves unexplored the material practices and technologies that buttress
literary accounts (e.g., the social location of the "biographer" or the ability to
control the ways in which a biographical subject actually appears and acts in his or
her world).[9] I have elsewhere considered the importance of material practices to
Beethoven's reputation;[10] here I shall consider more explicitly how a focus on

6. The commitment of Garfinkel's students to the incorrigible proposition that they were receiving "advice" is relevant. For another, simpler example, consider Wittgenstein's famous doodle of
what can be understood, depending on how one looks at it, as a rabbit or a duck (John Heritage,
Garfinkel and Ethnomethodology [Cambridge: Polity, 1984]), pp.86–87. In both cases, understanding
emerges from the ways that social actors draw together instances and theories. Practices of putting
theories and instances together are often a matter of routine. There are, in many situations, institutionalized patterns of practice, preferred and canonic forms of accounting, such as the musicological
institution of tripartite periodization in Beethoven scholarship. Alternative ways of accounting may
seem inadequate because they are not so well used, elaborated, and familiar within a community of
practice. But this does not mean that under different circumstances they could not have been equally
serviceable or that they are absolutely inferior.

7. Hugh Mehan, Alma Hertweck, and J. Lee Meihls, *Handicapping the Handicapped* (Stanford:
Stanford UP, 1986).

8. Aaron V. Cicourel, *The Social Organization of Juvenile Justice* (New York: Wiley, 1968).

9. Norman Denzin, *Interpretive Biography* (Newbury Park: Sage, 1989).

10. See my "Beethoven, the Viennese Canon, and the Sociology of Identity, 1793–1803" *Beethoven Forum* 2 (1993), 29–53. Literary representations are only one modality for the construction of
social reality, although some sociologists have tended to view all social construction as literary

biography as literature enriches Beethoven studies, and how this focus illuminates
the topic of Beethoven's early reputation in the Vienna of his contemporaries.

Twenty years ago, in his essay on Beethoven's creative periods, Maynard Solomon
described the three-stage notion of development as initially applied to Beethoven
during the 1830s, as elaborated during the 1840s and 50s, and as subsequently
institutionalized as a commonplace of musicological discourse. Solomon described
how the tripartite division of "stages" was available as an existing literary trope,
that it was as much applied *to* as derived *from* the particularities of Beethoven's life
and works.[11] Of course, this trope was mobilized to describe not only Beethoven;
teleological notions of development and of progress were currently being articulated in order to talk about the evolution of organisms and of societies as well.
Indeed, they are the linchpins of the modernist project within the social and
biological sciences.

Within developmental discourse, a variety of interpretive categories are interchangeably mapped on to each other: (1) childhood, manhood, old age; (2) beginning, middle, end; (3) early, middle, late; and (4), with regard to Beethoven,
imitation, heroism, reflection. The implications for the so-called first style period
are therefore fairly clear. Within this narrative structure, the years between 1793
and 1802 constitute a foreshadowing of what follows. Moreover, by implication,
Haydn and Mozart are retrospectively constructed as leading up to Beethoven.
According to A. Peter Brown, works have been ordered in Haydn chronology so as
to elucidate the movement of musical paths that *culminate* in Beethoven.[12]

A cursory survey of the Beethoven literature reveals some of the ways in which
the musical-developmental discourse has informed Beethoven studies. The late
1790s are referred to as: (1) "the Haydn years";[13] (2) the years of "imitation" as
opposed to the "experimental" middle period;[14] (3) or the years during which
Beethoven absorbed a Classical heritage and mastered the Classical models of
Mozart and Haydn.[15] Douglas Johnson considers these to be the years during

---

construction. Such a perspective fails to consider how social relations can be built into nonliterary
forms such as technologies (Latour, *Science in Action*, pp.141–70), and how the authority of specific
literary accounts is often related to the issue of who writes and reads them.

11. Maynard Solomon, "The Creative Periods of Beethoven," in *Essays*, pp.116–25.

12. A. Peter Brown, *Joseph Haydn's Keyboard Music: Sources and Style* (Bloomington: Indiana UP,
1986), p.113.

13. Solomon, "Creative Periods," p.122.

14. Joseph Kerman and Alan Tyson, *The New Grove Beethoven* (London: Macmillan, 1983), p.90.

15. Douglas Johnson, "1794–1795: Decisive Years in Beethoven's Early Development," BS III,
pp.1–28.

which Beethoven came "to grips systematically with the most sophisticated elements of Classical style."[16] Yet, Beethoven is by no means depicted during these
years as conforming ritualistically to prior models. The relationship between his
works and models is always depicted as dynamic. Indeed, there is a built-in paradox
in the way the first style period is conceptualized within the three-stage narrative,
one that both emphasizes Beethoven's continuity with previous masters and simultaneously differentiates and elevates Beethoven's accomplishments. This is most
visible in the types of stories that have been told about Beethoven's relationship with Haydn, where, on the one hand, there are successive renditions of the
"Haydn's hands" narrative and, on the other, stories of the falling out of Haydn and
Beethoven, when the former was reputedly unable to recognize the value of
Beethoven's more, as the story has it, artistically "adventurous" works.[17]

Rather than attempting to reduce what would have been a complex and, no
doubt, contradictory relationship into one or the other caricatures that these
opposing stories offer, we can account for the ambiguity of Beethoven's situation
in Vienna during the 1790s. To start with, there are alternative ways of coming to
know (constructing) the historical context of Beethoven's Vienna.

Interpreted from a sociological perspective, biographical material about Beethoven was already being collected and disseminated by his contemporaries during
the 1790s. Specifically, members of Beethoven's support network engaged in an
ongoing project of "writing" his biography, of updating it from moment to moment. This attempt to establish a "record" was simultaneously the creation of
resources for shaping future expectations of Beethoven's importance: Beethoven's
future importance was projected in reports about his *present* standing. These projec-
tions depicted Beethoven as "heir" to *and* transcender of the tradition of Viennese
classicism, as having both absorbed and transcended Haydn's and Mozart's own
innovations. By examining Beethoven's career during the 1790s, we can observe
the documentary processes that located Beethoven inside an interpretive framework that depicted him as revolutionary *and* traditionalist.

If, however, we view the years of the first style period through the lens of the
periodization narrative, many of these issues remain out of focus. It is time to

16. Ibid., p.2.

17. Count Ferdinand Ernst von Waldstein's entry in Beethoven's autograph book, 1789: "With
the help of assiduous labour you shall inherit Mozart's spirit from Haydn's hands." This is the first in a
series of tropes on this theme. See also James Webster, "The Falling-out between Haydn and
Beethoven: The Evidence of the Sources," in *Beethoven Essays: Studies in Honor of Elliot Forbes,* ed.
Lewis Lockwood, Phyllis Benjamin (Cambridge, Mass.: Harvard University Department of Music,
1984), pp.3–45.

reanimate the 1790s and to recover some of their social significance for the ideology of canonical music that was first articulated during these years. One way of doing this is to follow Beethoven and his contemporaries in action—to examine how these historical actors presented, re-presented, and occasionally squabbled over the value of Beethoven's work. To look at music history this way not only reanimates it socially, but makes it *palpable* because actors are involved in the dynamic process of defining and securing the contexts of their own activity.

We need to approach the 1790s as social ethnographers, to attempt to construct the context of social action from the assertions and points of view of its participants. The interpretive categories now used in music analysis must be exchanged for those of the social actors being studied; otherwise there is no basis for knowing whether our findings are a by-product of a retrospectively constructed accounting framework, or whether the things found in the history of Beethoven's life and works are the very things that our predecessors may have planted as "pointers" for both their contemporaries and posterity.

In short, we want to compare our own twentieth-century ways of seeing Beethoven with those of his contemporaries. Although an accord between these ways of seeing is possible, we must not assume, a priori, that we share a culture with these actors, or indeed, that we should think of a culture as "sharable" at all. Our own musicological discourse and its origins are problematic. We must attempt to distinguish between the usefulness of the periodization notion for music criticism and analysis (and its attendant concern with the search for Beethoven's models) and the usefulness of periodization as a sensitizing concept for social history. How can we begin to make this shift?

Charles Rosen has suggested that, with the "Hammerklavier" Sonata of 1817–18, "the emancipation of piano music from the demands of the amateur musician was made official, with a consequent loss of responsibility and a greater freedom for the imagination."[18] Statements such as this, which attempt to assess stylistic turning points in a composer's body of works, are problematic from a sociological point of view. From the vantage point of the late twentieth century (and faced with a relatively finite corpus of works by Beethoven),[19] it has become conventional to view the piano works of the 1790s as still within a "Classical" mold and oriented to

18. Charles Rosen, *The Classical Style* (New York: Norton, 1972), p.404.

19. It is "relatively" finite because the corpus can potentially be revised in light of new discoveries, redating and authentication, and, as has most recently been the case, "reconstructions" or, "constructions" of works from sketches, such as Barry Cooper's work on Beethoven's Tenth Symphony.

8 TIA DENORA

the demands of the amateur musician. It is also conventional, within the periodization paradigm, to view the "break" with classicism as coming later in Beethoven's
compositional development.[20]

Whereas assumptions such as these may be persuasive and accord with both
common sense and late twentieth-century music-analytical perspectives, they also
tend to close off potentially fruitful lines of historical research. This is the case for at
least two reasons. First, they treat (at least implicitly) classicism and musical "emancipation . . . from the demands of the amateur" as objective developments that can
be accurately dated, rather than as symbolic and as constructed out of socially and
historically located categories of analysis or "ways of looking" at music history.[21]
Second, these assumptions tend fallaciously to imply that at any point in the history
of Beethoven reception our twentieth-century analytical categories could be le-
gitimately applied to previous musical cultures, that they can serve as a legitimate
yardstick for assessing the musical past. The very notion that there is *one* history
rather than a multiplicity of narrative accounts from time-to-time and place-to-
place throughout the period is itself a resource for constructing this assumption.
This is not to suggest that we do not share a culture with Beethoven's contemporaries, but simply to suggest that we cannot accept in any a priori way that we do.[22]

To be sure, from a late twentieth-century point of view, we may assume that the
formal distance between the Piano Sonatas, op.2, and the music of not only Mozart
or Haydn but even Gelinek or Kozeluch is smaller or less significant than that
between op.2 and the "Hammerklavier." Although this may indeed seem right to
us, it is wrong to assume (without attempting to verify) that a hypothetical listener
in the 1790s would perceive Beethoven's early works as "not very different" from
works by Mozart. To do so would mean that we impute to the 1790s listener our
own retrospective frame of reference, that we assume 1790s listeners would hear
op.2 in light of subsequent music by Beethoven and other composers. The source
of our error here lies in failing to consider the *relativity* of reception (always a

20. Indeed, the very idea of "the Classical style" is a retrospective construct.

21. Leo Treitler develops an argument along lines similar to these in "The Politics of Reception:
Tailoring the Present as Fulfillment of a Desired Past," *Journal of the Royal Musical Association* 2 (1991),
280–98.

22. On this point, see Steven Shapin and Simon Shaeffer, *Leviathan and the Air-Pump* (Princeton,
N.J.: Princeton UP, 1985), chap.1. Historians, they suggest, "produc[e] accounts that are colored by
the member's self-evident method. In this method the presuppositions of our own culture's routine
practices are not regarded as problematic and in need of explanation . . . [they] start with the
assumption that they (and modern scientists) share a culture with Robert Boyle, and treat their subject
accordingly: the historian and the seventeenth-century experimentalist are both members" (p.5).

9 TIA DENORA

problem with historical research), the ways in which listeners' responses are constructed with reference to the contemporaneous categories of analysis and evaluation.[23]

This point is one of the fundamental lessons of social ethnography, interpretive
sociology, and critical discussions of method and measurement, all of which concern themselves with cultural relativity, multiple realities, and the social construction of the object. While music scholarship too is often concerned with
meaning and symbolic reality, the absence, until fairly recently, of bridges between
musicology and the human sciences has meant that the discourses of music analysis
have often made use of naively positivist narrative strategies. By the term *naive
positivism,* I mean modes of accounting that postulate categories of analysis as
historically transcendent. Naive positivist modes of accounting in music analysis
can perhaps be best viewed when analysts turn their attention to the issue of music's
social meanings. This is especially true of analyses that "read" musical texts as if the
referents of these texts were *in* the text as opposed to socially/culturally constructed through the interaction of text and recipient, as if the act of writing about
music were not part of the meaning construction process.[24] Once we realize the
importance of contexts of reception, however, we can consider conventional
musicological positions more critically and rethink the ways in which music reception is an important component of music history.

Thus, from a sociological standpoint, Beethoven's reception during the 1790s
and early 1800s emerges as arguably *the* most interesting period for Beethoven
research. How, then, was Beethoven's music during the 1790s experienced, not by
analysts of the late nineteenth and the twentieth centuries, but by members of the
Viennese concert and salon publics at the time of its composition?

With respect to the various turning points to be found in Beethoven's work, and
with regard to the status of the "first" or "imitative" style period, we need to
consider how the distance between early Beethoven and the so-called Classical
legacy may seem fairly small to us in retrospect, but may have been perceived quite
differently by those who were not granted the "benefit" of hindsight. We need to
appreciate the accounts his listeners actually offered about their responses to his
music, not as a window into the psychology of Beethoven reception, but as a way
of exploring the uses of that music in context. How was the social impact of

23. For a more thorough discussion of the theoretical basis of these points, see my "How is Extra-
musical Meaning Possible? Music as a Place and Space for 'Work'," in *Sociological Theory* (1986), 84–94.

24. See my "Musical Composition of Reality? Music, Action and Reflexivity," *Sociological Review*
(forthcoming).

Beethoven's music defined by specific individuals within a specific context? What was the repertoire of accounts that could be and were offered about Beethoven's output?

Table 1 lists some of the extant contemporary descriptions of Beethoven's music during the 1790s and the early 1800s. These sources at least implicitly compare Beethoven's work with that of his contemporaries. All are well-known sources, and many have been disseminated in the Beethoven literature. From the perspective of his contemporaries, the "departure" from the amateur tradition that Rosen perceives as having occurred at the time of the "Hammerklavier" Sonata (1817–18) can be construed as occurring far earlier in Beethoven's career, indeed as early as 1795. To be sure, from our late twentieth-century vantage point, this may not seem much of a departure at all. But the closer we get to the habits and modes of music apprehension relevant to 1790s Vienna, the more this break appears to be magnified: " 'One day,' reports Frau von Bernhard[25] . . . 'Streicher[26] put some things by Beethoven in front of her; they were the Piano Sonatas, Op.2, which had just appeared at Artaria's. He told her that there are new things in them which the ladies do not wish to play, because they are incomprehensible and too difficult; would she like to learn them'?"[27]

In a similar vein, Carl Czerny reports that

Mozart's clear and markedly brilliant playing . . . was more suited to the German Fortepianos which combine a delicate and shallow touch with a great clarity and thus are best adapted for general use and for use by children. . . . Beethoven, who appeared around 1790, drew entirely new and daring passages from the Fortepiano by use of the pedal, by an exceptionally characteristic way of playing, particularly distinguished by a strict legato of the chords and thus created a new type of singing tone and many hitherto unimagined effects. His playing did not possess that clean and brilliant elegance of certain other pianists. On the other hand, it was spirited . . . and, especially in the adagio, very full of feeling.[28]

25. Née von Kissow. She was in Vienna from 1796 to 1800 and lived at the home of a Russian Embassy Secretary (Thayer-Forbes, p.401).

26. To be discussed below. Johann Andreas was the husband of the piano maker Nanette Stein and manager of Geschwister Stein, Vienna's premier piano firm (Thayer-Forbes, p.189).

27. H. C. Robbins Landon, *Haydn: Chronicle and Works,* 5 vols. (Bloomington: Indiana UP, 1976–80), IV, 67.

28. Czerny, "Recollections from My Life," MQ 42 (1956), 302.

II TIA DENORA

Table 1: Contemporary Beethoven Reception, 1793–1802

Name	Date of contact	Date of event described	Date of writing	Nature of source; Original dissemination
A. Contemporary Accounts				
1. Junker	1791	1791	1791	Bossler's *Musikalische Correspondenz*
2. Haydn	1793	ca. 1793	1793	Letter to Max Franz, Elector of Cologne
3. Schönfeld	by 1796	by 1796	by 1796	Entry in *Jahrbuch der Tonkunst*
4. AmZ	1798	by 1798–99	1798–99	4 reviews in vol.1
5. AmZ	1799	by 1799–1800	1799–1800	2 reviews in vol.2
6. AmZ	1802	by 1801–02	1801–02	2 reviews in vol.4
B. Retrospective Accounts				
7. Schenk	1793–94	1793	1830	Autobiography (MS)
8. Seyfried	1799	1799	by 1832	*Beethoven's Studien*, 1832 Anhang
9. Moscheles	ca. 1808	1804	by 1841	Preface to Schindler (1841)
10. Czerny	ca. 1793 or later	1795–1805	1842	Autobiography (MS)
11. Tomaschek	1789	1798	1844	1845 in *Libussa*
12. Jahn		1787	by 1889	1889 biography of Mozart

As the composer Johann Wenzel Tomashek observed: "I admired his brilliant and powerful playing but I did not over-look his often daring leaps from one motive to another, whereby the organic connection and a gradual development of ideas is lacking. . . . Not infrequently, the unsuspecting listener is jolted violently out of his state of joyful transports. The most important thing in composition for him seems to be the unusual and original."[29]

Elsewhere I have compared in some detail the reception of Beethoven and his pianistic rival of 1799, Joseph Wölffl. According to Ignaz von Seyfried:

29. Robbins Landon, *Beethoven: A Documentary Study* (New York: Macmillan, 1970), p.104.

In his improvisations even then Beethoven did not deny his tendency toward the mysterious and gloomy. . . . It was the mystical Sanscrit language whose hieroglyphs can be read only by the initiated. Wölffl, on the contrary, trained in the school of Mozart, was always equable; never superficial but always clear and thus more accessible to the multitude. He used art only as a means to an end, never to exhibit his acquirements. He always enlisted the interest of his hearers and inevitably compelled them to follow the progression of his well-ordered ideas.[30]

Of course, these accounts are retrospective, and one could therefore argue that they are no better than the retrospective music analytical and music historical accounts that I have criticized from a sociological point of view. In other words, on what basis should we privilege *these* retrospective accounts?

We can compare these accounts, which were written by individuals who had contact with Beethoven during the 1790s, with those actually written in that decade. Here the evidence becomes more compelling. In his excellent book on the critical reception of Beethoven in the AmZ, Robin Wallace has documented how, until around 1802, there was critical opposition to Beethoven, primarily over the issue of his overly complex and too-learned music; moreover, this opposition was directed not only to Beethoven's more "serious" genres but also to his "lighter" and ostensibly more popular variations ("Herr v. B. may be able to improvise, but he does not understand how to write variations").[31] Indeed, when the AmZ began to recognize Beethoven as a special talent, it did so by creating a special category for him, by recognizing that Beethoven could actually be entitled to "go his own way."[32] The first intimation of this special treatment appears in the discussion of the Piano Sonatas, op.10, in volume 2 (9 October 1799), where Beethoven's music is described as oriented to the educated musician. Setting aside Beethoven as a composer of difficult and serious works, the anonymous Viennese correspondent to the AmZ (April 1799) described the Beethoven-Wölffl duels in a passage that, for the first time in the extant Beethoven reception, explicitly likens Beethoven to Mozart by emphasizing Mozart's ability to improvise:

> Opinion is divided here touching the merits of the two [Beethoven and Wölffl]; yet it would seem as if the majority were on the side of the latter

30. Thayer-Forbes, pp.206–07. See my "Beethoven-Wölffl Duel," in *Music in Austria, 1750–1800*, David Wyn Jones (Cambridge: Cambridge U P, forthcoming).

31. Robin Wallace, *Beethoven's Critics: Aesthetic Dilemmas and Resolutions during the Composer's ?time* (Cambridge: Cambridge U P, 1986), p.7.

32. Thayer-Forbes, p.278.

13 TIA DENORA

[Wölffl]. I shall try to set forth the peculiarities of each without taking part in the controversy. Beethoven's playing is extremely brilliant but has less delicacy and occasionally he is guilty of indistinctness. He shows himself to the greatest advantage in improvisation, and here, indeed, it is most extraordinary with what lightness and yet firmness in the succession of ideas Beethoven not only varies a theme given him on the spur of the moment by figuration (with which many a virtuoso makes his fortune and—wind) but really develops it. Since the death of Mozart, who in this respect is for me still the *non plus ultra,* I have never enjoyed this kind of pleasure in the degree in which it is provided by Beethoven. In this Wölffl fails to reach him. But W. has advantages in that he, sound in musical learning and dignified in his compositions, plays passages which seem impossible with an ease, precision and clearness which cause amazement (of course he is helped here by the large structure of his hands) and that his interpretation is always, especially in Adagios, so pleasing and insinuating that one can not only admire it but also enjoy. . . . That Wölffl likewise enjoys an advantage because of his amiable bearing, contrasted with the somewhat haughty pose of Beethoven, is very natural.[33]

Thus, while we may perceive continuity between Beethoven's early works and the works of his predecessors, and while Beethoven and his patrons sought to convince others that this continuity really existed ("Mozart's spirit from Haydn's hands"), we cannot afford to ignore the differences that Beethoven's contemporaries reported perceiving in his music. The issue should not revolve around whether Beethoven's works "really were" continuous with Mozart's or Haydn's. Indeed, this purely analytical question is far less interesting than the question of how Beethoven's perceived continuity/discontinuity with previous composers had political implications, how it affected the shape of musical reputations, and how particular interpretations of Beethoven's work and his relation to his predecessors were constructed and publicized over time. I have suggested elsewhere that we should be willing to consider how that process involved a reconceptualization of Mozart and Haydn in relation to Beethoven,[34] and how, more broadly, we can observe a partial eclipse of *Liebhaber* or amateur-oriented taste during the

33. Thayer-Forbes, p.205.

34. See my *Mozart's Spirit from Haydn's Hands?: The Social Bases and Social Consequences of Beethoven's Success and Vanguard Style during His First Decade in Vienna, 1792–1803* (Ph.D. diss., University of California, San Diego, 1989).

1790s, and an amplification of the popular/serious dualism that "waxed and waned over a long period of public and private music activities."[35]

Beethoven's music was perceived by its late eighteenth-century audiences as falling outside conventional boundaries of musical value. This perception of "difference," I believe, provided a potential resource for him.[36] To the extent that his music was accepted, Beethoven could become a force within the Viennese music world; his music could be upheld as an exemplar or new standard against which the works of his contemporaries and predecessors could be assessed. On the one hand, the more his works were praised, the greater the challenge their different aesthetic posed to conventional notions of musical value. On the other, Beethoven's differences were poised simultaneously as a potential liability; they were not designed for safe, routine, or inauspicious forms of success. In short, from the point of view of his contemporaries, his controversial and different music implied new criteria of value. When these new criteria were not invoked, Beethoven's music was placed in a weak position. But when they were developed and disseminated, Beethoven's music was empowered for reconfiguring the music-evaluative space. The oft-quoted review of the *Eroica* (possibly written by August von Kotzebue) of 1805 makes it clear that this point of view was discussed among Beethoven's contemporaries themselves:

> Beethoven's most special friends contend this particular symphony is a masterpiece, that it is exactly the true style for music of the highest type and that if it does not please now it is because the public is not sufficiently cultivated in the arts to comprehend these higher spheres of beauty; but after a couple of thousand years its effect will not be lessened. The other party absolutely denies any artistic merit to this work. They claim that it reveals the symptoms of an evidently unbridled attempt at distinction and peculiarity, but that neither beauty, true sublimity nor power have anywhere been achieved either by means of unusual modulations, by violent transitions or by the juxtaposition of the most heterogeneous elements. . . . The creation of something beautiful and sublime, not the production of something merely unusual and fantastic, is the true expression of genius. . . . The third, very small party stand in the middle. They concede that there are many beautiful things in the symphony, but admit that the continuity often appears to be completely confused and that the endless duration of this longest and perhaps most

35. Julia Moore, personal correspondence.
36. See my "Beethoven, the Viennese Canon," pp. 51–52.

difficult of all symphonies is tiring even for the expert; for a mere amateur it is
unbearable. . . . One fears . . . that if Beethoven continues along this road, he
and the public will make a bad journey. Music could easily reach a state where
everyone who has not been vouchsafed a thorough knowledge of the rules
and difficulties of the art will derive absolutely no pleasure from it.[37]

For his work to succeed, then, Beethoven's perceived differences had to be
protected from misapprehension, and a different evaluative frame (or frames) had
to be constructed. A consideration of how his work was protected and sponsored
by Beethoven's patronage network of aristocratic princes will lead us back from
ethnobiography and the ethnography of reception to the social history and sociology of cultural practice; more specifically, the goal is to raise questions about
musical taste and social structure, and the then changing organizational basis of
Vienna's high cultural music world.[38]

37. Robbins Landon, *Beethoven: A Documentary Study*, pp.153–54.

38. I use the term *organizational basis* in preference to *institutional basis*. The latter term implies
formalized and routine patterns of concert life. In Vienna during these years, after the decline of the
Hauskapellen, musical events were organized in an ad hoc way. The concert did not emerge as a
musical institution until well into the nineteenth century. Regarding music in Vienna at this time, see
my "Musical Patronage and Social Change in Beethoven's Vienna," *American Journal of Sociology* 97
(1991), 310–46.

CHAPTER 4

The musical composition of social reality? Music, action and reflexivity[1]

Abstract

Developments in the sociology of music during the 1980s have
brought the sub-field more firmly in to the center of sociological concerns. The 'worlds' concept, and the concern with music and social
status have helped to ground and specify links between music and
society. Meanwhile however, questions concerning music's social content have been sidelined. This paper explores music as an active ingredient in the constitution of lived experience. As with other
cultural/technical forms, music provides a resource for the articulation
of thought and activity. Bodily conduct and movement, the experience
of time, and social character within opera are used to illustrate this
point. Recent developments in feminist music analysis have been sug-
gestive for the ways in which music metaphorizes social processes and
categories of being. These developments can enrich the sociology of
music. However, as with all attempts to 'read' music's social content,
they should be conceived as claims made by analysts who are themselves engaged in social projects. Analytical readings of music have no
a priori claim of privilege. A constructivist sociology of music should
therefore be devoted to the question of how specific music users forge
links between musical significance and social life. A sociology of the
construction and deployment of musical realities is capable of avoiding the naive positivism otherwise implicit in attempts to 'read'
music's social content.

In recent years, the 'new' sociology of music has considerably
enriched our understanding of music's link to social formation,
opening up a range of new topics for sociological exploration. The
focus of this work has been directed at, among other things, the
social shaping of repertory (Gilmore, 1987, 1988 and 1990), the
construction of the musical canon as a cultural-entrepreneurial
strategy (DiMaggio, 1982; DeNora, 1991; Weber, 1992), reception

Tia DeNora

controversies (Pasler, 1987), music distribution (Blau, 1990), the international and occupational conditions of music production and collaboration (Abbott and Hrycak, 1990; Faulkner, 1971, 1983; Hennion, 1983), organizational constraints on music marketing (Peterson and Berger, 1974; DiMaggio and Hirsh, 1976), and arts audiences and taste publics (DiMaggio and Useem, 1978; Gans, 1974; Bourdieu, 1984).

The results of this work have been sociologically satisfying on a number of levels. Produced, for the most part, since Becker's now classic (1982) application of a 'studies of work' perspective to art, this research has effectively unhooked the sociology of music (and art more broadly) from the otherwise powerful ideology of 'Great' art. Simultaneously, it has led to a growing concern with demonstrably *grounding* statements about music's social qualities through accounts that stick close to the level of social action, the 'who, where, when, what and how' of Music and Society.

In these two respects, these (primarily American) attempts to develop a new trajectory for the sociology of culture provided an effective antidote, during the 1980s, to what Bennett Berger described as 'culturology' (1985 ms) by which he meant a 'sociology' of art devoted to the production of 'readings' of art works or styles in order to uncover (decode) the ways that they reflect or run parallel to 'Society' (to, that is, ideology or relations of production).

Perhaps not surprisingly, this 'Grand' tradition of sociology of art often exasperated music historians. In an article that sought to reassert the value of grounded historical work in musicology (at a time when the field had begun to move toward social theory), the music scholar Hans Lenneberg baldly complained that, 'one cannot say a *Zeitgeist* reached a composer or other artist unless one can show the means by which it did' (1988: 419).[2] From the music historian's point of view, 'readings' of cultural works, or observations of how one thing (music) 'reflects' another (society), did not problematize the *processes* of encoding and decoding. Analytical attempts to decode works of music suffered from the fallacy of the 'missing middle'; they did not attempt to describe the processes by which the social actually comes to be inscribed in the musical and they were unable to describe *how* homologies between art works and social formations come to be generated, reproduced and transformed. As the poet Ed Dorn once – perhaps more eloquently – put it (in reference to a very different set of concerns), culturological readings

Music, action and reflexivity

left the sociology of art stranded in, 'that great Zero/Resting eternally between parallels' (1978: 73).

It was this 'gap' that the Art Worlds perspective attempted to fill by focusing on artistic production as it occurs within art 'worlds' – intermediate or 'meso' structures (Gilmore, 1990; Clark, 1990)[3] poised between large-scale notions such as 'Social Structure' or 'Ideology' and individual art workers. As Howard S. Becker put it in his 'Letter to Charles Seeger':

> Sociologists working in this [the Art World's] mode aren't much interested in 'decoding' art works, in finding the work's secret meanings as reflections of society. They prefer to see those works as the result of what a lot of people have done jointly (1989: 282).

Back to the music

To be sure, the Art World's focus militated against long-distance research relationships with empirical materials. Indeed, with regard to musical topics, the 'worlds' approach has provided an increasingly recognized basis for discussion and collaboration between music history and sociology of music.[4] Paradoxically though, this 'journey into context' has simultaneously been a journey away from a concern, however conceived, with the social *presence* of the artistic text or object. By concentrating upon how art is made, contested, distributed and purchased, the 'new' sociology of culture has specified many of the ways that art works are 'shaped' by the social organization, interests, conventions and capacities contained within specific Art Worlds. But the 'career' of an art work, a particular symphony or pop tune, for example, is by no means 'over' once concerts are given or LP's, CD's and Singles are distributed to outlets, played on radio stations and purchased for home consumption. Nor after critics have pronounced (perhaps especially in the case of 'popular' forms and the cultural studies work described below).

There is therefore much to be learned through in-depth focus on the points where musical 'texts' and social actors/auditors meet, on *how* this process is situated in ordinary life. In this paper I suggest it is now time to think systematically about how we might return to a concern with music's social *meaning* – its effects – and, equally importantly, how we might make this

Tia DeNora

return journey without having to leave the ground of social action, the real time level on which social life actually happens. Specifically, I want to consider the ways that music, like other technical forms, is 'implicated in the redrawing of boundaries and relationships' (Moores, 1994). In what follows I develop *one* way of exploring this issue: whether it is possible to speak of a *musical* definition of the situation, and if so, how such a process can be described. For this task, I suggest, we should view musically 'finished' products – compositions – as *resources* for producing things other than music. The question I am asking is not only about how the social 'gets into' the musical (the social provenance of a musical work), but also about how the musical 'gets into' the social. In short, I am asking about the musical composition of social reality.

But what kinds of things can music possibly help to compose? Social structure? Solidarity? Subjectivity? Legitimation? And if any or all of these things can be counted as, to use Simon Frith's famous phrase, 'sound effects', *how* is their efficacy achieved? Is the relationship between music and its effects determinate? Is it constructed? Answers to these questions have been extremely elusive for socio-musical studies. Yet music (and often the music of others) features largely in everyday life, whether or not we care to listen. In public, it is often emitted, as if part of the air conditioning, in shops, waiting rooms and elevators. On trains and buses it often seeps from other peoples' headphones. It is as if everyone, analysts included, 'knows' intuitively that music is socially meaningful, yet attempts to specify *how* this is so remain fragmentary and speculative. How then, can we begin to specify and observe the actual 'import-export' business as it is transacted between music and social life? How can we talk about music as having social 'content' – or, more particularly, as informing the social – without falling into 'that great [culturological] Zero'?

From macro structure to ethnography – homology and cultural practice

Socio-musical analysis got off to a good start during the 1970s in the ethnographically-oriented work produced by affiliates of the Birmingham Centre for Contemporary Cultural Studies. The 'Birmingham School' provided a more dynamic context for the homology concept by focusing on the (subcultural) *use* of music,[5] the ways that music could be used to articulate particular values or social arrangements.

298

Music, action and reflexivity

For example, in a study of bikeboy culture, Paul Willis' observed that the songs the boys preferred were fast-paced and characterized by a clearly defined beat. In describing how this music 'resonated' with bikeboy culture, Willis' work demonstrated how music was not merely 'representative' of the bike boys' cultural values but was rather *constitutive* in the sense that it helped to create and enforce those values which were 'almost literally *seen in* the qualities of their preferred music' (p. 63 [emphasis in original]). The boys' preferred music didn't leave listeners 'just sit[ting] there moping all night' (1978: 69). Rather, it invited, perhaps incited, movement. In the words of one of the boys, 'if you hear a fast record you've got to get up and do something, I think. If you can't dance any more, or if the dance is over, you've just got to go for a burn-up [motorcycle ride]' (Willis 1978: 73).

Although Willis was interested in the homological relation between music and social structure, his work respecified the analytic means to such an end. In *Profane Culture*, homologies were discoverable in and through situated members' attempts to constitute the 'cultural field' of their group: 'objects, artifacts and institutions do not, as it were, have a single valency. It is the act of social engagement with a cultural item which activates and brings out particular meanings' (193). Thus, the focus of Willis' work was directed to the ways particular actors made connections or parallels between music and society. Willis therefore problematized the issue of *how* cultural 'resonances' are made.

This theme, of how agents attach connotations to musical forms, was further developed by Stuart Hall (1980; 1986) in his discussion of 'articulations'. By articulation, Hall meant the 'work' of drawing together cultural forms (like music) and social topics,[6] music, movement and social identity for example. This shift, from a focus on cultural *codes* to a focus of cultural *practice*, activated the notion of homology and rendered it sensitive to intra-cultural diversity. The point then, was two-fold: (a) cultural forms do not necessarily reflect 'Society'; indeed the various encodings produced by members of any given 'society' may be so diverse as to undermine the notion of *a* single society and (b) the ways in which forms are perceived is dependent upon the *activity* of perception. This focus on practice left room for a poststructuralist (and interactionist) concern with how the subject is constructed through interaction with textual forms – how representations become resources for the formulation of desires, feelings, ambitions, interests, and so on.

299

Tia DeNora

In short, if we assume cultural forms are various, it becomes less interesting to speak of parallels that a given social *analyst* might observe between music and 'Society'. Of greater interest is to observe the ways in which lived connections are made between a potential plurality of cultural forms (eg, musics) and a plurality of social formations. What is of interest is, in other words, not so much *what* can be said about culture, but rather what articulation *achieves* for its speakers. And for this reason, the creative work of accessing and using culture (and the social shaping of this process) becomes a focal point for socio-cultural studies.

In a sense, then, one could argue that Willis and Hall were developing a 'worlds' (subcultures) approach to the cultural artifact and its consumption at the same time that American scholars were elaborating the 'production' emphasis. Within the Willis/Hall approach, the notion of homology was relocated to the level of subcultural (ie, socially specified) stylistic *practice*. To speak of 'music' and 'society' in the singular, therefore, is to miss both the fundamentally dynamic nature of social formation *and* the constitutive nature of analytical description, the ways in which analysis constructs its object by writing 'about' it.

Willis' work is typically read as a discussion of how subcultural and marginalized groups create symbolic 'solutions' to material problems (ie, solutions that ultimately reconcile agents to oppressive social relations). Music and fast riding, for example, don't really 'get' the boys out of anything; at the end of the night, they deliver the boys back to their original social locations. Indeed, this focus on the simultaneous resistive and conciliatory feature of culture is one of the distinguishing features of Willis' work *as sociology*: Willis attempts to make links between cultural practice and social structure.

But this is not the only way to read *Profane Culture*. It can also be read, for example, as describing a link between music and social activity. One of its most striking (and usually underplayed) points is that we *do things to music and do things with music*: dance and ride in the case of the bike boys, but beyond this, many of us may (at least occasionally) eat, fall asleep, dance, daydream, exercise, celebrate, commemorate, even procreate, to music. Things get done to music, moreover, as it plays both in real time, *and* as it is played and replayed in memory and imagination. As one of the bike boys observes, 'you can hear the beat in your head, don't you . . . you go with the beat, don't you' (Willis 1978: 72).[7]

Music, action and reflexivity

Getting into the music

If we take them at their word, then, the bike boys tell us that they enter *into* the music and 'go with it' or let it take them (rather as one might 'take' a train or a bus) from one state (sitting around) to another (dancing as the music plays) to another (riding as the music plays in memory). Music, in this sense, is a cultural *vehicle*, a way of getting from one situation to another, and of 'getting through' a particular situation. The bike boys' music did more than 'refer' to a mode of activity. It provided a referent *for* a mode of activity, a working or candidate model for the temporal ordering (coordinating) of the evening and for the ways in which other events were arranged and experienced. In this sense, music can be said to 'impress' itself on action (Witkin: 1974). For example, one actor might say to another, 'we'll go like *this*' (the 'this' being a musical example) or s/he might make use of a musical metaphor in order to outline a line of action (eg, 'faster, smoother, and all in unison'). The point is that music provides common mediators for social experience; music therefore provides *resources* for collective (ie, concerted) activity. Exploring how musical resources come to be mobilized, then, provides an entrée into the non-verbal bases for, in Becker's terms, 'doing things together'. In this latter respect, the sociology of music could learn from previous research on skill and how skills are taught and acquired (Sudnow, 1978; Witkin, 1974; Jordan, 1990; Shapin, 1989).[8] This work has examined the importance of tacit, embodied, non-rational referents (touch, movement, imagery) in the teaching of other kinds of embodied skills (eg, the plastic arts, surgery, music, dance, sports, mechanics, cookery, laboratory science).

Put differently (and in a way that 'modulates' this discussion into a more sociological key), to enter a piece of music is to enter a form of 'textual time' (Smith, 1990: 74). That is, in providing non-verbal resources for activity, music also provides non-verbal resources for the clarification of perceived reality. It is to enter an arranged medium for notating (and therefore experiencing) time's passage. What then, does it mean to speak of the musical construction of time? To discuss this issue I will make use of a very mundane example.

Tia DeNora

Digression: The musical composition of temporal experience

When I work at home and want to log on to the mainframe computer, there is always a short delay after the telephone connection is achieved and before I am connected to the terminal server. It is from this server that I can then call up the machine I use. I'm almost always in a hurry when I dial up (having waited until the end of a work session), and, though the delay is only five or six seconds, it can *seem*, given the context of my up-till-then rapid typing (and my eagerness to see any computer mail), like a *long* time. When initially instructed on how to log on, I'd been told that I should repeatedly press the 'Enter' key until connected to the server so, for a number of months when logging on, I pressed the key as fast as I could, impatiently and certainly with no particular 'music' in mind. Then, one day, during a week when I had been reading an essay about Bizet's opera, *Carmen* (to be discussed below), I pressed the key to the repeated rhythmic phrase that appears in the opening four bars of the Habañera (see below). And even before Carmen had begun to sing the words, 'L'amour est un oiseau rebelle . . .', I was on the mainframe. Somehow, this 'playing' of Carmen became a habit, and now when I dial up from home, the interval which I once perceived as 'a long time' ('endless' repeated pressing of the enter key) has been reconstructed *in musical terms* as 'no time at all'.[9] Indeed, sometimes nowadays, even in my eagerness to log on to

Figure 1   George Bizet, "Habañera" from *Carmen*

302

Music, Action and Reflexivity

the mainframe, I feel slight regret that I have to stop replaying the aria in my mind!

This example from ordinary experience illustrates *one* way music as a form of textual time can be understood to have effects. In this example, music had the effect of *translating* time as I experienced it. That is, imaginatively replaying music during the wait for the mainframe 'marked time' by providing a *ground*, 'pathing device' or contrast structure (Smith, 1978; Woolgar, 1989) against which the passing of time could be observed and (re)evaluated. It was to reconstruct the time in musically pro-vided terms – to think, in other words, *in* music, as opposed to thinking about music. To think in music is to be enrolled into (or to tuned into – cf. Schutz) another way of experiencing time. To enter textual time, then, is, as Smith observes (1990), to be located within a virtual reality, to perceive 'reality' through a medium that can be used to construct time's meaning. In more conventional sociological terms, I am describing how a 'definition of the situation' can be accomplished through *musical* means. The Habañera provided a *different* way of experiencing the inter-val of a few seconds. It did this by recontextualizing that inter-val, by subsuming it as 'part' of a more complex temporal process – the playing out of a musical phrase.

Musically composed reality

Thus, music can be used, as Willis' bike boys described it, to realign bodily activity (speed up the motion of bodies). It can also be used (as I described in the case of my imaginative replay-ing of Carmen's aria) to realign the experience of time's passage (and, with it, in this example, to *slow* bodily motion, ie, the finger pressing the 'Enter' key – so that I pressed it only eight or ten times during the interval rather than twenty to twenty five). In both these examples, extra-musical phenomena (eg, courses of action, experience of time) came to be oriented in *musical* terms. Actors were, in other words, musically enlisted which is to say that music became (was mobilized as) a ground against which other things were experienced or conceptualized.

In short, these two examples highlight how music can be understood as a non-conceptual, non-verbal, non-pictorial *resource* for constructing the shape and speed of social activities,

Tia DeNora

mental and physical. They show how music can be used as an analogue for non-musical activities and, equally importantly (as I'll discuss in the final part of this paper), for the social *distribution* of activities between actors.

To say this is to open up the possibility of a 'strong' program for socio-musical studies. By this I mean it provides a way of conceptualizing music as far more than a 'reflection', 'resonance' or 'embodiment' of social relations. Instead, music can be conceived as a constituent part of the process of reality construction. But what *is* musical reality? In other words, what is it about music itself that is referred to when music becomes a resource for the construction of non-musical things like the experience of time or the course of an action or (see below) social characterization and literary narrative.

If, as I have suggested, music is able to become a ground for action or conception, how can we perceive and describe that ground? One way of answering this question is to speak about the ways that particular listeners/analysts experience musical structure, how musical elements themselves can be used in order to clarify musical realities. To speak of this issue is to describe the ways that listeners come to clarify musical realities through reference to other examples of music, ie, by understanding music in terms of its conventional devices – publicly recognizable features that are familiar because they are understood to be part of a stock of musical customs. The rhythm of the Habañera, for example, combined with the way it sketches the octave, can be understood as typical of (though by no means exclusive to) a musical genre[10] – 'Latin' dance music, and the repeated harmonic sketch, a typical 'introduction'. That is, even without technical musical knowledge, many listeners will be able to *guess* that there is something 'familiar' about the Habeñera (but *only* to guess, because as the music unfolds it could turn out to be something different),[11] and it is therefore possible to be 'knowing' about it – to know that the music is making use of enlisting devices (that it is signifying) – even as one resists being enlisted by it. Thus, to the extent that we can speak of recognized musical signs or devices (and – at least some of – their associated expectations), we can speak of musical realities, either in the terms of the music analyst or in the vocabulary available to non-musicians.[12]

From the viewpoint of the latter, for example, the repeated rhythm and emphasized beat of the Habeñera's introduction can be understood as a reference to dance or to 'moving the body

Music, action and reflexivity

with the music').[13] Beyond this contagiousness, the rhythm creates musical suspense because, in repeating itself, it sets itself up as something that is *continuing* as part of a background (rather than something that is working toward a resolution)[14] leaving the listener free (if s/he is so inclined) to wonder what will happen next, what will come to be juxtaposed with the ground. Harmonically, it is as if each four note unit (each repetition) contains an 'opening' and a 'closing', (it 'goes up and then comes down') and the fact that both pitches and rhythms are repeated over a two beat passage sets up a period of waiting, a feeling of things 'ticking along' and a feeling that something is about to happen if the listener 'sticks around'. Thus one might suggest that the opening of this music isn't 'about' waiting; rather the music itself is in waiting, and it is in waiting in order to do the musical work of paving the way for the melodic passage that will follow a few seconds later when Carmen starts to sing.

To a music analyst, the 'catchy' rhythm (emphasized beat) can be understood as achieved through the sixteenth note (the second note of each bar). In real time, this note lasts about .20 of a second (the other three notes in each bar as twice as long), and it comes after a gap equal to its length. Because of this gap, and because the note is half as long as the one that follows it, it may be conventionally perceived as if it is associated with (leading to) the following note which occurs on the second beat.[15] It therefore emphasizes that following note and with it, the second beat; it is heard as 'going' toward the second beat. Moreover, because its duration is brief (both relative to the notes in its immediate vicinity and in real time terms) it has the effect of implying that the listener could expect some quicker rhythmic movement to follow (which of course it does when Carmen begins to sing), but meanwhile the rhythm repeatedly moves forward (on the second note, the sixteenth note) only to fall back (with the final eighth note of the bar). Meanwhile, harmonically, each bar outlines a tonic-dominant[16] movement, and melodically, each bar sketches the octave ('do' to 'do'). The combination of these harmonic and melodic elements provides a pitch compass for whatever follows.

Taken together, then, and repeated three and a half times before Carmen sings, rhythmic, harmonic and melodic elements create a sense of latent musical energy: a sense of musical movement being held 'in check'. In short, the first three bars of this piece set up a logic of expectancy – rhythmic and harmonic. This is musical waiting, it can be experienced as pleasurable because

Tia DeNora

one knows it is a prelude to what will follow, one knows or can
guess that the wait will be no more than a few bars long, that the
'wait' is an integral part of the piece as a whole.[17] This is an
example of how one might, as an analyst or lay-listener, experience the musical reality of Carmen's song. But how can it be
used to compose other examples of extra-musical reality?

Musical mappings: the case of music, gender and sexuality

So far, I have considered two examples of how music can be
used for organizing experience: (1) an analogue for the speed of
bodies on dance floors and bikes and (2) an analogue for the
passing of a five second interval. These examples have been simple ones, but they help to establish that music can be used as a
basis for action or experience, that music can be used to project
structure on action, experience and events.

I have been concerned, in both examples, with how music can
become a *referent* for action/conception. I have deliberately
refrained from attempting to talk about how music *signifies*
extra-musical issues. The question of 'what' a music signifies (of
what it 'represents'), asked without a corresponding attempt to
situate music in a context of use, leads away from more fruitful
sociological exploration of the links between artifacts and action.
By contrast, I am trying to outline a way of doing socio-musical
analysis that circumvents the issue of what or how music *ultimately* signifies in favor of an approach that focuses on the ways
music is *used*: responded to, acted to. I am less interested in what
music 'simulates' than in what is 'done to' music, and by 'doing
things to music' I include discussions (lay and analytical) of
'what' music signifies: how do actors orient to what music does
in order to 'do' or 'get through' other things? Music can best be
understood, I am suggesting, as a cultural 'work space' for the
articulation of meaning and action, a real structure upon which
one can 'map' or 'hang' non-musical associations and activities
(DeNora, 1986).

The notion of musical 'mappings' has been taken up recently
by music scholars, primarily at the instigation of Susan McClary
(McClary, 1991; 1992). In the remainder of this paper, I want to
suggest that McClary's work is useful to sociologists of music for
the ways it attends to *musical* reality but that, as a program of
research, McClary's perspective needs to be developed in ways

Music, action and reflexivity

that take it further afield from music analysis. And to these ends, I want to return, once again, to *Carmen*.[18]

Who sings what in *Carmen*? As it turns out, according to McClary's often persuasive analysis (1991; 1992), Bizet's opera maps musical structures on to social roles in a way that results (musically and socially) in horizontal and vertical segmentation. In other words, a musical division of labour or 'who sings what kind of material' is associated with aesthetic and social distributions of status and identity. Throughout the opera, for example, Carmen's arias are dance tunes (Habañera; Seguidilla) which, as I began to discuss above, emphasize the musical pulse and invite listeners to move (and therefore assert and remember) their bodies, and dance music, within the canonic paradigm of 19th century music aesthetics, is viewed as 'lower' than more abstract forms. Moreover, because Carmen's music is highly chromatic (ie, it uses the notes 'in between' the notes of the scale), it creates musical ambiguity or tonal 'slippage' (ie, it elides tonal closure [McClary, 1991: 571]. In *musical* terms, these elements are indiscrete, and in need of resolving. These musical characteristics in turn highlight and bring into greater relief the ways in which Carmen's social character is 'deviant'.

Musically, in other words, Carmen is a disordering force. Both musically and socially, her character does things that 'nice girls' shouldn't do. This moral lesson is further underlined through the ways that Bizet contrasts Carmen's music and character with those of Micaëla, the demure childhood sweetheart of the principle male character, Don José. As a contrast structure to Carmen, Micaëla sings diatonic, non-pulsating melodies. Thus, the imagery of 'nice, steady girl' versus 'unpredictable and "slippery" transgressing woman' is musically constructed.

In another example, McClary examines the ways in which Don José's desire for Carmen, as expressed through his words, is further articulated by the ways in which words are mapped with music. In his famous 'Flower Song', McClary argues, the infatuated Don José:

> sets up a pitch-ceiling that constricts his melodic line (thus recreating in sound the experience of frustration), which he penetrates on 'te revoir, ô Carmen' . . . Following this explosive moment, his energy gradually seems to subside almost to a kind of whimpering. But as he sings of submitting himself masochistically to her power . . ., he rises again – this time

Tia DeNora

through an unaccompanied scale – and attains climax on
b [flat], the highest, most vulnerable pitch in the aria.

In *Carmen*, musical structure effects characterization; it is used
to organize the various character's identities, and through this, to
advance a gendered narrative structure. McClary's achievement
has been to show us how this is done. As with the two examples
I offered at the start of this paper, we can view Bizzet's music as
a ground against which to make sense of characters and action.
Telling us how these associations are made (and helping us to see
the *musical* segmentation which underlines and helps to constitute
this social segmentation) is where McClary excels.[19]
But (and McClary does not consider this issue) conversely, we
can use the action to make sense of the music.[20] The one provides a map (or referent) for the other. Each sets us up to perceive aspects of the one in the other: we look for ways that the
music 'illustrates' character and plot and we look for how plot
and characterization help to clarify the dramatic import of the
music. Music and text are, in other words, *co-productive* of each
other.
Mapping is about the creation of links; it is articulation in
Hall's sense. In her examination of Bizet's music, McClary
observes how links between words, music and characterization
are forged. The point, however, is that music may be used as a
map, but it does not specify in itself what it is a map *of*.[21] In
musical terms, breaking through a pitch ceiling ('penetration')
and singing a scalar passage up to a note that is both difficult to
sing *and* the highest note in the aria ('climax') are not *necessarily*
sexual (which is by no means to say that they are not or have
not come to be associated with a particular manner of fulfilling
desire); rather, they connote a manner of sexual activity *when we*
(learn to) *hear them* as making that kind of representation, when
we map sexual activity on to music, and vice versa. To speak, in
other words, of *musical* realities is to speak about the ways these
come to be articulated with social realities, to describe how music
actually comes to be positioned as analogous for extra-musical
activity.
Thus, to provide a reading of what music signifies (what it is a
map of) is to 'frame' music, to presume that one knows what it
stands for. It is to hypostatize the musical object.[22] Thus, it may
or may not be fair to suggest, as McClary does at the end of her
(1991) analysis of Carmen, that:

Music, action and reflexivity

the aspects of Carmen I have just discussed – namely these particular constructions of gender, the ejaculatory quality of many so-called transcendental moments, the titillating yet carefully contained presentation of the feminine 'threat', the apparent necessity of violent closure – are all central to the great tradition of nineteenth-century 'Absolute Music'. We can easily find both the characterizations and plot lines of *Carmen*, *Salome*, or *Samson et Dalila* exquisitely concealed in the presumably abstract, word-less context of many a symphony (67).

Doing things to music: mapping the music-society interface

To make such claims is to take an analytical short-cut, one that socio-musical analysis does not *need* to take. Indeed, it goes against the grain of the very powerful form of observation that McClary otherwise develops for Carmen. It is to shift from a focus on how music is used as a referent (how it can be used by actors to define or get through other things) to a focus on what *music* signifies. To make this shift, ie, to shift the analytical focus from how articulations are made between music and activity (the social) to a focus on what types of activity music *represents*, is to sidestep the articulations of (situated) others (whom the analyst might have observed) and to present the analyst's own articulation or 'map' as an exclusive analytic perspective. To take this sidestep privileges the analyst's viewpoint: and her/his own ground or referent for the music. Instead of focusing on what music constructs by looking at how others make use of music as a map for other things, focus is shifted back to the ways that an analyst 'reads' (ie, 'imputes') meanings by bringing to bear upon the musical object interpretive resources from within his/her own external vantage point. To be sure, McClary is right to criticize musicologists for ignoring the issue of musical signification:

> most people who have not been trained as academic musicians (who have not had these responses shamed out of them) believe that music signifies – that it can sound happy, sad, sexy, funky, silly . . . or whatever. Oblivious to the skepticism of music theorists, they listen to music in order to dance, weep, relax or get romantic . . .

But attempts to 'discover' what music signifies elide the more

Tia DeNora

sociologically interesting topic of how the musical (fast paced music/musical time/musical segmentation) 'gets in' to the social (fast riding/re-experiencing the meaning of a five second wait/social characterization) and vice versa, how social connotations get aligned with musical structures. In either case, this is not a question for music analysis but a question for ethnographically oriented socio-musical analysis which leads away from reports of what music 'contains' and toward examinations of how music is acted toward and with, and how it is perceived. This is by no means to say that certain works or passages may not come to have long-standing, seemingly 'fixed' connotations:

> [h]owever arbitrary musical meanings and conventions are – rather than being 'natural', or determined by some human essence or by the needs of class expression – once particular musical elements are put together in particular ways, and acquire particular connotations, these can be hard to shift. It would be difficult, for instance, to move the 'Marseillaise' out of the set of meanings sedimented around it . . . which derive from the history of the revolutionary French bourgeoisie (Middleton, 1985: 9).

Some pieces, Middleton suggests, carry their connotations with them. With other musics, preferred readings may be encouraged through the use of, for example, liner or programme notes, music criticism. But there are also many musical works that do not come equipped with 'user's guides' or 'directions' for reading/ decoding (or they may come with several alternative and perhaps contradictory guides) and even with those that do, music can be 'mis-read' (see Sue Wise's idiosyncratic reading of Elvis Presley – Wise, 1984) or 're-read' when something different is provided as a map for its apprehension. Think for example, of the feminist reappropriation of Tammy Wynette's 'Stand By Your Man' (see Scott, 1993) or the Jimi Hendrix version of the 'Star Spangled Banner' (DeNora, 1986) or, to return to the 'Marseillaise', the English schoolboy version of that tune ('a Frenchman went to the lavatory . . .'), all examples of 're-mapping' music. Musical borrowings, also, attest to the ways in which musical connotations can be renewed or exchanged, sometimes dramatically (DeNora, 1986).[23]

In short, focus on the musical text is necessary, but it is not enough. We need to focus as well on the *practice* of approaching

Music, action and reflexivity

music for social activity (consumption) and the *practice* of appropriating the non-musical as a resource for musical composition (production). The social is not 'in' the text; rather it is 'in' the interaction between text and actor. And we have to regard music criticism as part of this interactive, constitutive process. As Henry Kingsbury has observed, 'musicological discourse is not simply talk and writing "about music", but is also constitutive of music' (1991: 201). Musical/textual analysis, in other words, cannot 'tell' us 'about' music what ultimately signifies. But it can help to provide a ground, against which musical meaning can be clarified.

If music provides a means for the construction of time, bodies, and courses of action for bodies and minds – for the construction of grounds for action – then *neither* textual analysis nor poststructuralist theory is enough. Neither will tell us how the work of signification actually happens, how it is done by real, socially located people. Instead we need to consider 'naturally occurring' examples of how music is used and oriented to, how it is constructed as a 'work space' for the continuation of social life. To ask about the uses to which music is put is to ask about how people connect with or 'get into' music, how musical realities get converted into social ones. Exploring this topic will require far closer, ethnographically motivated attention to music as it features in the everyday lives or ordinary people, a project traditionally beyond the purview of both musicology and the sociology of music.

Exeter University   Received 4 June 1993
                                           Accepted 6 February 1994

Notes

1 An earlier version of this paper was presented at the Annual Meeting of the American Musicological Society, Pittsburgh, PA, November 1992 as part of the Special Session, 'Musicology and Sociology in Dialogue' and, in a slightly different form, to a staff seminar, Department of Music, University of Wales, Cardiff.

2 Sadly, Lenneberg was evidently ignorant of the move within Sociology over the past decade *away* from the 'Grand' tradition.

3 For example, networks (Becker, 1982), organizations (Dubin, 1988) or fields (Bourdieu, 1978).

4 See, eg, Leonard Meyer's 1986 article on 'Innovation and Choice' – written when Meyer was still at the University of Chicago and collaborating with Becker, then at Northwestern University.

311

Tia DeNora

5 Or, as Willis put it, the 'continuous play between the group and a particular item which produces specific styles, meanings, contents and forms of consciousness' (Willis: 191).

6 For a summary of the concept articulation, see Hall 1986. My understanding of articulation has profited greatly from Shaun Moore's forthcoming discussion of the general theoretical issues that inform his on-going research into the domestic consumption of Satellite TV (Moores forthcoming a and b). For a discussion of how the Birmingham studies did not go far enough in letting members speak for themselves, see Dyer. For a critique of the gender bias of these early studies, see McRobbie 1980.

7 In a socio-music analysis workshop recently with final year sociology undergraduates in a course I teach on 'Gender and Society', students made the following observations in the course of a discussion of the Lenny Kravitz ('hard rock') song, 'Are You Gonna Go My Way':

> First Student: It's not the kind of song you'd want to hear in the morning just before you leave the house.
> Me: Why is that?
> First Student: You find the song stays in your head all day. You can't get it out of your head. The beat stays with you and it's annoying.
> Me: Can you think of any situations where you'd like to listen to this song?
> Second Student: You might listen to it if you were getting ready to go out to a party.
> First Student: Or if you have to make a long drive late at night. It keeps you awake and energized.

(At the time of this discussion, the student was not acquainted with Willis' essay on bikeboy culture.)

8 Shapin has referred to skill as 'knowledge without a voice' that is, knowledge of 'how to' that is not spoken for through words and therefore may not occupy a seat in the assembly of consciousness.

9 Alternative approaches to pain management (eg, visualization) make use of this type of 're-visioning' of physical phenomena; the patient attempts to align her/his consciousness with the visual image, and to perceive the pain through it. (See Trotter and Chavira, 1981).

10 I do not wish to imply that there exists any one-to-one correspondence of musical gesture to musical function. The same gesture may in different musical contexts come to connote different, even musical associations. Moreover, I do not wish to imply that all listeners will recognize the musical/conventional reality of a piece in the same way. In earlier work I have argued against this line of thinking and indeed, it is just this unsociological perspective that I am attempting to criticize in this paper.

11 As further information is added, previously recognized meanings are 'adjusted' or realigned to 'fit' the new context.

12 I do not mean to suggest here that music analytical vocabularies and those of the lay listener are distinct. There is indeed a good deal of overlap and the notion of professional distinction must be treated as a status claim. I separate the two here for descriptive purposes only.

13 Indeed, the music provided me with a way of organizing the movement of my finger on the 'Enter' key; the repeated rhythmic unit gave that finger something fairly easy, definite and physically gratifying to do (a repeated rhythm that played with but returned to and emphasized a definite beat).

312

Music, action and reflexivity

14 Within Western reception conventions that is.

15 Because our habits of hearing have a bias in favour of forward motion, or movement into what follows, a bias in favour of where the music is going as opposed to, for example, what is brought back to a static ground (as in, for example, medieval Cantus Firmus).

15 The chords based on the first and fifth notes of the scale, 'do' and 'sol' which are the two strongest chords in functional tonal music, the dominant chord being understood as 'leading back to' the tonic or final chord.

17 One way of testing whether a piece of music sets up this kind of expectation is to see what happens if the introduction is repeated for more than a few bars. When performers use this over-repetition as a 'trick', live audiences usually find this device humorous because it defies expectation, it sets up the listener to expect 'something' and then nothing is forthcoming. It is an example of a musical joke, a joke whose humour is constituted in *musical* terms.

18 In brief, the plot of the opera is as follows: A soldier, Don José becomes infatuated with Carmen, a gypsy who works in a cigarette factory. She is arrested. He helps her to escape. They become lovers. She persuades him to join her in the roving Gypsy life. He becomes possessive. He is approached by Micaëla, his childhood sweetheart, who begs him to return to his native village where his mother is dying. Carmen, meanwhile, begins to tire of Don José. She is courted by the bullfighter, Escamillo. Don José pleads with Carmen not to leave him. She refuses. He kills her and then himself. The libretto is based on a novel by Merimée. The character of Micaëla was added to placate family audiences at the Opéra Comique, where Carmen was first performed in 1874.

19 Charles Ford's, *Cosi? Sexual Politics in Mozart's Operas* attempts a similar kind of analysis. Ford examines the gendered division of musical labour in order to suggest that the feminine in Mozart is a topos or empty space (ie, melodically and harmonically ambiguous) that is given meaning by the more directed movement of the masculine voice parts. For example, Ford suggests that the music actually undermines, in places, the illocutionary force of what female characters say, such that, in extreme cases, a female character's verbal 'no' to a male character's advances can be read, musically, as a 'yes'.

20 Nor does she consider that either text or music can be made sense of through resort of other types of grounds. See below.

21 This is a point long recognized within both the sociology of scientific knowledge and ethnomethodology. See, for example, Barnes (1983) on classification (eg, Barnes, 1983). See for example Heritage's 1984 discussion of the sentence, 'I have a red sweater here' where the predicate (the category 'red' for example) is completed by the putative red-ness of the sweater. In both research strands, the point revolves around the reflexive constitution of instance and category.

22 I am grateful to the music historian Dexter Edge for this observation (personal correspondence, 1991).

23 I do not mean to suggest that connotations aren't often, perhaps most often, a matter of routine. That is, I do not mean to imply instrumentality or hyper-alertness as the normal pattern of reading (eg, Machiavellian readers on the look-out for ways of appropriating texts). Rather, I mean to suggest that it isn't useful to assume that there is only one preferred or most routine reading. There may be a variety of routine responses.

313

Tia DeNora

References

Abbott, Andrew and Alexandra Hrycak, (1990), 'Measuring Resemblance in Sequence Data: An Optimal Matching Analysis of Musicians' Careers', *American Journal of Sociology*, 96: 144–85.

Barnes, Barry, (1983), 'On the conventional character of knowledge and cognition', 19–54 in Knorr-Cetina and Mulkay, (eds), *Science Observed*, London and Los Angeles: Sage.

Becker, Howard, S. (1982), *Art Worlds*, Berkeley and Los Angeles: University of California Press.

Berger, Bennett, (1985), 'A Proposal for the Sociology of Culutre'. Circulated manuscript, Department of Sociology, University of California, San Diego.

Blau, Judith, (1990), *The Shape of Culture*, Cambridge: Cambridge University Press.

Bourdieu, Pierre, (1984), *Distinction*, Cambridge: Harvard University Press.

Clark, Adele, E., (1990), 'Symbolic Interactionism in Social Studies of Science', pp. 179–214 in Michal M. McCall and Howard S. Becker, (eds), *Symbolic Interaction and Cultural Studies*, Chicago, University of Chicago Press.

DeNora, Tia, (1986), 'How is extra-musical meaning possible? Music as a place and space for "work"'. *Sociological Theory*, 6: 2: 84–94.

DeNora, Tia, (1991), 'Musical Patronage and Social Change in Beethoven's Vienna'. *American Journal of sociology*.

DiMaggio, Paul, (1982), 'Cultural Entrepreneurship in Nineteenth-Century Boston: the Creation of an Organizational Base for High Culture in America'. *Media, Culture and Society* 4: 35–50 (part I) and 4: 303–322 (part II).

DiMaggio, Paul and Paul Hirsch, (1976), 'Production Organizations in the Arts'. *American Behavioral Scientist*, 19: 6: 735–742.

DiMaggio, Paul and Michael Useem, (1978), 'Cultural Democracy in a Period of Cultural Expansion: the Social Composition of Arts Audiences in the United States'. *Social Problems*, 26.

Faulkner, Robert, (1971), *Hollywood Studio Musicians*, Chicago: Aldine.

Faulkner, Robert, (1983), *Music on Demand*, New Brunswick, NJ: Transaction Books.

Gans, Herbert, (1974), *Popular Culture and High Culture: An Analysis and Evaluation of Taste*, New York: Basic Books.

Gilmore, Samuel, (1987), 'Coordination and Convention: the Organization of the Concert World'. *Symbolic Interaction*, 10: 209–27.

Gilmore, Samuel, (1988), 'Schools of Activity and Innovation'. *Sociological Quarterly*, 29: 203–19.

Gilmore, Samuel, (1990), 'Art Worlds: Developing the Interactionist Approach to Social Organization', 148–78 in H.S. Becker and M.M. McCall, (eds), *Symbolic Interaction and Cultural Studies*, Chicago: University of Chicago Press.

Hall, Stuart, (1980), 'Encoding/Decoding', pp. 128–38 in S. Hall *et al.* (eds), *Culture, Media, Language: Working Papers in Cultural Studies, 1972–79*, London: Hutchinson.

Hall, Stuart, (1986), 'On Postmodernism and Articulation: An Interview with Stuart Hall'. *Journal of Communication Inquiry*, 10 (2): 45–60.

Hebdige, Dick, (1979), *Subculture: The Meaning of Style*, London: Methuen.

Hennion, Antoine, (1983), 'The Production of Success: An Antimusicology of the Pop Song'. *Popular Music 3*.

Music, action and reflexivity

Heritage, John, (1984), *Garfinkel and Ethnomethodology*, Oxford: Blackwell.

Jordan, Brigitte, (1990), 'The Role of Touch in Midwives' Practice'. Paper prepared for the Conference on Rediscovering Skill in Science, Technology and Medicine, Bath, 1990.

Kingsbury, Henry, (1991), 'Sociological Factors in Musicological Poetics', *Ethnomusicology* 35.

Lenneberg, H., (1988), 'Speculating About Sociology and Social History', *Journal of Musicology*, (IV): 4: 409–420.

McClary, Susan, (1991), *Feminine Endings*, Minneapolis: University of Minnesota Press.

McClary, Susan, (1992), *George Bizet's Carmen*, Cambridge: Cambridge University Press.

McRobbie, Angela, (1980), 'Settling Accounts with Subcultures: A Feminist Critique', *Screen Education*, 34.

Middleton, Richard, (1985), 'Articulating Musical Meaning/Re-constructing Musical History/Locating the "Popular"', *Popular Music*, 5: 45–80.

Moores, Shaun, (1990), 'Texts, readers and contexts of reading: developments in the study of media audiences', *Media, Culture and Society*, 12: 9–29.

Moores, Shaun, (1993), *Interpreting Audiences: Ethnography and Media Consumption*, London: Sage.

Moores, Shaun, (1994), 'Satellite TV as cultural sign: consumption, embedding and articulation', *Media, Culture and Society*.

Pasler, Jann, (1987), 'Pelleas and Politics', *Nineteenth Century Music*.

Peterson, Richard and David Berger, (1975), 'Cycles in Symbol Production: The Case of Popular Music'. *American Sociological Review*, 40: 1975.

Schutz, Alfred, (1978), 'Making Music Together'. Collected Papers, Vol. 2, The Hague.

Scott, Derek, (1993), 'Sexuality and musical style from Monteverdi to Mae West', 110–27 in *The Last Post: Music After Modernism*, Manchester: Manchester University Press.

Shapin, Steven, (1989), 'The Invisible Technician'. *American Scientist*, 77 (November–December) 554–603.

Smith, Dorothy, (1978), 'K is mentally ill', *Sociology*.

Smith, Dorothy, (1990), *Texts, Facts and Femininity: Exploring the Relations of Ruling*, London: Routledge.

Sudnow, David, (1978), *Ways of the Hand*. Cambridge MA: Harvard University Press.

Trotter, Robert and Juan Antonio Chavira, (1981), *Curanderismo: Mexican American Folk Healing*, Athens, GA: University of Georgia Press.

Weber, William, (1992), *The Rise of Musical Classics in 18th Century England: A Study in canon, Ritual and Ideology*, Oxford: Clarendon Press.

Willis, Paul, (1978), *Profane Culture*, London: Routledge and Kegan Paul.

Witkin, Robert, (1974), *The Intelligence of Feeling*, London: Heineman.

Woolgar, Steve, (1989), *Science: The Very Idea*, London: Routledge.

CHAPTER 5

The biology lessons of opera buffa: gender, nature, and bourgeois society on Mozart's buffa stage[1]

Now would I have a book where I might see all characters and planets of the heavens, that I might know their motives and dispositions . . . nay, let me have one book more, and then I have done, wherein I might see all plants, herbs and trees, that grow upon the earth. Goethe, *Faust*

Opera buffa in Mozart's Vienna has typically not been considered in the context of its participation in a wider intellectual and creative milieu. Even musicologists with overt interests in context typically leave unexamined the ways in which opera interacted with endeavors in culture-producing fields beyond the most obvious. Yet disciplinary boundaries in the late eighteenth century were permeable, and exponents from a variety of intellectual and creative enterprises met regularly to exchange ideas. Circa 1789 it was possible to believe that the world's knowledge could be contained encyclopedically, and well-educated amateur could still reasonably expect to keep abreast of developments in both science and art. Indeed, in his youth, even Da Ponte dabbled in the study of "human nature" by writing a Rousseau-inspired essay entitled, "Whether man is happier in an organized society or in a simple state of nature."[2] Given this lively cross-fertilization of cultural practice, interdisciplinary perspectives would seem to be indispensable to the study of opera. That these perspectives have so far been underrepresented is perhaps due to the fact that musicologists rarely employ the notion of

---

1 I would like to thank Miss Sylvia Fitzgerald, Chief Librarian and Archivist at The Royal Botanic Gardens, Kew, for help with locating works by and about the von Jacquin family. Thanks to Bruce Alan Brown, Frankie Peroni, Ronald J. Rabin, John A. Rice, Douglas Tudhope, and Robert Witkin for "fruitful" discussions.
2 Nicholas Till, *Mozart and the Enlightenment* (London: Faber and Faber, 1992), p. 240.

intellectual and artistic "worlds"[3] – networks of interdependent actors who import and export aesthetic materials and ideas from one field to another in the course of carrying out their cultural work.

What, then, was the nature of the cultural field that opera buffa inhabited? And how can an awareness of opera buffa's location in a wider cultural terrain enrich our understanding of the social and cultural role of musical theatre? In the eighteenth century, opera was the most elaborate kinesthetic form available for the depiction and discussion of social life. In its shift away from stories of gods, kings, and mythological topics, opera buffa was expressly oriented to the representation of "ordinary" life. To what extent, then, is it possible to observe ideas and images from other cultural enterprises – science and social philosophy for example – being acted out, elaborated, transposed, and clothed in the form of human situations on the buffa stage? This essay attempts to address these questions by considering some of the links between opera buffa and a crucial and, even controversial, science in late eighteenth century Vienna – botany. I suggest that opera buffa was a "cultural workspace" wherein new lessons concerning, among other things, social and sexual relations could be registered imaginatively through sight and sound.

"AGOG WITH THE VEGETABLE KINGDOM AGAIN" – BOTANY IN EARLY MODERN EUROPE

In *The Order of Things*, Michel Foucault outlined the eighteenth-century emergence of a particular mode of thought or *episteme* which he dubbed "Classical," contrasting it with an earlier "Renaissance" mode. With the notion of *episteme* Foucault attempted to map out a history of epistemology, to convey a sense in which the form and style of knowledge production has varied

---

3 See Howard S. Becker, *Art Worlds* (Berkeley: University of California Press, 1982) and Pierre Bourdieu, "Intellectual Field and Creative Project," *Social Science Information* 8.2 (1969), 89–119.

over time and place. His contrast between the "Renaissance" and emerging "Classical" episteme is intended to highlight a shift – away from knowledge characterized by analogy and interpretation and toward a concern with classification and taxonomy.[4] Foucault characterizes the pursuit of knowledge in eighteenth century Europe as increasingly concerned with delineating, describing, and ranking the contents of the natural world. The ambitious scholarly projects of this time – such as the *Encyclopédie* and Johnson's Dictionary – exemplified this concern, as did, perhaps most strikingly, the development of a taxonomy and nomenclature for the so-called "three kingdoms of nature" ("Animal, Vegetable, and Mineral") in Carolus Linnaeus's *Systema naturae*.

Linnaeus's work initially appeared in 1735 as a modest folio of twelve pages. By 1766, in its twelfth edition (the last one to be revised by Linnaeus himself), it had swelled to a 2,400-page, three-volume set.[5] By the late 1770s, his reputation and system were secured within the natural science worlds in Paris, London, Vienna, and Berlin. Thus, in the heyday of opera buffa, Linnaean classification provided the working basis for (in Thomas Kuhn's terms) the "normal sciences" of zoology, mineralogy, and botany.

Of these, botany was perhaps the most socially salient. It was linked, on the one hand, to foreign exploration and colonial expansion; on the other, its proliferation gave rise to botanical gardens where rare and exotic plants were brought "home" and exhibited to the public.[6] That the pleasure garden emerged at this time in the British Isles and on the continent (Viennese examples include the Prater and the Augarten) attests to the eighteenth-century fascination with nature – albeit the socially arranged nature of the garden or pleasure ground. Among aristocratic ladies, botanical science became a fashionable pastime, particularly in England, while on the

---

4 Michel Foucault, *The Order of Things* (New York: Pantheon, 1970), pp. 46–77.
5 Londa Schiebinger, "Why Mammals Are Called Mammals: Gender Politics in Eighteenth-Century Natural History." *American Historical Review* 98.2 (April 1993), 383.
6 Lucile H. Brockway, *Science and Colonial Expansion: The Role of the British Royal Botanic Gardens* (New York: Academic Press, 1979).

continent it was pursued by leading literary and political figures. "I am agog," wrote Goethe to his intimate friend Frau von Stein in 1786, "with the vegetable kingdom again ... the enormous realm is simplifying itself out in my soul, so that I will soon be able to see through the most difficult problems straight away."[7]

At this time, Vienna was in the forefront of botanical practice, enjoying what has subsequently been referred to as the "golden age" of Austrian botany.[8] Its chief exponents were Nikolaus Joseph Baron von Jacquin (1727–1817) and his eldest son, Joseph Franz (1766–1839). The elder Jacquin was born in Leyden, the son of a cloth merchant of French origin. He became a protégé of Gerhard van Swieten, Maria Theresa's personal physician (and father of Mozart's and Haydn's patron Gottfried van Swieten). He studied in Antwerp, Louvain, Leyden, and Vienna. He went to Paris in 1750 and returned to Vienna in 1752, whence he embarked on a scientific expedition to the Antilles, from 1755 to 1759. He spent most of the 1760s in Schemnit. He returned again to Vienna in 1769 as professor of botany and chemistry at the University of Vienna, where he remained until he was succeeded in his post by his son. He designed both the Rennweg Botanical Gardens and the Schönbrunn park, and published seventeen books between the years 1760 and 1811 (he made his reputation as a taxonomist with *Selectarium stripium americanum* in 1763). He was ennobled in 1806.

Nikolaus Jacquin was known as the "Austrian Linnaeus"; he became one of the staunchest supporters of the so-called Linnaean "reform." In return he received the following accolade from Linneaus after one of his collecting expeditions: "We [that is all naturalists and scientists] receive and honor you as the ambassador of Flora itself, bringing us the treasures from foreign worlds, so far neither heard of nor seen."[9]

---

7 Nicholas Boyle, *Goethe: The Poet and the Age*: vol. 1: *The Poetry of Desire (1749–1790)*, (Oxford: Clarendon Press, 1992), p. 386.

8 Frans A. Stafleu, *Linnaeus and the Linnaeans: The Spreading of their Ideas in Systematic Botany 1735–89*. (Utrecht: A. Oosthoek's Uitgeversmaatschappij N.V. for the International Association for Plant Taxonomy, 1971), p. 185.

9 Ibid.

The career of Joseph Franz was perhaps less illustrious than his father's, though it demonstrates the international character of botany during the late eighteenth century. Joseph Franz published five works between 1784 and 1825 and is perhaps best known for his tour of European botanical centers, begun in 1788. He traveled to Prague, Karlsbad, and Dresden, where he was much taken with the gardens of the Elector (Kurfürst) whom he viewed as a "passionate botanist."[10] He then moved on to Leipzig, Halle, Berlin, Göttingen, and Leyden, arriving in London (which he considered to be the leading European center for botany) at the end of the year. He was invited to become an associate of the recently formed Linnean Society, and his father was simultaneously invited to hold the post of honorary president of the botanical side of the same organization.

The Jacquins were active in Vienna's social and cultural scene. Their home was the setting for a group of artists and scholars who met weekly for discussion, music making, and light entertainment. Among those who attended regularly was Mozart, who became acquainted with the Jacquins in 1783 (he dedicated the Notturnos K. 436–9 to his close friend Gottfried Jacquin, the younger brother of Joseph).[11]

The extent to which this group directed their attention to the latest developments in botany will probably never be resolved. That these meetings occurred at the Jacquin household would suggest, however, that botanical matters were aired at least occasionally,

---

10 A. B. Rendle, "Letters of J. F. von Jacquin (1788–90)," *The Journal of Botany* 61 (1923), p. 288.

11 Would Da Ponte also have been part of this group? It does not seem implausible, given that Mozart and Da Ponte met at the house of Baron Wetzlar (a member of the so-called "second society" of ennobled professionals and merchants) and that the Jacquin salon was an upper-middle-class (professional) salon. We know that Mozart's young friend Gottfried Jacquin took an interest in his success since Mozart wrote to him twice from Prague to describe how his works were faring abroad. We also know that Wetzlar volunteered to underwrite *Le nozze di Figaro* if the emperor would not sponsor it; (Wetzlar would have arranged to have it produced in France or London – see Lorenzo Da Ponte, *Memoirs of Lorenzo Da Ponte, Mozart's Librettist*, trans. L. A. Sheppard (Boston and New York: Houghton Mifflin, 1929), p. 129.

especially given the social status of the science. For example, the elder Jacquin's course of lectures was published in German in 1785 (*Anleitung zur Pflanzenkenntniss nach Linnés Methode* [*Lessons on Botany according to Linnaeus's Method*]). This was the only one of his seventeen publications to appear in German rather than Latin, then as now the official scientific language of botany. That this work was published in the vernacular suggests it was intended to be quasi-popular, a precursor of modern popularizations of science.[12] One can speculate that it might at least have been mentioned within a circle devoted to the discussion of intellectual and social matters of the day, particularly as it had been written by a hosting member.[13] What then, did this book contain that would have held the interest of non-scientists and, more to the point, opera librettists and composers? What was it about botany in the 1780s that held its observers, practitioners, and non-practitioners, so "agog"?

THE "MANLY" AND THE "WOMANLY" IN PLANTS

"Plants," as the elder Jacquin's course of instruction tells us, "feel nothing...[they] have no heart, no lungs...no mind, no stomach, no urinary tract, no anus."[14] Astonishingly, however, plants do possess,

12 It was reissued in 1792 and 1798. The second edition appeared in 1800, with a preface signed by Joseph Jacquin, who made some corrections. The third edition was published in 1840.

13 Joseph Franz Jacquin's entry in Mozart's autograph album refers obliquely to matters botanical. He wrote (in Latin), "To thee who canst 'gently move the attentive oaks with thy melodious strings'. In token of friendship. Joseph Franz Jacquin, Vienna, 24 April 1787." Otto Erich Deutsch, *Mozart: A Documentary Biography* trans. Eric Blom, Peter Branscombe, and Jeremy Noble (Stanford: Stanford University Press, 1965) p. 29. The quote is from Horace.) We know that Mozart took at least some interest in natural history as the list of books owned by him contains two works (written for children) on nature, F. Osterwald's *Historical Description of the Earth for the Benefit of the Young* (published in Strasburg in 1777) and Johann Jakob Ebert's *Natural Science for the Young* (published in Leipzig, 3 vols., 1776–78). See Deutsch, *Mozart: A Documentary Biography*, pp. 601–02.

14 Nikolaus Jacquin, *Anleitung zur Pflanzenkenntniss nach Linnés Methode: Zum Gebrauche seiner theoretischen Vorlesungen* (Vienna: Christian Friedrich Wappler 1785), pp. 5–6.

like humans, sexual organs ("*Fortpflanzungsorgane*"). In a section entitled "The sexuality of plants," Jacquin observes that "the Ritter von Linnaeus called his system of plant classification a sexual system [*Geschlechtssystem*] . . . in plants the male and female genders are represented, and fertility [*Fruchtbarkeit*] is created between them."[15]

Linnaeus was originally introduced to the idea of plant sexuality in 1727 by a fellow scientist, Johann Rothman. At the time this idea was little known and not widely accepted,[16] but Linnaeus employed it from the start of his publishing career in *Systema naturae*. According to his system, plants were categorized first into *classes* and then into the subcategory of *orders*. Classes, the higher category, were derived according to the relative proportions and positions of the *male* parts of flowers, the stamens. Orders, which were subdivisions of the various classes, were based on the proportion and position of the flower's *female* parts, the pistils. (A flower could thus possess both male and female parts in various proportions.) Thus, the female attributes of plants were classified in relation to male attributes and the female properties of plants were rendered subordinate to the male. Further distinctions – genera, species, and variety – were in turn based upon differences between the gender-neutral calyx, flower, fruit, leaves, and a variety of other characteristics.

As Londa Schiebinger has observed in "The Private Life of Plants," Linnaeus's so-called "scienticization" of botany during the eighteenth century "coincided with an ardent 'sexualization' of plants."[17] Thus, in taking up and helping to elaborate Linnaeus's *systema sexuale*, Nikolaus Jacquin was simultaneously involved in a larger, pan-European, project of sexualizing nature. Sex, in Mozart's Vienna, had been introduced as the very essence of vegetable life.[18]

15 Jacquin, *Anleitung*, p. 164.
16 Tore Frängsmyr, ed., *Linnaeus: the Man and his Work* (Berkeley: University of California Press, 1983), p. 64.
17 Londa Schiebinger, "The Private Life of Plants: Sexual Politics in Carol Linnaeus and Erasmus Darwin," in Marina Benjamin, ed., *Science and Sensibility: Gender and Scientific Inquiry 1780–1945* (Oxford: Blackwell, 1991), p. 123.
18 Stafleu, *Linnaeus and the Linnaeans*, p. 55.

But sex of what kind? Or rather, according to what conventions did flowers conduct their amorous affairs? Crucial to the project of botany in the 1780s and 1790s were debates about the shape and conduct of plant sexuality, and the metaphors employed in describing the "nature" of this conduct represented rival attempts to inscribe plant life with human values. According to Linnaeus, the proper location for vegetable love was in the "lawful marriage" of plants or "plant nuptials." Schiebinger recounts how, in describing the sexual relations of plants, Linnaeus did not use the terms "stamen" and "pistil," but employed instead the Greek terms *andria* and *gynia* – husband and wife. Trees and shrubs donned floral "wedding gowns," while the anatomy of flowers burgeoned with sexual metaphor. The calyx, or "nuptial bed," was compared to human *labia majora* and foreskin; the corolla, or "bridal curtains," to *labia minora*. All were described as conspiring with the verdant bridegroom, preparing him "to embrace his beloved bride and offer her his gifts."[19]

The rigidly binary character of sexual difference that Linnaeus imposed upon plants thus paved the way for the heightened notions of sexual difference in human beings. Different however was the degree to which plants, but not humans, were understood as engaging in the legitimate pursuit of a variety of reproductive modes. Unlike the "lawful marriages" of humans, only one order of plants, the "one-husband" or *monoandria* class – the *monoandrian-monogynias* – practiced monogamy. Other plant classes and genera possessed flowers containing two or more "husbands" (stamens) and two or more "wives" (pistils). In other words, plants reproduced in a variety of polygynous and polyandrous relations, one bride with several bridegrooms or vice versa, or indeed, several of each.

To some observers and scientific commentators such as William Smellie, chief compiler of the first edition of the *Encyclopaedia Britannica*, Linnaean botany went "beyond all decent limits,"[20] while to others, it did not go far enough. In *The Loves of Plants*, pub-

19 Linnaeus, quoted in Schiebinger, "Private," p. 127.
20 Schiebinger, "Private," p. 130.

154 | *Tia DeNora*

lished in 1789 and again in 1791 along with *The Economy of Vegetation* (the two were collectively entitled *The Botanic Garden*), Erasmus Darwin popularized Linnaeus's ideas in passages that advocated the "free" expression of plant/human sexuality in a plethora of forms. Darwin – who viewed sex as "the cordial drop in the otherwise vapid cup of life" – poeticized the "wanton" nature of plant conduct in a way that invited human parallels to be both drawn and acted upon. His project, as he described it in an advertisement for *The Botanic Garden*, was to "inlist Imagination under the banner of Science."[21]

While Darwin is by no means the only creative artist to be so explicit about the project of popularizing or imaginatively re-clothing science, it is relatively rare for developments in science or technology to be so directly employed, and in so didactic a manner, as the basis for artistic work. As a number of cultural historians and science studies scholars have documented,[22] the interrelationship between the arts and sciences is typically complex and hard to trace. This is certainly the case with opera buffa and the late eighteenth-century biological sciences. Nevertheless, it is possible to view opera buffa as partaking of a culture in which vegetation and the metaphors of plant life were socially salient, sexually charged, and controversial. What, then, was the relationship between opera buffa and botanical imagery?

"HAN PIÙ FOGLIE CHE FRUTTI"? – WOMEN AND MEN IN THE BUFFA GARDEN

Come, lovely joy, do not delay. Come where love calls you to delight . . .
Flowers smile, the grass smells fresh; everything quickens the pleasures

21 Quoted in Maureen McNeil, *Under the Banner of Science: Erasmus Darwin and his Age* (Manchester: Manchester University Press, 1987), p. 184.
22 See Svetlana Alpers, *The Art of Describing: Dutch Art in the Seventeenth Century*, (Chicago: University of Chicago Press, 1983); Gordon Fyfe and John Law, eds., *Picturing Power: Visual Depiction and Social Relations*, (London: Routledge, 1988); Robert W. Witkin, *Art and Social Structure* (Cambridge: Polity Press, 1995).

of love. Come, my beloved, through these dark trees. I long to crown your brow with roses.

Le nozze di Figaro, IV.10 (trans. Mann, p. 431)

In Act II of *Le nozze di Figaro*, Cherubino leaps from a balcony outside the Countess's boudoir and lands in the garden below. We are meant to hear the sound of breaking glass – a cloche or cold frame perhaps, for a non-indigenous planting sheltered by the castle wall?[23] We learn later that it was a pot of carnations. Antonio – Head Gardener at Aguasfrescas – presents it indignantly to his employers. People are always flinging things out of the windows, he complains, but this is the first time a human being has been jettisoned.

As others have observed,[24] the garden provides a frequent setting for opera buffa. It is perhaps fitting that Cherubino – or *Cherubin d'amore* as he is called on one occasion by Basilio – makes his escape to the garden, since gardens in Mozart have scenic specificity; they are nearly always erotically charged. For example, Susanna (the gardener's niece) arranges to meet Almaviva in the shadowy evening garden, "beneath the pines of the grove" as she and the Countess put it in the letter they compose together. Later, in the crepuscular atmosphere of the evening garden, she describes how nature "conspires with the secrets of love": the flowers smile, the grass smells fresh. "Come, my beloved," she sings, ostensibly to Almaviva but in truth to Figaro, "through these dark trees. I long to crown your brow with roses."

As Wye Allanbrook has observed,[25] the pastoral features prominently in Mozart's operas. Both musically and poetically, it provides a natural-historical backdrop for love in all its guises. More specifically, she has suggested that the pastoral is a *topos* associated with the feminine and feminine sexuality (and the grace of sexual

---

23 Beaumarchais mentions melons.
24 Wye J. Allanbrook, "Human Nature in the Unnatural Garden: *Figaro* as Pastoral," *CM* 51 (1993), 82–93; *Rhythmic Gesture*; Mary Hunter, "Landscapes, Gardens, and Gothic Settings in the *Opere Buffe* of Mozart and his Italian Contemporaries," *CM* 51 (1993), 94–104.   25 Allanbrook, *Rhythmic Gesture*.

expression within the bonds of love). It is also associated with feminine inconstancy.

Opera buffa was by no means the only cultural form to be pre-
occupied with women, love, and sex. During Mozart's adult life-
time blurred genres abounded; for example, social-scientific
"lessons" concerning sexual, reproductive, and familial relations
were often presented through the media of fiction (e.g. Rousseau,
Bernardin de Saint-Pierre) and painting (e.g. Greuze, one of
Diderot's favorite painters).[26] As Ludmilla Jordanova has observed,
natural history cast its net widely during the eighteenth century.
The specific interest in reproduction within the natural sciences
spiralled back into the growing preoccupation with human sexuality as an object of scientific study. The result blended biology and
eroticism.[27] At one level, then, opera provided yet another cultural
"workspace" in which questions concerning nature and human
nature could be debated and dramatized. At another level, opera
could depict particular configurations of the erotic, as these arose
from and could be justified by "scientific" knowledge. Of special
interest, however, is that in company with a number of other cultural enterprises – anatomy, physiology, fiction, and social theory –
the natural history lessons of opera buffa were drawn from an
interrogation not of *human*kind, but specifically of *women*.

As a number of cultural historians have observed, woman
increasingly came to be associated with "the natural" – with being
less rational and less physically disciplined – during the eighteenth
century. "Man is more solid; woman is softer. Man is straighter;
woman is more supple. Man walks with a firm step; woman with a
soft and light one. Man contemplates and observes; woman looks
and feels" – these, according to Lavater in 1775–78, were the differences between the sexes.[28] In his *Dictionnaire de la conservation de
l'homme*, L. C. H. Macquart suggested that women were more sen-

---

26 L. J. Jordanova, "Naturalizing the Family: Literature and the Bio-Medical
    Sciences in the Late Eighteenth Century," in L. J. Jordanova, ed., *Languages of
    Nature: Critical Essays on Science and Literature* (New Brunswick, NJ: Rutgers
    University Press, 1986), p. 90.   27 Jordanova, *Naturalizing*, p. 87.
28 Quoted in Jordanova, *Naturalizing*, p. 92.

sible (sensitive or sensitized) than men – in fact they were like children in this regard – and also more passionate because of "the great mobility of their fibres, especially those in the uterus; hence their irritability, and suffering from vapours."[29] According to Linnaeus, woman's ability to lactate placed her closer than man ("homosapiens" [*sic*]) to other mammalian creatures.[30] In choosing the breast as the key distinguishing feature of mammals and in rejecting earlier distinctions, such as the one based on a creature's number of legs, Linnaeus's system reflected his current preoccupation with the breast and breast-feeding, and his involvement in anti-wet-nurse campaigns.[31] Moreover, as with his system of plant classification, Linnaeus introduced sexual difference as a salient feature of life itself.

In examining the cultural history of the breast, we can follow ideas about gender being imported and exported in a convoluted journey from social campaign to scientific classification and back again to social campaign, as a range of writers (as, for example, Rousseau) were quick to capitalize on the idea of the breast as "nature's sign" and the essential basis of woman's nurturant social role. Through such mutual referencing and borrowing between different branches of the social and natural sciences, cascades of biological inscriptions accrued in ways that eventually came to locate women (of all classes)[32] both within their naturally "rightful" place within the private sphere of the family[33] and within the

29 Ludmilla Jordanova, *Sexual Visions: Images of Gender in Science and Medicine between the Eighteenth and Twentieth Centuries* (Madison: University of Wisconsin Press, 1989), p. 28.   30 Schiebinger, "Mammals," pp. 393–94.

31 Ibid.

32 The "bourgeois" family ideal articulated by thinkers such as Rousseau applied to aristocrats as well. For example, Linnaeus suggested that baby farming, namely lower-class milk, could corrupt upper-class babies (Schiebinger, "Mammals," p. 407.)

33 The word family (*Familie*) was virtually unknown in the German-speaking world until around the second half of the eighteenth century. Ute Frevert, *Women in German History: From Bourgeois Emancipation to Sexual Liberation*, trans. Stuart McKinnon-Evans (Oxford: Berg, 1989), p. 14, has described how it is first listed in Krünitz's *Oeconomische Encyklopädie* in 1788 ("married couples and their children").

purview of the emerging "clinical gaze" of the newly mobilizing profession of medicine.[34] "By around 1800," Thomas Laqueur has observed, "writers of all sorts were determined to base what they insisted were fundamental differences between the male and female sexes, and thus between man and woman, on discoverable biological distinctions . . .".[35]

Thus, in a range of eighteenth century texts woman's anatomy and physiology made her more "natural" than man;[36] her bodily parts, her cycles, indeed, her very fibers rendered her less predictable and hence more subject to nature's laws. Woman was posited as natural and beautiful, but also as wild, dark, and dangerous. In short, woman was a potential bundle of troubles, emotionally and sexually unstable, medically problematic, and in need of scientific scrutiny. What better way of underscoring the instability of woman-as-nature than by associating her with that highly eroticized and sexually variegated entity – the flower?

"FIOR DI DIAVOLO" – OR, WHAT KIND OF FLOWER IS WOMAN?

You are the flowers of life . . . You civilize the human race . . . You are the Queens of our beliefs and of our moral order.
        (*Bernardin de Saint-Pierre, from the 1806 preface to* Paul et Virginie)[37]

34 See Anne Witz, *Professions and Patriarchy* (London: Routledge, 1991); Jean Donnison, *Midwives and Medical Men: A History of the Struggle for the Control of Childbrith* (2nd edn.), (London: Historical Publications, 1988), especially ch. 3, "The Ascendancy of Men" pp. 53–71; Barbara Ehrenreich and Deirdre English, *Witches, Midwives and Nurses: A History of Women Healers* (Old Westbury, NY: Feminist Press, 1973); William Ray Arney, *Power and the Profession of Obstetrics* (Chicago: University of Chicago Press, 1982); Ann Oakley, *The Captured Womb: A History of the Medical Care of Pregnant Women* (New York: Blackwell, 1984).
35 Thomas Laqueur, *Making Sex: Body and Gender from the Greeks to Freud* (Cambridge 1973, MA: Harvard University Press, 1990), p. 5.
36 Jordanova, *Sexual Visions*, ch. 2, *passim*.
37 Ibid., p. 34.

The association between women and flowers was hardly new to the late eighteenth century; indeed, its origins were pre-Linnaean.[38] New, however, was the overtly sexualized character of flowers. Given the social salience of botany in the 1780s, it seems reasonable to suggest that aristocratic and upper-middle-class audiences would have been at least vaguely aware of this new, anthropomorphic and overtly sexualized addition to flower imagery. If so, they would no doubt have appreciated its uses in opera.

The woman-flower comparison is frequently employed by Mozart and Da Ponte. For example, in Act I of *Le nozze di Figaro*, a chorus of flower-bearing country people describes how the Count's magnanimity in rescinding the *droit de Seigneur* has preserved for them "the divine innocence of an even lovelier flower." As Allanbrook has observed, the most musically "florid" part of the text they sing begins with the word *fiore*.[39] Later, a chorus of peasant girls presents flowers to the Countess – it is perhaps no accident that Beaumarchais named her Rosina; nor perhaps that nearly half the female characters in Mozart's buffa works have flower names.[40] In the Beaumarchais version, Figaro's famous monologue was a diatribe about politics. In the Da Ponte version political satire is removed. Instead, in Act IV, Figaro turns his attention to women ("Aprite un po' quegl'occhi, uomini incauti e sciocchi" – "Open your eyes a little, you incautious, silly men"). Angered and exasperated, Figaro compares women to a range of natural and supernatural entities: witches, sirens, owls, comets, vixens, she-bears, and malign doves. He also compares them to "thorned roses."

What kind of flower, then, was woman? And how was she to be

38 We can see it in Shakespeare, for example, in *The Winter's Tale*, where Perdita ushers in summer wreathed in flowers: "Here's flow'rs for you / Hot lavender, mints, savory, marjoram, / The marigold, that goes to bed wi' th' sun / And with him rises weeping; these are flow'rs / Of middle summer and I think they are given / To men of middle age" (IV. 4). The garden is also featured in this play as the setting for a woman's trial.

39 Allanbrook, *Rhythmic Gesture*, p. 92.

40 Rosina in *Le nozze di Figaro*; Rosina in *La finta semplice*; Violante in *La finta giardiniera* (and also the Count "Bel Fiore"); Fiordiligi in *Così fan tutte*; Giacinta in *La finta semplice*.

160 | *Tia DeNora*

classified? Women, as Bernardin de Saint-Pierre put it in the 1806 preface to *Paul et Virginie*, may be the "flowers of life," but like all natural objects, they are subject to laws that lie outside human convention. On the one hand woman/nature could bestow grace upon men, and shelter them from the exigencies of mundane life. We see this point clearly illustrated in the finale of *Le nozze di Figaro*. When all the confusion is sorted out, properly individuated love is protected by the efforts of women and is secured within the "lawful" institution of bourgeois companionate marriage.[41] On the other hand, love (and woman) are morally vulnerable and both can be "led astray" by an excess of desire. Woman was paradoxically configured as moral garantor on the one hand and temptress on the other. Within this paradox, nature and culture (social convention) could come into conflict when woman's sensual vulnerability led to the transgression of convention and the traduction of men (as Figaro observes in the conclusion of his Act IV monologue). Woman therefore required study – she could be controlled through understanding of the laws governing her behavior. "What kind of animal," asks Don Alfonso in Act I of *Così fan tutte*, "are these beauties of yours?" ("Che razza d'animali son queste vostre belle?"). As we have seen, this concern with taxonomy was characteristic of eighteenth-century thought; it should therefore not seem surprising that buffa plots abound with interrogations of woman's nature, and, within this enquiry, convey an almost obsessive interest in woman's sexual weakness.

One of these interrogative modes was the seduction plot, a creature of the late eighteenth century (e.g. Laclos, *Les Liaisons dangereuses*, 1781).[42] It consisted of a contrived or *man*-made environment in which the controlled or quasi-experimental proce-

---

41 We know this was a preoccupation of Mozart himself. As he wrote to Gottfried Jacquin on 4 November 1787, "Surely the pleasure of a transient, capricious infatuation is as far removed as heaven from earth from the blessed happiness of a deep and true affection." *Letters*, p. 913; *Briefe*, vol. 4, p. 59.

42 Nineteenth-century commentators found it repugant. H. C. Robbins Landon, *Mozart: The Golden Years* (New York: Schirmer, 1989), p. 177.

dure of testing women could be carried out in clinical detail.[43] The proving ground for man's observation of woman was, perhaps not surprisingly, often the garden – nature's laboratory. Mozart's and Da Ponte's *Così fan tutte* is a prime example of a seduction plot. Here, two gardens ("a garden by the seashore"/"a pretty little garden") provide the backdrop for women's temptation, resistance and eventual seduction. Dorabella and Fiordiligi ("lily-flower" – Da Ponte doled out flower symbolism with a heavy hand [lily=purity] for this more resistant sister) are described by Despina as "poor fools...wandering in the garden" ("Le povere buffone / stanno nel giardinetto" [1.12]). In Act II, scene 3, Don Alfonso calls the sisters to come at once to the garden where, in scene 4, Ferrando and Guglielmo arrive by boat, distributing garlands of flowers. Their servants distribute further flowers. The disguised lovers and the sisters then pair off and stroll in the garden. Later, when the men reconvene to discuss the sisters' behavior (Dorabella has succumbed to Guglielmo's advances), Ferrando, who has remained unsuccessful in his attempts to seduce Fiordiligi, tells his friend that she is "chaste as a lily" ("pura como columba" [literally, any plant from the arum family, such as jack-in-the-pulpit or calla lily]). When Fiordiligi objects to Dorabella that she doesn't understand how the heart can change in only one day, her sister replies, "Now you're being ridiculous! We're women!" ("Che domanda ridicola! Siam donne!"). Later still, after Fiordiligi has finally responded to Ferrando's wooing, Guglielmo refers to her as "flower of the devil" ("fior di diavolo").

This investigative attitude toward women (and the trial of women in gardens) is by no means unique to Mozart's operas. It is also featured in Da Ponte's and Martín y Soler's reworking of the plot of *L'arbore di Diana* (first produced in 1787; it was the work Da Ponte himself considered to be his best). As Mary Hunter has

43 Andrew Steptoe, *The Mozart-Da Ponte Operas: The Cultural and Musical Background to Le nozze di Figaro, Don Giovanni and Così fan tutte* (Oxford: Clarendon Press, 1988), p. 123.

observed,[44] the text was reworked from a 1721 *festa teatrale* by
Metastasio. A magic tree in Diana's garden lights up and plays
music when pure nymphs walk beneath it, but its fruit blacken and
pelt impure nymphs who pass under it. After Cupid's three youthful helpers have seduced all of Diana's nymphs, and eventually even
the Goddess of Chastity herself, the garden is transformed into a
palace of love. In Da Ponte's reworking of the story, the obstacle to
the union of Diana and Endimione is no longer his inexperience,
but Diana's commitment to virginity which, of course, is then duly
tried and eventually vanquished in the course of the opera, underscoring once again the emerging modern notion of woman's
paradoxical character as both virtuous and vulnerable to temptation.

Of course, not all women are so weak. In the Da Ponte–Martín y
Soler *Una cosa rara* (performed first in the autumn of 1786), a beautiful "girl of the mountains" loves a mountaineer but is pursued by
an infatuated Infante of Spain. She resists the Infante's advances
(both before and after her marriage) and for this (apparently astonishing) "virtuous" female conduct, she is awarded the appelation
"cosa rara" or "rare thing," following, as Da Ponte tells it, the
famous line of the satirist, *"Rara est concordia formae atque pudici-
tiae"* – "rare is it that beauty and virtue go together." She could
perhaps just as easily have been referred to as a "flower of grace and
virtue" ("Fior di grazie, e di virtu") – Rusticone's words in the 1789
Da Ponte–Salieri work, *La cifra*.[45]

To what extent are the "biology lessons" of opera buffa conveyed, not only through plot and librettos, but also through musical
characterization? In recent years this important question has been
addressed by several pioneering scholars. Of these, Gretchen
Wheelock's analysis of the gendered distribution of musical
material in Mozart's operas is highly compelling. Wheelock has

44 Mary Hunter, "Some Representations of *Opera Seria* in *Opera Buffa*," *COJ* 3 (1991),
    101–05.
45 John Platoff, "The Buffa Aria in Mozart's Vienna," *COJ* 2 (1990), 99–120. According
    to Da Ponte, *Una cosa rara* was a particular favorite of the ladies. Lorenzo Da
    Ponte, *Memoirs*, p. 149.

described how the social force of Mozart's female characters is musically undermined by the use of the so-called weak and unstable realm of the minor mode – a predominantly feminine musical medium. Wheelock's work speaks clearly to sociologists and others who are interested in the non-cognitive means through which social classifications are achieved and reinforced.[46]

Charles Ford has suggested that musical femininity in Mozart is achieved through fluid, aperiodic and functionless musical material which demarcates the feminine as a "sub-style," removed from the more musically purposive "public discourse" of diatonic musical masculinity. According to Ford, the chromatic color and nuance characteristic of Mozart's female vocal lines inscribes the feminine as, musically, a private world of feeling and sensibility; this is, of course, as Ford points out, a *male* representation of feminine sensibility.[47] The musical unpredictability of so much of Mozart's feminine musical material, particularly when women are undergoing seduction, Ford suggests, renders woman as "an empty but plenitudinous space," one in which the Enlightenment, in the form of its many projects and spokesmen, can project its classifications and "scientific" claims.

These specifically musicological explorations, which attempt to document musical constructions of gender differences, illuminate music as a crucial medium in the articulation of modern gender imagery. It should therefore come as no surprise that the biology lessons of the Enlightenment era were echoed and given further substance through the text and tones of opera buffa.

Woman as natural, as unstable, as in need of surveillance, as belonging in the realm of the private sphere – woman in this set of representations was deprived of participation in the then emerging realm of public life. At the same time the household or "private

---

46 "*Schwarze Gredel* and the Engendered Minor Mode in Mozart's Operas," in Ruth A. Solie, ed., *Musicology and Difference: Gender and Sexuality in Music Scholarship*, (Berkeley and London: University of California Press, 1993), pp. 201–21.

47 *Così? Sexual Politics in Mozart's Operas* (Manchester: Manchester University Press, 1991), p. 138.

sphere" was being transformed. Not only a locus of reproduction and physical maintenance, it increasingly came to be viewed as a feminine haven of feeling, warmth, and individuated love. Thus, the eighteenth-century obsession with woman, worked out in a range of media, provided a means for articulating and publicizing the bourgeois notion of marriage and its various antagonisms. To be sure, these views did not pass uncontested. Mary Wollstonecraft's *Vindication of the Rights of Woman* (1792) is perhaps the best-known work today to object to the gender bias of Enlightenment thought – its implicit pairing of woman with the private, and man with the public, sphere.

During the 1780s, dicta concerning the nature of woman and the social shape of love were being reinforced in a variety of cultural media. Opera buffa provided yet another "workspace" for the imaginative elaboration of gender difference as it was initially articulated in its modern, bourgeois form.[48] Of course, opera is impoverished if it is reduced to a mere venue for the rehearsal and mobilization of social imagery and sexual politics. But restoring opera's links to the social, scientific, and cultural contexts in which it was produced and consumed can also empower opera studies. Opera buffa gave dramatic, scenic, and musical flesh to the peculiarly Enlightened obsession with woman and her nature. Conversely, when nature and social convention are depicted as poised in harmony (through the medium of woman's constancy), as at the end of *Le nozze di Figaro*, opera buffa served as a crucial medium for the celebration (and modern articulation) of the fragile but glorious joys of love.

48 Perhaps because of its highly sensuous nature (dramatic action, music, scenery, costume, sound effects and props, poetry) opera is one of the most persuasive media. To look at how twentieth-century music scholars themselves have not been immune to opera's seductive and sometimes insidious "biology lessons" would no doubt be instructive. For example, whatever could William Mann (whose writing on Mozart's operas is often delightful) have been thinking when he wrote, ". . . it would be beneficial to [Donna Anna's] personal growing-up if she had been pleasantly raped by Don Juan"? Mann, *The Operas of Mozart* (New York: Oxford University Press, 1977), p. 468. (This passage is also quoted in Ford, *Così?*, p. 185.)

CHAPTER 6

Music and Erotic Agency – Sonic Resources and Social-Sexual Action

How does the cultural configuration of being and body happen? Just how are cultural products mobilized and how *do* texts, images, sonic structures and representations inform and thereby 'get into' action? These are key questions for cultural studies, sociology and social psychology. They have so far not been addressed head on, and they by no means entail a mere 'empirical implementation' of an otherwise already complete theorization of agency. In this article, I suggest that a good theory of agency can be developed through specific considerations of particular social realms, and with reference always to particular cultural materials. To this end, after some initial theoretical clarification of the links between culture, nature and social agency, I focus on the *erotic*, in order to pursue a more general concern with the interrelationship of expressive media and social agency (Witkin and DeNora, n.d.). More specifically, I consider the question of how erotic agency may be 'musically composed' (DeNora, 1995a), by which I mean how agency may take shape with reference to musical media.

Culture into Agency

The Social Structure of Sexual Experience

The erotic is one of the best available building sites for cultural constructivist theory because the emotions, pleasure and desire have consistently been brought to the fore in current sociocultural analysis. This attention arose as part of an effort to redress the often 'disembodied' character of classic social theory (Turner, 1984; Featherstone et al., 1991) and to address the historical, geographical and scenic specificities of sexual pleasure (Gagnon and Simon, 1973; Plummer, 1975; Jackson,

1978, 1982; Foucault, 1981, 1987; Weeks, 1981, 1985; Simon and Gagnon, 1984; Snitow et al., 1984; Greenberg, 1988; Seidman, 1992). Thanks to works like these, it is now commonplace for sexual activity to be theorized as something that takes shape in and through reference to culture – imageries, representations, metaphors, sexology manuals, narrative structures, medical and scientific classifications, and so on. Cultural materials are herein understood as providing possibilities for the 'disciplinization' of bodies, hearts and minds to the extent that culture is understood to offer a range of (potentially contradictory) physical and emotional ways of being, sexual being included (Coward, 1984; Betterton, 1987; de Lauretis, 1987; Rakusen, 1989; Irvine, 1990; Bartky, 1990; Hall, 1991; Birke, 1992a, 1992b; Laqueur, 1990; Jackson, 1996; Jeffreys, 1990).

It is one thing to illuminate the cultural construction of sexual *representations*, and to allude to their constitutive role as 'technologies' of gender (de Lauretis). It is quite a different, and perhaps equally challenging, matter to describe how these representations actually 'get into' and inform real lines of erotic conduct. What has been missing within sociocultural studies so far is a focus on the social, social-psychological and micro-political *processes* through which desire and socially situated sexual action actually come to be culturally informed (see Jackson, 1994 on this point). Conversely, we also know little about how cultural forms come to be occupied by real-time residents. These matters are far from trivial: for real social actors – social analysts included – the idea that culture can be mobilized in ways that generate erotic agency is well known, albeit not necessarily in these specialist-analytic terms. In erotic play, in daydream and in more strategic forms of sexual conduct, actors can be seen clearly to mobilize culture; they (we) may resort to diverse images, scripts, values and ideas of all kinds in order to 'do' being erotic and being sexual. In this respect, 'passing' and 'getting through' the erotic is similar to the accomplishment of any other scenic social activity. At times, these mobilizations are accompanied by considerable self-awareness; at other times, actors resort to particular cultural forms as a matter of practical action or routine. Whatever the level of reflexive awareness, culture clearly provides constituent ingredients for the configuration of (erotic) feeling, situations and agency.

How, then, do cultural forms get 'under the skin' in ways that animate actors, 'nature' and natural-social scenarios? And what, if any, are the limits of cultural construction?

A convenient entry into these issues as they apply to the social/physiological event of orgasm is supplied by Travers (1993). Travers depicts orgasm as fraught with a peculiar kind of tension, one generated from an often conventional demand in sexual interaction for contradictory forms of sincerity – social versus bodily. On the one hand, sexual actors may be constrained by the need 'to please' each other through the mutual communication of bodily (i.e. 'natural') pleasure.[1] To accomplish this 'social' form of sincerity, actors employ a range of gestures and devices garnered from more and less conventional etiquettes and images of nature/pleasure.[2] For example, they may feel obliged to enact preferred semblances of 'dissolution of the self into bio-forces beyond its control' (Travers, 1993: 137). On the other hand, bodily sincerity, or 'sincerity of the flesh' as Travers puts it – may not resemble culturally preferred and publicized images of sexual climax. Thus, Travers concludes, 'a faked orgasm [i.e., one accompanied by canonic orgasmic insignia] is often more real than a real one' (1993: 137), the 'real' one being improperly socialized (and therefore not ceremonially pleasing but rather, socially insincere) when unaccompanied by canonic orgasmic insignia. These contradictory demands on the social and physical body are generated by physical versus social ceremonial forms of sincerity. This contradiction is perhaps an existential feature of (late 20th century?) 'intimacy' – the need for (creatively misplaced?) trust because, as Travers puts it, 'no matter how loud the cries, how inevitably *accelerando* the climax, how transported the facial features, there is no guarantee that all the signs are not empty, as in *When Harry Met Sally*' (1993: 137). I now want to use and critique Travers's insights in order to move beyond what I regard as 'weak' versions of cultural constructivism.

Disentangling Culture, Nature and Agency

By portraying the ceremonial features of sexual occasions, Travers's consideration of orgasm highlights some of the ways in which bodily processes and bodily responses are socially 'disciplined', how the body and its activities may be structured and presented in ways that 'live up to' social expectations, values and taboos. Just as Elias (1939) documented the disciplinization of a range of bodily minutiae, Travers points to sexual 'climax' and sexual narrative as similarly socially disciplined. In this respect, he is not alone (see Gardetto, 1988). In what follows, I suggest that a focus on bodily dramaturgy, and the cognitivist bias this project entails, unnecessarily juxtaposes the bodily and the social (as if the social merely 'clothed' the body). Such a project is simply not bullish enough about culture's powers, it does not specify adequately what is meant by culture, nature or social agency and it cannot therefore examine the actual character of the interrelationship between these terms. To lay the groundwork for this 'strong' theory, via musical examples, of how culture gets into action and 'nature' and, conversely, how nature and culture are the achievements of social action, I attempt, in the next two sections to disentangle culture, nature and agency.

46 ■ Body and Society

Disentangling Culture and Agency
Interactionist perspectives on sexuality are sometimes criticized for failing to theorize the role of cultural and social *structures* and for failing to consider the social
provenance of aesthetic structures such as, for example, sexual 'scripts' (see, e.g.,
Walby, 1990: 115). This criticism is only partially correct. It imputes to interactionist conceptions far too much regard for 'free' agency and it fails to appreciate
the implicit structuralist character of many symbolic interactionist treatments of
sexuality.

It is true that dramaturgical and other actor-centred approaches to sexuality do
not usually consider the question of where particular sexual-cultural forms come
from (e.g. where did the 'twin-set and pearls' femininity to which Garfinkel's
'Agnes' aspired actually come from? And *who says* orgasmic cries will be
meaningful or 'realistic' only if they involve *accelerando*, particular facial features
or *crescendo*?). But it is not true that actor-centred approaches ignore the supra-
individual features of culture. Indeed, their failure to develop the concept of
culture derives less from a denial of culture than from an implicit tendency to
presume cultural structures while at the same time failing to describe the mechanisms through which culture actually informs action. Culture, in other words, bears
a great deal of weight in many actor-centred approaches, but it is rarely positioned
in the limelight.

For example, the Goffmanian – and, on occasion, even the Garfinkelian –
subject, is obliged to respect, realize and maintain the ceremonial order of a
'normal, natural world', that is the world of social forms. As a case in point,
Travers's depiction of social and sexual social agency dwells almost exclusively on
the mobilization of preferred signs. It purports the acting subject as concerned
with 'getting it right' in terms of gesture, with 'passing' and with being 'pleasing'.
In sexual situations, for example, it may be polite and indeed expected, that one
groan! Thus, what dramaturgical and some ethnomethodological accounts fail to
address is also what structuralist and poststructuralist accounts themselves often
omit: cultural innovation, challenge, resistance, change and – perhaps equally
importantly – the ways in which what comes to pass as cultural 'stasis' is a
dynamic social achievement (Hays, 1994; Barnes and Loyal, forthcoming).

These are important matters because cultures are never fully formed, never
ineluctable, and therefore themselves topics of investigation *and* manipulation
(just as it is political to depict 'natural reality' so too it is political to make claims
about 'what a culture is' [Barnes, 1982; Bourdieu, 1984; Tudhope et al., 1995]).
This point is underscored when the indexical properties of concepts, rules or conventions are recognized (Barnes 1982). If it is in and through practical instantia-
tions that cultures and traditions are realized, then a space is left for creative forms

of agency and, thus, for social and cultural challenge and change. As one com-
mentator has put it, the Goffmanian, dramaturgically engaged subject is, 'committed to the conventional order, not distanced from it' (Witkin, 1995: 183). The
focus of dramaturgical sociologies is therefore implicitly directed to actors as *enactors* of the ceremonial.

Thus culture is not the sole author of action. Dramaturgical perspectives may
tell us about how culture disciplines action, but they celebrate cultural stability
and underemphasize the ways in which cultures are often packed with tension.
Dramaturgical perspectives are thus of little use for nuanced examinations of the
dynamic quality of the culture–agency relationship, examinations that recognize
the reflexive relationship between the ways that agents invoke and mobilize cultures and cultural forms themselves.

Indeed, the ability to be conscious of culture as something to be used, shaped
and mobilized, and the ability to comment reflexively upon culture, implies that
agents have degrees of distance from cultural resources. Recently these issues have
been reinvigorated within the literature on 'modernity'. A range of commentators
have suggested that the ability to stand askew from cultural forms, and to mobilize those forms deliberately in favour of specific activities, are cardinal features
of late 20th-century life (Giddens, 1990, 1991; Baudrillard, 1983; Lash and Urry,
1993; Witkin, 1995), though the historical nature of this claim has not gone unchallenged (Douglas, 1993). This heightened reflexivity, and the often *removed* quality
this reflexivity lends to real-time experience, is a function of the plurality and
availability of (often contradictory) discourses that characterize the so-called
'postmodern condition'. 'Simulation', 'virtuality', 'hyperrealism' – these terms
index a purportedly *modern* form of symbolic mobility wherein an entry into a
cultural form is like making a 'trip' (Urry, 1990; Frisby, 1985; Lash and Urry,
1993). This mobility is itself viewed as a testimony to the heightened role played
by culture and the imaginary in modern life.

In short, if we are to gain explanatory benefit from the idea of cultural construction as it occurs at the ground-level of social agency, then the study of how
cultural forms 'get into' action needs to be built upon a conception of agency and
culture as distinct but reflexively linked. This reflexive linkage can be understood
as occurring in two directions. First, in and through the ways that action mobi-
lizes culture, it 'fills in' or creatively elaborates the very forms that enable and constrain it. Second, a plurality of cultural forms may be available for action, and these
forms may have contradictory implications for action's outcomes. The perception
of this plurality, and the potential contradictions engendered by it, in turn
lengthen the distance between actors and the cultural forms in and through which
action is configured.

Disentangling Culture and Nature

A similar type of reflexivity applies to the interrelationship of culture and nature. It can be illuminated by considering the *limits* of cultural constructivism. These limits need to be specified if the power of culture is to be fully investigated and if we are to specify what it means to say that bodies and bodily processes are inextricable amalgams of nature/culture (as I do below by considering the ways in which culture may provide crucial ingredients for the organization of bodily processes). Thus, it is necessary to recover, albeit only temporarily, the now-often discarded culture/nature dichotomy.

Sexual action and bodily response can occur outside or askew from narratives and classification systems. That is, sexual experience may be meaningful to bodies without necessarily being meaningful to linguistic or imagistic consciousnesses. In a variety of ways, bodies and bodily sensation can and will exist outside of culture – bodies can warm, cool, exude, swell, feel pain or be itchy, and so on. These phenomena may be ascribed with a variety of meanings, and they may remain 'meaningless', i.e. without socially recognized implication (Hilbert, 1984, 1986). Indeed, the non-linguistic *materiality* of sex – its specific sensual properties, such as smells or sounds – constitute some of its distinguishing features and may serve to sexualize otherwise non-sexual circumstances.

I am suggesting that the cultural construction of 'culture/nature' is not, as is sometimes implied, a one-way process; non-cultural, bodily materiality provides enabling/constraining resources for the generation of 'new' cultural forms. This is true for sexual culture but also for many other forms of culture production. For example, in an earlier study (DeNora, 1995b) I have discussed how Beethoven's bodily approach to the piano keyboard provided a somatic basis for his musical style. In a different context, I have also described how, within a culture of 'alternative' contraceptive practice, material aspects of the fertile female body have been identified in ways that access them as 'natural resources' for the articulation of gendered accounts of bodies, reproduction and sex (DeNora, 1996). Similarly, others have described how the materiality of bodies can 'disrupt' social relations and this disruption may provide space within which to resist a 'given' cultural regime (Holland et al., 1994: 23); particular bodies, in other words, do not only give rise to particular desires, they may also *intrude on* desire, whether actors' own or the desires of others (Holland et al., 1994: 23). Indeed, the very point that cultural representations are *political* rests upon the assumption that representations interact with, and make demands on, their subjects in different and consequential ways. Cultural forms may configure nature, but they do so by marginalizing and ranking *non*-cultural features (e.g. of bodies). To speak of the 'politics of representation' presumes, in other words, a negotiation between cultural forms and

Tia DeNora ■ 49

the subjects and materials to which these forms apply. This presumption implicitly rests on actors' real experiences of tension between culture and non-culture, between forms of culture and *something else*.

The point, then, is that culture is not totalizing in its disciplinary properties over nature; rather it facilitates the process of bringing *semblances* of the material body to life. Culture vivifies and disciplines the body, yes, but it does not create bodies *ex nihilo*. This point is illustrated clearly in the cultural history of anatomy. A number of distinguished scholars have recently demonstrated that anatomical classification systems have politics in and through the ways they discipline what counts as the body and its workings (Jacobus et al., 1990). Nowhere is this point more vividly illustrated than through the vicissitudes of the clitoris and its career in the annals of 'orthodox' medical taxonomy (Moore and Clarke, forthcoming). Nonetheless, and without denying the serious consequences of anatomical/cultural politics in this regard, women may experience sexual pleasure whether or not they have read *Gray's Anatomy* because (1) the body is *more* than a mere cipher and (2) because there are cultures of the body and bodily practice that do not owe their existence to public descriptors.

One does not, in other words, require adjectives – or, for that matter, concepts – for bodily experience, though cultures provide often robust, compelling resources for facilitating and organizing bodily experience and its perception. Bodies – not just actors – can *act*, and can do so in unruly, un-cultured ways; bodies are not just culture disciples and because of this, they may betray actors just as actors may betray bodies.

In short, 'nature' – when it consists of unanticipated and undefined bodily manifestations – may provide resources for cultural discovery, for the creative production of new and 'alternative' accounts of 'how nature works'. Indeed, this is the liberatory feature of culture; that new and 'alternative' forms can be created and adapted in innovative ways, by individuals and collectivities. Cultures are living; they are public conveniences and as such can be tailored to the perceived exigencies of local, practical and material circumstances. The perception of the 'reality' of these circumstances is never entirely dependent upon the viewpoints that cultures provide. To believe otherwise is to be a 'cultural dope'.

'Nature' has been recently disempowered within sociocultural theory. It has too often been reduced to an empty space, one merely awaiting cultural configuration, a mere 'raw and pliable material' for meaning construction. It is as if so-called 'nature' were only knowable in and through culturally constructed forms. This position is crude and is well-illustrated by considering the erotic realm.[3] It is not currently popular to maintain that 'nature constructs culture'. To do so – to refer to bodily 'realities' – is often viewed as dangerously essentialist, as leading away from or ignoring constructivist understanding. This need not be the case. The creation and mobilization of culture and its resulting 'natural histories' may be structured by the specific material features of 'nature' (nature may greet social actors without having been formally [culturally] introduced). Moreover, to maintain that culture constructs nature, without simultaneously maintaining the opposite, smuggles an unwarranted form of theoretical asymmetry into an otherwise useful understanding of nature and culture as reflexively linked. As Carole S. Vance (1992) suggested some time ago, we can and should incorporate, 'bodily sensation and function into a social constructivist frame while still acknowledging that human experience of the body is always mediated by culture and subjectivity, and without elevating the body as deterministic' (Vance, 1992: 140).

The human sciences should not be shy of the idea that there is an extra-cultural dimension to human social activity. Indeed, entertaining such a notion creates conceptual space within which to explore with far more nuance the interrelationship between culture, nature and agency. That relationship is currently (and oxymoronically) depicted as simultaneously too tight and too loose. It is too tight because it will not admit the possibility that action may escape *discursive* construction but may nonetheless be social (in ways that highlight the physicality, the animal-sociality of human action). It is too loose because it is unable to retain a principle that cultural construction can apply not only to meaningful action, but to human physicality (e.g. the physiological human body) as well. If this statement appears paradoxical it is only because of social theory's current inability to conceive of culture as simultaneously *more* powerful and *less* ubiquitous than it is currently understood to be. One may be an agent without necessarily being a *cultured* agent because resources and structures for agency may derive from physical and environmental features of action's settings and from actors' bodies as these interact with settings. *Bodily* business may be transacted outside culture ('nature may inform culture') and also outside the modes of consciousness that culture generates. Conversely, the body and its business are both heightened and suppressed by culture; actors/bodies live up to cultural expectations and engage in the moral work of producing a 'natural, normal world'. Sexual bodies, like bodies in general, are thus neither full-time consumers of, nor fully consumed by, cultures. Cultures arise from bodies as much as vice versa. (Think, for example, of the links over time between '*cuisine*' and what historically/geographically located human bodies can chew, swallow, tolerate and digest.)

As Haraway (1985) has suggested, the body can be usefully viewed as a cyborg ('cybernetic organism'), a compound of hybrid techno-organic embodiment and textuality. Bodily potentialities are made manifest through the ways they *interact with* the symbolic and material cultures that repress, liberate and otherwise

Tia DeNora ■ 51

discipline them. These configuration processes are rarely smooth, indeed they are mostly 'lumpy' (Haraway, 1985) because the cultural resources that discipline bodies are often inimical. But it is through these configuration processes that anatomy and physiology – as we know them – are assembled.

In sum, good constructivist theory can acknowledge material realities without hypostatizing them and without reverting to essentialism. The recognition of bodily realities only strengthens the power of constructivist paradigms, particularly when we can cite cases where bodies are culturally configured and where particular aspects of bodily reality are culturally suppressed. Culture clearly facilitates/constrains the transaction of bodily business; it constructs bodily reality to the extent that body and embodied action are reflexively oriented to the terms, models and structures culture provides. For example, how many individuals 'know' their gallbladders in the ways they 'know' their genitals? Because we have learned a range of conventional accounts for the latter – accounts which provide simultaneously a medium of surveillance – we mistakenly assume that there is less to know about the former (or that such knowledge is less accessible – even when they give us 'trouble' we learn about our gallbladders through the intermediaries of X-rays, experts and scans). Thus, to tighten up the looseness of cultural constructivism, and to loosen up the tight bits, we need to accept that (1) even highly cultured, well-disciplined and vigilantly surveilled entities like genitals may 'act' in ways that escape cultural frameworks, and (2) even un-cultured things like the gallbladder may be phenomenally amplified in and through the creation of culture. 'Culture', then, is a resource for the *realization* of particular semblances or aspects of 'nature', and, conversely, bodily materiality may provide a resource for culture creation.

Returning now to Travers's dramaturgical portrayal of the orgasm helps to clarify this point. Distinguishing, as Travers does, between the 'real' (physiological) and 'fake' (i.e. social) features of orgasm pre-empts investigation of the *interaction* between the semiotic and physiological body. The nature/culture distinction that dramaturgic considerations of the body preserve make it impossible to consider that bodies may in fact *become* the forms that depict them. It may, in other words, be sociologically disempowering to conceive of a non-interactive relationship between body and culture. Although culture is not the only resource for social and/or sexual agency (I have described above some of the ways that 'nature' may intrude on social action in ways that lead to cultural innovation), culture and body may interact. Actors are often aware of the 'uses' of culture and they often make and mobilize culture in ways that allow them to 'get things done'. Indeed, the culture/body dichotomy is precisely what actors are often attempting to bridge, either by trying to align nature with culture (e.g. through exercise or plastic surgery) or culture with nature (e.g. by engaging in activities to alter representations and conventions). In these ways, actors may be engaged routinely in the personal and social projects of establishing more intimate links between the bodily (*their* bodies) and the cultural. Culture is thus not only good to think with, it is something within which one can be a body of quality. Both in their technical details and in the responses that come to be associated with these details, cultural forms bear traces of bodies – *the* body, perhaps, but also particular bodies as these appear within 'idiocultures' (Fine, 1986). Bodies come alive and are configured through culture; indeed, sometimes, bodies can only be or do things when culture is there to help.

For example, in the now-classic piece, 'Sensual Uncertainty, or Why the Clitoris is not Enough', Lynne Segal (1983) can be read as elaborating this theme. In autobiographical mode, Segal describes how the fantasies which she has always needed, 'to come to orgasm, by any methods, are . . . tedious and obnoxious. . . . I resent the effort I have to make to produce them, and the disconnection which occurs with lovers who, at least recently, are most caring, gentle and as extensively physically stimulating as I could wish' (1983: 42). Segal describes the way in which, for her, culture (images and ideas) are part of an erotic technique of arousal and satiety. That is, fantasy is a device that generates explicit 'fixations' for imaginative and real-time sexual processes. In this sense, then, culture is a 'fix' and Segal, in these circumstances, a 'culture addict' who needs the (what she considers to be) unwholesome cultural substance of masochistic imagery, without which she can't get to and through 'orgasmic sex'.

Both Travers and Segal show us how culture is 'used' to accomplish sex. Both allude to how cultural materials – images ideas, and texts – are brought into the bedroom where they function, as they would in any other setting, as part of a 'toolkit' (Swidler, 1986) for social action, as a means or medium for the accomplishment of scenic (Travers) and bodily (Segal) specificity. Cultural materials – things from outside the real-time event – provide cues and means for the organization of lines of conduct and bodily process. A focus on how culture gets into (sexual) action, therefore, is a focus not only on the semiotic and ethnomethodological 'work' of sex, but also on the cultural creation of the body and thus, on body politics. In recognizing culture's limits (in relation to the nature and to agency), and that it may apply to social locations and actors with varying degrees of intensity, culture's constitutive and disciplinary powers are significantly extended into the realm of human physicality. Thus, finally, a theoretical foundation for a 'strong' version of cultural construction has been established. In the remainder of this article I build upon this foundation by developing a theory of how culture, here specifically *music*, 'gets into' and 'composes' action, here erotic action.

Music and Aesthetic Agency

How can music be examined for the ways in which it is implicated in the constitution of aesthetically reflexive subjects? When actors employ music in the context of erotic activity, to what extent can this resort to culture be understood as part of a process of constituting an aesthetic-erotic environment and a set of parameters (a partial pre-design or stylistic signalling) for the organization of erotic interaction and its embodied beings? How is music a resource for the configuration of bodies/minds?

Music as a Social 'Force'

There is a venerable tradition within musical theory that depicts music as active in the production of emotion, thought and conduct. From Plato's strictures against particular melodies to the Parents' Music Resource Center (Baker, 1994), the notion of musical *affect* is prominent. Because of its conventional and often repeated character (notated, orally or mechanically reproduced), music is a purposeful, though not necessarily instrumental-rational activity. Can bodies, then, be understood to pass through sonorous fields, and if so, how? Can music's 'traces' be perceived in acting bodies? How, more specifically, do actors (and their bodies) *use* musical culture in real-time experience?

It seems obvious that music is effective (that for its listeners it is infused with *affect*), and that, at least on occasion, music channels action (to the extent that it is oriented to and articulated as meaningful). I have addressed this issue in earlier work (DeNora, 1995a) using Willis's (1978) study of the 'bikeboys'. Willis describes how these boys thought of their music as emblematic of their non-musical cultural practices. For the bikeboys, music was not merely 'representative' of professed values/acts. Rather, music was *constitutive* of social life in the sense that the boys referred to their music in order to create and enforce a way of life that was, 'almost literally *seen in* the qualities of their preferred music' (1978: 63, emphasis in original).

Music and Temporality

Within Bikeboy culture, music provided a cultural *vehicle*, a means of transport from one situation to another, a way of 'getting through' a particular situation. To say that the Bikeboy's music provided a referent *for* a mode of activity, is to say that it provided a working or candidate model for the temporal/spatial ordering (coordinating) of the evening. For example, referring to a musical passage, an actor might say to another, 'We'll go like *this*', or s/he might make use of music as metaphor to allude to a line or style of action (e.g. 'faster', or 'smoother', or 'in

54 ■ Body and Society

unison'). The point here is that music provides non-propositional *resources* for collective (i.e. concerted) physical activity. For the Bikeboys, music provided a guide/model for how to move bodies (on/off bikes). As with dance (Thomas, 1993), then, music can be understood as providing a referent to be taken up in and through bodily conduct. Music can thus provide a catalyst for body transformation (slow to fast, sitting or standing, standing to dancing, clipped to fluid and so on). Music is by no means the *only* referent for body transformation – one can also move 'like treacle' or run 'like the wind'. Moreover, music – like treacle, wind and poetry, 'makes nothing happen' (as Auden once put it), but is nonetheless, 'a way of happening/a mouth'. As a candidate way of happening, music (treacle, wind, poetry) provides models, means, motives, agendas and opportunities for ways of social and social-sexual happening.

For example, like other cultural materials (Adam, 1991), music can provide resources for the articulation of temporal process. At a basic level, music can be used to measure time. (Toscanini's rendering of Mozart's overture to *Le Nozze de Figaro* is often described as the perfect egg-timer – if you want a very soft boiled egg.) Music can also be used to map or *mark* the phenomenological experience of time's passage (for example, a 'long time' can be turned into 'no time at all' through the introduction of music [DeNora, 1995a]). Musical translation of time occurs when music is perceived as providing a *ground* against which time's passing can be observed, (re)evaluated and (re)experienced. Through the ways time is musically 'chunked', linear or serial time can be converted in to cyclical time, time can be heard to be repeating itself, recoiling, retracting or retreating. It can also be understood as compressed or decompressed (e.g. 'cut time' or 'double time'). Music can make time 'fly', it can make us 'forget time' and it can also 'drag time out'. Music can also annul time: for example, Adorno (1974) considered Stravinsky's use of 'primitive' rhythms (i.e. dance rhythms) degraded the time of the bourgeois subject through its abandonment of overarching rhythmic patterns in favour of sheer pulse. In Adorno's view, this was one aspect of the 'sacrifice' of the subject which he so disdained in Stravinsky. In the celebration of the musical unit of the pulsating instant, historical structures and historical consciousness were forsaken. This, Adorno believed, led to the 'forgetful' mindset that was the bedrock of the 'ontological ideology'.

Specifying the 'Music' of Sexual Action – Music as Metaphor
I have described how music 'chunks' and rechunks time and how actors may play or imaginatively replay music in ways that enable them to transcend other time claims. I have also alluded, via Willis (1978), to how music may be used to realign bodily activity (speed up/slow down the motion of bodies). These are examples

of how music provides non-conceptual, non-verbal, non-pictorial *resources* for the constitution of agency. In them, music can be seen as a resource for producing activity that has narrative structure and timing. In these two senses, music provides technologies for the production of occasioned social realities.

Music may also be used as a metaphor or analogue for non-musical events, concepts and activities. For example, one might attempt to *think* 'symphonically' or 'contrapuntally'. Or one might 'trumpet' one's message. One might speak of 'feminine' and 'masculine' cadences (weak vs strong closure to the tonic key) or feminine and masculine themes, as is all too common in music commentary. One might also say that the music of Beethoven conveys, as Adrienne Rich once put it, 'sexual messages' (quoted in McClary, 1991: 129). For Susan McClary, at least, Beethoven's characteristically powerful, boisterous and sometimes obsessive forms of musical closure (e.g. the finale of the Fifth Symphony) are phallocentric (McClary, 1991). In all of these examples, music is being *read* – by social actors – as a metaphor, simulation or sublimation of social life. In the act of these readings, actors mobilize music as a resource for action, argument and for the constitution of social reality.

How social representations are inscribed into and read off from 'disinterested' music is of course of considerable interest to analysts of culture. But it is important here that we do not treat these readings as resources, but rather consider them as members' accounts. To remain in our interpretive armchairs dictating claims about just what music metamorphoses is simply authoritarian (DeNora, 1986, 1995a), overlooking as it does the often rich diversity of cultural practice and consumption through which texts of all kinds are 'made habitable' (de Certeau, 1984). To claim for example, that Beethoven's music is 'masculine' because it is 'powerful' (i.e. loud, emphatic *tutti* finales) not only skips a logical step, it simultaneously grounds itself on unwarranted assumptions about the 'nature' of the feminine. For these reasons, it is clearly turned away from the interactionist concern with the ways actors co-produce both themselves through objects and, conversely, produce objects through themselves.

Music is a key cultural resource for the disciplinization of body, emotion and action. It is a form of culture closely linked, through movement and dance, to body conduct. As with all forms of culture, however, its link to agency (and to the interpretations it inspires) is contingent upon local circumstances of use. Particular musics may conspire with or against particular bodies, they may constrain and/or enable particular desires and forms of conduct.

Of sociological interest, then, is the question of how, with reference to musical forms, nature/culture amalgams are forged by real actors. To ask this question is simultaneously to ask about how music is a constituent ingredient in actors' productions of their agencies. In what follows, I suggest that we can do this not by considering whether music simulates erotic activity, but rather by considering how and when erotic activity simulates music. Can/do we (ever), for example, hear (feel? experience?) music in sex? To ask this question is to ask whether music and sex are ever or can ever be co-productive. To address these questions means that we need to consider much more closely what it means to say that music organizes the body. To do so is to examine Raymond Williams's proposition that:

> rhythm is a way of transmitting a description of experience, in such a way that the experience is re-created in the person receiving it, not merely as an 'abstraction' or an emotion but as a physical effect on the organism – on the blood, on the breathing, on the physical patterns of the brain . . . it is more than a metaphor; it is a physical experience as real as any other. (1961: 66–9 and quoted in McClary, 1991: 23)

Issues like these can only be explored through qualitative studies of music and everyday life. They *cannot* be addressed through social theory alone. In the remainder of this article, I draw on a few tentative examples of some of the myriad ways in which music may be used as a structuring device for erotic interaction. These examples should not be considered as ethnographic data (though an ethnographic investigation is currently ongoing); they are used only for the heuristic purpose of formulating topics and questions for the investigation of music-in-action.

Music in Everyday Life – As Soundscape for Erotic Action

Here are the musical-erotic experiences of four social actors, each of whom had been involved in at least one sexual situation where music played a constitutive, organizing role. All four of the accounts concern heterosexual encounters, all of which occurred at the male participant's dwelling. Perhaps unsurprisingly, therefore (but also in keeping with studies of gender and domestic technology [Jackson and Moores, 1995]), in each case, it was the *male* partner who selected the 'background' music.

In the first example, a female respondent described how she 'went home with' a man who put on a recording of Bach's *Saint Matthew Passion*. The choice of music bemused her because she thought it seemed inappropriately pious for what she regarded as a 'casual' encounter. It was as if the male participant was trying to use the music to signal their union as spiritual ('love'), on a high emotional plane. Thus the music 'made' assumptions about the quality of the relationship, insofar as the action which it accompanied was coloured by its inflections.

In another example, a female participant described how a man she knew liked to play symphonic music during sexual encounters. She described the music as 'intruding' on their interaction, saying that, 'it was like he was getting off on the music' (rather than really interacting with her). This she found offensive because,

'I don't like having sex to music because I don't like sex aids of any kind.' In this second example, music is not only used to signal the quality of the sexual encounter, and to comment on its 'seriousness'; beyond this, the music came to function as a device for the enhancement of the erotic occasion.

Conversely, music can depress sexual excitement. One woman (musically trained) described how she had gone home with a man (also a university trained musician), with whom she was already acquainted sexually. He put Alban Berg's *Wozzeck* on the stereo.[4] In the course of the evening, they quarrelled, and she left. Later, attempting to account for that evening's 'troubles', he suggested that 'he should never have played *Wozzeck*' because it altered the scene in ways that led to their sexual disconnection.

These examples raise the issue of how music may be used as a structuring device in sexual situations, in particular, how it may provide resources for the establishment of scenic specificity (e.g. what kind of sexual situation?). In each case, music was understood as providing a means for cueing into a particular (sexual) 'conduct register', ('spiritual' in the one case, as a 'sexual aid' in another, 'depressing' in the third). Within at least the first two situations, wherein music was used strategically as a way of constructing an environment or habitat for erotic activity, there were clearly interpretive politics at work concerning just what the music connoted (e.g. was the Bach sublime or ridiculous? was the symphony erotic or was it a distraction?).

Of course, actors may not be fully conscious of what they are trying to 'do' with music. Nonetheless, once introduced into an environment, music may establish parameters (albeit blurred and elastic) for action – how intense, how much languor, with what kind of pacing, how varied, for example, but also what types of participants and with what degree of playfulness, seriousness, and so on. It is important to realize that actors need not be deliberate about the ways they mobilize music. Indeed, they may mobilize certain musics without being conscious of why they do so. This is because music is often meaningful to actors in ways that by-pass rational consciousness. To explore the social uses of music in a level of detail that exceeds that of this article, we would need to develop a theory of aesthetic knowledge.

In short, music is an active, but perhaps often unacknowledged, ingredient in the practical management of 'tuning in', sexual or otherwise; it allows actors to introduce generic activity structures into (and adapt according to) local sexual situations. Musical devices are thus resources (enabling/constraining) for the semiotic configuration of sex, just as they are resources for the configuration of other forms of agency (e.g. the long tradition of 'songs for work', the semiotic repertoires of music for the film, the role of muzak in organizational culture).

Musics provide materials with which actors may allude to styles and genres of activity. They also provide a means of contextualizing actors and of creating a 'background' to which actors may relate in order to discipline, meaningful feeling and bodily form.

The fourth example, in which Ravel's *Bolero* was used as an accompaniment to erotic activity, illustrates, perhaps most clearly, the ways in which music may be used to discipline bodily conduct. This piece was composed in 1928 and it became, as Donald Grout once observed (1973: 658), 'the musical equivalent of a best-seller'. In the example relayed to me, it was put on the stereo as background music by a man in his early 20s, the first time he and his partner (of the same age) had sexual intercourse. After the film *10* (and the British ice-skating duo Jane Torvill and Christopher Dean who skated to *Bolero* in the Olympic games), the choice may appear somewhat hackneyed,[5] but this is precisely why it can also seem 'correct'. *Bolero*'s highly publicized sexual and frankly coital associations thus brought to the foreground music as a simulation of sex. Indeed, in choosing it as 'background' music, the male partner in the example I have been discussing was proposing it as a model *for* sex in the sense that activity and desire were inserted into the narrative form it offered. The piece played an overt role in the process of occasioning.

It is worth developing this example for its heuristic value, in order to consider how music (whether heard in real time or remembered) may provide a ground or candidate model for structuring the incarnate practices of erotic conduct. The piece begins quietly, sustains a regularly repeated pulse throughout and rises steadily to a crescendo. The same melody is reiterated throughout and is stated initially by solo flute (an upper-range instrument conventionally associated by both 'expert' and 'lay' listeners with both 'pure' and 'open' tone colour and also an instrument typically used to register the feminine in music – the silvery gurgling of water, as in the opening of Smetana's *Moldau*, or delicate bird song as in Beethoven's *Pastoral Symphony*, or languor, as in Debussy's *L'après-midi d'un faune*). The melody is played in the flute's (and flautist's) most relaxed-sounding, 'coolest' lower register, in the key of C, beginning on the C above middle C and ending on middle C, the instrument's lowest note.[6] Ravel intended the piece to sound like a pipe organ, growing steadily louder as stops are pulled out. The lower brass instruments are the last to enter and the use of glissando (tonal sliding) in the upper-register trombone plays a special role in that it introduces, frankly, the sexualized body by introducing a particular kind of 'grain' (Barthes, 1985). Glissandi are, within the discourse of 'classical' music, often construed as 'unclean' that is, as part of different and 'less tasteful' musical discourses (such as jazz). At the approaching climax of this piece, then, preferred and dispreferred discourses come to be melded together. Earlier in the work, the way is paved for this liminality by the saxophone, an instrument outside the traditional 'classical music' orchestra. The work ends abruptly after its tonal apex is reached.

As an icon of erotic temporality, *Bolero* can stand for the tone, pacing and duration for the real time sexual event. The work lasts about 15 minutes. Is 15 minutes 'long enough'? 'Too long'? And for whom? One might argue[7] that, for a man in his early 20s, the 15-minute format of the piece provided a device for *prolonging* the event. *Bolero* retranslated the young man's bodily tempo in ways that slowed it down. One could also argue that for the woman, the piece made a statement about the shape and content of the sexual event. For example, the ineluctable quality of its melody may have provided a means of holding her in, symbolically, to the regular thrust of what the man defined as the 'sexual event'. In this sense, music can come to carry moral-stylistic force, though it would be un-useful to posit this force as deterministic, as McClary has at times implied with reference to, for example, Beethoven. These matters cannot be 'read in to' real life events but must be seen in the interaction and/or its accounts.

The Musical Construction of Physiological Response
Music's role as an active ingredient in social formation may also at times encompass the physiological body itself. That is, the physical body can itself be a semiotic achievement and music provides one set of cultural materials for that kind of semiotic work. For these reasons, the question of how people negotiate 'background music' for sex may be an important part of the study of the politics of sexual pleasure.

For example, music may inspire and interact with physical-cultural practices, in ways that Dyer alludes to in his personal responses to disco, pop and rock (Dyer, 1990) and their relation to 'scene culture'. Dyer suggests that rock's 'repeated phrases keep you in their relentless push' whereas pop is 'disembodied' – about psychological yearning rather than bodily activity, and disco is 'whole body' in the sense that it implies sinuous movement as opposed to sheer thrust. It is of course key to underline that these musical 'forces' are only activated in and through the ways that users (listeners, dancers, sexual actors) *interact* with musical forms.

Musics may also provide resources for synchronizing embodied action, as in dance, by imposing/offering narrative structures on/for that action. These first two forms of musical disciplinization are illustrated in the *Bolero* example discussed above. They concern bodily *conduct*. But music may enlist bodies in ways that may at times come to discipline not just conduct, but, more profoundly, the quantity and quality of *physiological response* as well. For example, it may be reasonable to suggest that orgasms can be 'musically constructed', *if* music provides structures into which actors' perceptions of their bodies are translated and which, in turn, establish non-cognitive forms of 'bio-feedback' that come to structure body sensation.[8] Here music provides structural materials for the psychological sources of sensation, its phenomenological features such that the experience of sexual sensation itself can be understood as 'musically composed'. This is to say that the physical-cultural practices of body conduct that emerge from human-music interaction affect bodily sensation and physiological response (e.g. bodies – not just actors – may imitate and fall into musical rhythms and textures in ways that heighten or suppress sensations).

Music is by no means unique as a medium for the reconstruction of bodily materiality. That culture can construct or reconstruct physiology is increasingly recognized by alternative approaches to pain management and medical treatment (e.g. visualization, bio-feedback) where culture's structuring capacity is employed strategically to alter body perception. For example, with visualization, patients learn how to align their awareness of the 'painful' phenomenon with an image. This activity relieves pain (or lowers blood pressure) by translating it into different imagistic terms (see Trotter and Chavira, 1981; Sharma, forthcoming). This process recontextualizes the pain in ways that reconfigure it as 'something else'.

There is clearly a parallel to be drawn here with Becker's classic work on marijuana use (Becker, 1953). As Becker puts it, the drug's so-called 'effect', is something that, 'emerges from an interaction between culture and chemistry'. One has to *learn* categories for perceiving the drug's effects. One enters in to a symbolic world of categories that construct 'getting high'. The 'drug' then, is culture/cannabis.

Lynda Birke (1992a: 75) has suggested that:

> what you are now – your biological body – is a product of complex transformations between biology and experiences in your past. And these transformations happening now will affect any such transformations in the future. Biology, in this view, does have a role: but it is neither a base to build on nor determining.

Culture, through the ways it interacts with the body, may heighten or bring into focus both body and bodily experience. To say this is not to deny the materiality of the body (e.g. erection, lubrication, the emission of semen and so on), but it is to admit, at the very least, that whatever comes to count as 'evidence' of a 'bodily event' (even when we are dealing with a body's testimony to itself) is a matter of cultural construction and, at the most, that, as Birke puts it (1992b), materiality itself is a hybrid of nature/culture.

Conclusion

To be sure, music is, as Richard Leppert has put it, 'a well-practised device for the production of desire' (1993: 7). The question of just what, at the level of lived desire and erotic conduct, this statement actually means has been under-explored. The point of this article has been to initiate a discussion on this neglected topic and, to pave the way for a 'strong' cultural constructivist position by disentangling agency, culture and nature (while at the same time appreciating their reflexive links).

As a form of textual time and textual architecture, music provides non-propositional, non-depictive terms through which physiological processes can be perceived. Played in either real time, memory or imagination it can provide parameters through which and into which sexual response is shaped. It can provide a way of marking sexual time. Examining human–music interaction provides a clear entry into the question of how culture/nature amalgams are actually put together over time and space and how agency is configured with reference – often reflexive – to aesthetic forms.

Music can thus be employed in ways that enable/constrain (and establish claims about) the shape and duration of sexual activity. It provides just one of the potentially wide range of resources for action and experience, one which can be mobilized with varying degrees of deliberation. Music is, moreover, a resource, an often under-acknowledged resource, one that can easily slip past rational awareness but nevertheless engage the body. These are practical matters and they require further investigation.[9] Music's role in the configuration of agency has, as I have attempted to describe, implications for sexual differences (individual differences and generic-class differences) between participants (in both heterosexual and homosexual encounters) and in this respect, it is potentially sexual-political. The constitutive role of cultural resources such as music may, moreover, have special salience in non-intimate sexual partnerships where, as with mechanical modes of production in factories, offices, sites and classrooms, generic parameters provide crucial resources for coordination and expectation.

In short, questions about how music is used in erotic situations, how fore-grounded/backgrounded it is, and the peculiarly modern use of electronically reproduced music (CD player, personal stereo, muzak and so on) are all potentially informative for the historically changing character and the politics of 'intimacy'. There are many issues concerning human–music interaction that should be explored and they will add considerably to our knowledge of how culture 'gets into' action. Simultaneously the profile of socio-music studies will be significantly heightened when we can at last begin to *explain* what it means to speak of music's 'power'.

62 ■ Body and Society

Notes

Earlier versions and parts of this article were presented to the 1994 Annual Conference of the British Sociological Association (Preston), the 20th Anniversary Conference of Social Theory Politics and the Arts (Baton Rouge), the LAMS Seminar, University of Milan, the 1996 American Sociological Association (New York), and the 1996 ISA RC 37 Committee Conference (Brussels). Thanks to Paul DiMaggio, Giampietro Gobo, Antoine Hennion, Alberto Melucci, Richard Peterson, Douglas Tudhope, Anna Lisa Tota, Gretchen Wheelock, Robert Witkin and Vera Zolberg for critical feedback.

 1. Here Travers's portrayal of sexual action coincides with Simon and Gagnon's notion of 'cultural scenarios' (Simon and Gagnon, 1984).
 2. Of course these gestures also serve as orientational devices and facilitate the mutual tuning in process of (sexual) interaction; they are one sort of building material for the construction of shared social space and time.
 3. So far, a space for 'nature' has been reserved within social theory only by certain post-Lacanian, 'gynocentric' feminists such as Luce Irigaray in *This Sex Which Is Not One* (1980). But in Irigaray's work, the 'nature' of the female body is hypostatized. Irigaray conflates bodily materiality with bodily meaning (i.e. the feminine imaginary) in order to articulate ontological characteristics of female sexuality. She does not problematize the very anatomical categories from which her account of that sexuality is derived.
 4. Written in 1921, *Wozzeck* is an atonal work. It is about an imperial Austrian army soldier who is subjected to sadistic treatment by his army doctor and captain. He lives with a 'licentious' woman who deceives him with a drum major. On discovering this, he stabs her and then drowns himself.
 5. A 1994 Valentine's Day issue of *Cue* magazine published a series of responses to the question, 'What music gets you in the mood for . . . [sex]?' and listed the first names and ages of respondents. One, 'Colm, age 22' said, 'Ravel's Bolero. Never fails. Actually that's not true. It never fails in *theory*. The practice is another story. Put it this way, for everyone apart from me it never seems to fail, so I'd recommend it. But maybe I should recommend something else to myself because it's not getting me anywhere' (pp. 70–1). Thanks to Elizabeth York for bringing this article to my attention.
 6. Professional model flutes usually have a 'B key' as well, so that their lowest note is B natural. But the instrument is understood to be 'in the key of C' that is, the most natural scale pattern that can be played, with one finger being lifted after the other (thus shortening the pipe) is the scale of C major. The 'B key' is mainly added to give tonal depth to the lower register.
 7. Thanks to a member of the audience in the BSA conference session on aesthetics and sexuality, Preston, 1994.
 8. When I presented this paper at the 1994 Social Theory, Politics and the Arts conference in Baton Rouge I was told of yet another, perhaps far more obsessive, example of this 'Bolero phenomenon': a man who took pleasure in coordinating his own sexual climax with the musical climax in the work.
 9. We need to consider, for example, how actors 'switch on or in' to music and we need to consider the degree of consciousness with which music as erotic technology is mobilized (e.g. the less deliberation, the more likely actors are being mobilized by [as opposed to mobilizing] cultures, the more likely they are enactors).

References

Adam, Barbara (1991) *Time and Social Theory*. Cambridge: Polity.
Adorno, Theodor (1974) *Philosophy of Modern Music*. New York: Seabury Press.
Baker, Mark (1994) The Parents' Music Resource Center: Symbolic Conflict Amidst Structural Decay in the United States', unpublished PhD Dissertation, Department of Sociology, University of Exeter.

Tia DeNora ■ 63

Barnes, Barry (1982) 'On the Extensions of Concepts and the Growth of Knowledge', *Sociological Review* 30(1): 23–44.

Barnes, Barry and Steven Loyal (forthcoming) 'Agency as a Red Herring in Social Theory', unpublished manuscript, Department of Sociology, University of Exeter.

Barthes, Roland (1985) *The Responsibility of Forms: Critical Essays on Music, Art and Representation*, trans. Richard Howard. New York: Hill and Wang.

Bartky, Sandra (1990) *Femininity and Domination*. London: Routledge.

Baudrillard, Jean (1983) *Simulations*. New York: Semiotext(e).

Becker, H.S. (1953) 'On Becoming a Marijuana User', *American Journal of Sociology* 59: 235–42.

Betterton, Rosemary (1987) *Looking On: Images of Femininity in the Visual Arts and Media*. London: Pandora.

Birke, Lynda (1992a) 'In Pursuit of Difference: Scientific Studies of Men and Women', pp. 81–102 in G. Kirkup and L. Smith Keller (eds) *Inventing Women: Science, Technology and Gender*. Cambridge: Polity.

Birke, Lynda (1992b) 'Transforming Biology' pp. 66–77 in H. Crowley and S. Himmelweit (eds) *Knowing Women: Feminism and Knowledge*. Cambridge: Polity.

Bourdieu, P. (1984) *Distinction: A Social Critique of the Judgement of Taste*. Cambridge: Polity.

Coward, Rosalind (1984) *Female Desire*. London: Paladin.

de Certeau, Michel (1984) *The Practice of Everyday Life*. Berkeley and London: University of California Press.

de Lauretis, Teresa (1987) *Technologies of Gender*. Bloomington: Indiana University Press.

DeNora, Tia (1986) 'How is Extra-musical Meaning Possible? Music as a Space and Place for "work"', *Sociological Theory* 2(2): 84–94.

DeNora, Tia (1995a) 'The Musical Composition of Reality? Music, Social Action and Reflexivity', *Sociological Review* (May): 296–315.

DeNora, Tia (1995b) *Beethoven and the Construction of Genius: Musical Politics in Vienna 1792–1803*. Berkeley and London: University of California Press.

DeNora, Tia (1996) 'From Physiology to Feminism: Reconfiguring Body, Gender and Expertise in Natural Fertility Control', *International Sociology* 11(3): 359–83.

Douglas, Mary (1993) 'Reconstituing the Cosmos', paper presented to the International Conference on De-traditionalization: Authority and Self in an Age of Cultural Uncertainty, Lancaster University, 8–10 July.

Dyer, Richard (1990) 'In Defence of Disco', pp. 410–18 in S. Frith and A. Goodwin (eds) *On Record: Rock, Pop and the Written Word*. London: Routledge.

Elias, Norbert (1939) *The Civilising Process, Vol. 1: The History of Manners*. Oxford: Blackwell.

Featherstone, Mike, Mike Hepworth and Bryan S. Turner (eds) (1991) *The Body: Social Process and Cultural Theory*. London: Sage.

Fine, Gary Alan (1986) 'Idioculture and Little League Baseball', *American Sociological Review* 44: 733–45.

Foucault, Michel (1981, 1987) *The History of Sexuality*, Vols 1 and 2. Harmondsworth: Penguin.

Frisby, David (1985) *Fragments of Modernity*. Cambridge: Polity.

Gagnon, John and William Simon (1973) *Sexual Conduct: The Social Sources of Human Sexuality*. Chicago, IL: Aldine.

Gardetto, Darlaine (1988) 'The Social Construction of the Female Orgasm', paper presented to the American Sociological Association, Atlanta, Georgia (August).

Giddens, Anthony (1990) *The Consequences of Modernity*. Cambridge: Polity.

Giddens, Anthony (1991) *Modernity and Self-Identity*. Cambridge: Polity.

Greenberg, David (1988) *The Construction of Homosexuality*. Chicago, IL: University of Chicago Press.

64 ■ Body and Society

Grout, Donald J. (1973) *A History of Western Music*. New York: Norton.

Hall, Lesley A. (1991) *Hidden Anxieties: Male Sexuality, 1900–1950*. Cambridge: Polity.

Haraway, Donna (1985) 'A Manifesto for Cyborgs: Science, Technology and Socialist Feminism in the 1980s', *Socialist Review* 80: 65–107.

Hays, Sharon (1994) 'Agency and Structure and the Sticky Problem of Culture', *Sociological Theory*.

Hilbert, Richard (1984) 'The Acultural Dimensions of Chronic Pain: Flawed Reality Construction and the Problem of Meaning', *Social Problems* 31: 365–78.

Hilbert, Richard (1986) 'Anomie and the Moral Regulation of Reality: The Durkheimian Tradition in Modern Relief', *Sociological Theory* 4(1): 1–19.

Holland, Janet, Carolyn Ramazanoglu, Sue Sharpe and Rachel Thomson (1994) 'Power and Desire: The Embodiment of Female Sexuality', *Feminist Review* 46: 21–38.

Irigaray, Luce (1980) 'This Sex Which Is Not One', in E. Marks and I. de Courtivron (eds) *New French Feminisms*. London: Schocken.

Irvine, Janice M. (1990) *Disorders of Desire: Sex and Gender in Modern American Sexology*. Philadelphia, PA: Temple University Press.

Jackson, Stevi (1978) 'On the Social Construction of Female Sexuality'. London: Women's Research and Resources Centre.

Jackson, Stevi (1982) *Childhood and Sexuality*. Oxford: Basil Blackwell.

Jackson, Stevi (1993) 'Even Sociologists Fall in Love', *Sociology* 27(2): 201–20.

Jackson, Stevi (1996) 'Heterosexuality as a Problem for Feminist Theory', pp. 20–38 in Diane Richardson (ed.) *Theorizing Heterosexuality*. Milton Keynes: Open University Press.

Jackson, Stevi and Shaun Moores (eds) (1995) *The Politics of Domestic Consumption: Critical Readings*. London: Harvester Wheatsheaf.

Jacobus, Mary, Evelyn Fox Keller and Sally Shuttleworth (eds) (1990) *Body/Politics: Women and the Discourses of Science*. London: Routledge.

Jeffreys, Sheila (1990) *Anti-Climax: A Feminist Perspective on the Sexual Revolution*. London: The Women's Press.

Laqueur, Thomas (1990) *Making Sex: Body and Gender from the Greeks to Freud*. Cambridge, MA: Harvard University Press.

Lash, Scott and John Urry (1993) *Economies of Signs and Space*. London: Sage.

Leppert, Richard (1993) *The Sight of Sound: Music, Representation and the History of the Body*. Berkeley and London: University of California.

McClary, Susan (1991) *Feminine Endings: Music, Gender and Sexuality*. Minneapolis: University of Minnesota Press.

Moore, Lisa Jean and Adele E. Clarke (forthcoming) 'Clitoral Conventions: Twentieth-Century Anatomical Representations', *Feminist Studies*.

Plummer, Ken (1975) *Sexual Stigma: An Interactionist Account*. London: Routledge.

Rakusen, Jill (1989) 'Relationships and Sexuality', pp. 11–270 in *The New Our Bodies Ourselves*, (2nd British edn) by Angela Phillips and Jill Rakusen. Harmondsworth: Penguin.

Rich, Adrienne (1980) 'Compulsory Heterosexuality and Lesbian Existence', *Signs* 5(4): 631–60.

Segal, Lynne (1983) 'Sensual Uncertainty, or Why the Clitoris is not Enough', in S. Cartledge and J. Ryan (eds) *Sex & Love*. London: The Women's Press.

Seidman, Steven (1992) *Embattled Eros: Sexual Politics and Ethics in Contemporary America*. London: Routledge.

Sharma, Ursula (forthcoming) 'Bringing the Body Back into the (Social) Action. Techniques of the Body and the (Cultural) Imagination', manuscript in preparation, Department of Sociology and Social Anthropology, University of Keele.

Simon, William and John H. Gagnon (1984) 'Sexual Scripts', *Society* 22: 53–60.

Smith, Dorothy (1990) *Texts, Facts and Femininity: Exploring the Relations of Ruling*. London: Routledge.

Snitow, Ann, Christine Stamsell and Sharon Thompson (eds) (1984) *Desire: The Politics of Sexuality*. London: Virago.

Swidler, Ann (1986) 'Culture in Action', *American Sociological Review* 51: 273–86.

Thomas, H. (ed.) (1993) *Dance, Gender and Culture*. London: Macmillan.

Travers, Andrew (1993) 'An Essay on Self and Camp', *Theory, Culture & Society* 10(1): 127–43.

Trotter, R.T. and Juan Chavira (1981) *Curanderismo: Mexican American Folk Healing*. Athens: University of Georgia Press.

Tudhope, Douglas, Carl Taylor and Paul Beynon-Davies (1995) 'Taxonomic Distance, Classification and Navigation', *Proceedings of the International Conference on Interactivity and Hypermedia in Museums*, San Diego, CA (October).

Turner, Bryan (1984) *The Body and Society*. Oxford: Blackwell.

Urry, John (1990) *The Tourist Gaze*. London: Sage.

Vance, Carole S. (1992) 'Social Construction Theory: Problems in the History of Sexuality', pp. 132–45 in H. Crowley and S. Himmelweit (eds) *Knowing Women*. Milton Keynes: Open University Press.

Walby, Sylvia (1990) *Theorizing Patriarchy*. Oxford: Blackwells.

Weeks, Jeffrey (1981) *Sex, Politics and Society: The Regulation of Sexuality since 1800*. London: Longman.

Weeks, Jeffrey (1985) *Sexuality and its Discontents: Meanings, Myths and Modern Sexualities*. London: Routledge.

Willis, Paul (1978) *Profane Culture*. London: Routledge and Kegan Paul.

Williams, Raymond (1961) *The Long Revolution*. London: Cox and Wyman.

Witkin, Robert (1974) *The Intelligence of Feeling*. London: Heinemann.

Witkin, Robert (1995) *Art and Social Structure*. Cambridge: Polity.

Witkin, Robert and Tia DeNora (n.d.) 'Art as social agency', paper presented to the American Sociological Association, Washington DC (August 1995).

Tia DeNora teaches sociology at the University of Exeter. Her publications include *Beethoven and the Construction of Genius* (University of California Press) and a number of articles on music and society. She is co-editor, with Pete Martin, of the 'Music and Society' series (Manchester University Press).

CHAPTER 7

The concerto and society

As something 'that people do',[1] music shapes and takes shape in relation to the social settings where it is produced, distributed and consumed. Within those settings, music may provide exemplars and resources for the constitution of extra-musical matters. Through the confluence of performance and reception, musicking makes and partakes of values, ideas and tacit or practical notions about the social whole, agency and social relations; in this respect, music is an active ingredient of social life.[2]

The concerto – the form par excellence of *contrast* – provides a useful case in point for socio-musical exploration. Following its vicissitudes will reveal music's role as a medium of social values and as a medium enabled and constrained by practical, conventional, material and organizational factors. This chapter explores the concerto and its link to society from two interrelated perspectives, the focus on local and pragmatic features of musicking and music's role as a meaningful medium and a medium of social change. I use three case studies to explore the concerto's social features, in especial relation to the keyboard concerto – Bach's Brandenburg No. 5, Mozart's career as a concerto composer/performer in 1780s Vienna, and Beethoven's innovations in keyboard performance and their connections to the gendering of the repertory during the early nineteenth century.

Case study one: Bach's Brandenburg Concerto No. 5

J. S. Bach's six Brandenburg Concertos, written separately but collected as a set and dedicated to Christian Ludwig, Elector of Margrave, Brandenburg, in 1721, constitute a milestone in the concerto's history,[3] not least because of the degree of virtuosity they displayed and demanded of the players. The fifth Brandenburg, for a combination of flute, violin and harpsichord, merits special attention, not only because it 'marks the beginning of the harpsichord concerto as a form'[4] but because it opens up a range of themes within music sociology. It has already been the subject of socio-cultural analysis[5] and this account can be used as a springboard for further exploration of the concerto as a social medium.

The stylistic strategies Bach appropriated in this work, Susan McClary argues, can be read as embodying social values.[6] In particular, his

20 Tia DeNora

adoption of the Italian concerto style, via Vivaldi, makes greatest use of
what McClary sees as the bourgeois properties of tonality more generally
('values ... held most dear by the middle class: belief in progress, in expansion, in the ability to attain ultimate goals through rational striving, in the
ingenuity of the individual strategist operating both within and in defiance
of the norm') so as to depict and celebrate values associated with the new
individualism ('virtuosity, dissonance and extravagant dynamic motion').[7]

In Brandenburg No. 5, which begins ostensibly as a concerto for flute
and violin, the harpsichord is initially presented as a 'darkhorse compe-
titor for the position of soloist'.[8] During the course of the first movement,
the harpsichord comes to occupy an extreme foreground position in the
extended cadenza ('delivered by a frenzied continuo instrument'),[9] the
longest cadenza then known, lasting roughly a quarter of the entire
movement's length. As McClary puts it: '[T]he harpsichord, which first
serves as continuo support ... then begins to compete with the soloists
for attention ... and finally overthrows the other forces in a kind of
hijacking of the piece'.[10]

McClary's essay illustrates an interesting and important analytical
approach to the Concerto–Society topic, namely, narrative analysis. She
considers in particular the disruption of convention, represented by the
prominence of the harpsichord as a solo instrument (the harpsichord had
hitherto played the background role of continuo, namely blending into
the background to provide harmonic and rhythmic stability). By bringing
this 'service' instrument to the limelight and allowing it to indulge in 'one
of the most outlandish displays in music history',[11] Bach, McClary argues,
musically presents (and in an extreme form) then-emerging notions of
individual freedom of expression:

> In the eighteenth century, most musical genres testify to a widespread interest
> in integrating the best of both those worlds into one in which social harmony
> and individual expression are mutually compatible. The concerto, the new
> formalized opera aria, and the later sonata procedure all are motivated by
> this interest.[12]

As McClary observes – and this is at the heart of her semiotic method –
the strategies of an individual piece (such as in Brandenburg No. 5) can
only be perceived as significant if they are held against a backdrop of
musical norms and conventions. Such a method, she observes, is:

> both ad hoc ... and dialectical in so far as its strategies take shape in relation
> to the specific demands of particular compositions and in so far as the
> method seeks to account for the ways that particular compositions relate to
> the norms and conventions that enable and constrain the compositional
> process.[13]

All methods of analysis reveal and conceal, and semiotic methods are by no means immune to this predicament. The semiotic toolkit consists of a catalogue of conventions, an understanding of the history of ideas, politics, economics and some astute interpretative observation. At the same time, the analytic strategy of reading musical works may promote a kind of theorizing that is disconnected from the *actual* mechanisms through which music plays a mediating role in social life. Elsewhere, I have suggested that semiotics is useful but not sufficient as a method of socio-musical analysis and that semiotic analytical strategies occupy what the novelist and philosopher Iris Murdoch has described as 'a wrong level of generality',[14] one that foregrounds analytical concepts such as style, compositional strategy and idea but leaves in shadow the rather more 'down-home', and more overtly sociological, matters of music's material culture and physical practice, custom and local meanings, networks, occupational worlds and structures, and pragmatic and mundane matters.[15]

In short, reading music for its ideological content implies a conception of the music–society nexus in terms of homological relationships between *macro* historical trends and developments in musical *works*. However, social life (for example, what Bach did in Brandenburg No. 5) happens in the here-and-now and is embedded in local conditions. It is at this *local* level that large-scale social trends are *mediated* by what is 'do-able'[16] – by material culture, by the specific concerns of patrons and other local contextual issues such as occasion and dedicatee, and by an individual composer's particular appropriation of ideas, models and working materials.

In short, there is no one-to-one connection between musical forms and the world of ideas (for how does the genie of 'The Social' actually get into the music and how, even more complicatedly, does the music inform the social – what are the *mechanisms*?). Rather, there are always a multiplicity of connections and possibilities and it is only at this level of actual doing that what we describe as social structure is produced and reproduced.[17] The particular pathway through these possibilities taken by a particular composer at a particular time is thus shot through with layers of significance that cannot be reduced to the history of ideas. It is only through an appreciation of the myriad conditions of a work's genesis (and regenesis via performance, reception, scholarship and other cultural practices) that it is possible to begin to describe how it is *actually* linked to society.

Again, Brandenburg No. 5 provides a case-in-point. Looking closely at the specific features of Bach and the local musical worlds in which he operated extends our understanding of music–society connections by

22 Tia DeNora

helping to explain why, *in this case*, Bach came to position the harpsichord so prominently in the musical limelight.

Prior to his move to Cöthen, Bach's experience at Arnstadt (1703–7), Mülhausen (1707–8) and Weimar (1708–17) was – in both church and court contexts – as an organist. As such, Bach was intimately acquainted with musical instrument technology. He was frequently called upon, for example, to test new organs, such as the one in Halle in 1716 about which, in company with Johann Kuhnau and Christian Friedrich Rolle, he produced a highly detailed report.[18] Bach was also familiar with the convention of dedicating a new instrument; he was present for the dedication of the Halle organ (two weeks after the report was filed), and he served as the soloist at other organ dedications.

On such occasions, flamboyant display was *de rigueur*, so as to display the instrument's capacities and, as a by-product of that primary display, inevitably also the capabilities of the performer. Also, during these years just prior to the composition of Brandenburg No. 5, musical skill was conceived as a kind of sport; Bach took part or was scheduled to take part in various musical tournaments for the amusement of aristocratic patrons. Improvisation would be fundamental to both types of occasion and, of course, Bach was a master improviser, praised by virtually all who came into contact with his art.

> Enter the arrival of a new harpsichord in 1719:
> On 1 March 1719 Bach travelled to Berlin to acquire a splendid new harpsichord for the Köthen court – 'The great harpsichord or Flügel with two keyboards, by Michael Mietke'. It has been suggested that he may have had this instrument in mind when he conceived two of his most brilliant harpsichord works – Brandenburg Concerto No. 5 in D major BWV 1050, and the Chromatic Fantasia and Fugue in D minor BWV 903. . . . According to Forkel, 'When he played from his fancy, all the 24 keys were in his power. . . . All his extempore fantasies are said to have been of a similar description'.[19]

Christoph Wolff has also suggested that Brandenburg No. 5 was written to inaugurate the new harpsichord, as has Malcolm Boyd, who reasons that, '[p]ossibly it was with this new and unprecedentedly elaborate cadenza that Bach celebrated the arrival of the new instrument from Berlin'.[20]

Bach spent a good deal of time in Berlin negotiating for the new harpsichord (between June 1718 and March 1719). During this time he played for and came to know Christian Ludwig, Elector of Margrave, to whom Bach dedicated the Brandenburg Concertos in 1721. The harpsichord would have loomed large for Bach during this phase of his life and it seems reasonable to suggest that it would have loomed not only as a 'dark horse' figure in Concerto No. 5 (possibly the last to have been composed)[21] but behind the entire set on which he worked during these years.

In this context, and bearing in mind Bach's intimate knowledge of keyboard instrument technology, the predominant display of the harpsichord no longer seems, in McClary's terms, 'deviant' but rather, within the musical culture of Bach's world, appears as a fitting practice, one devoted to celebrating the new instrument. This would have been even more the case if the first performance were indeed the instrument's 'inauguration', where an extended unaccompanied frenzy would allow the instrument to be put through its paces (simultaneously allowing Bach, who apparently premièred the work, to display his own abilities). And indeed, the *type of frenzy* in that extended cadenza (numerous scales up and down the keyboard, the chromatic passages) seems precisely to place on public trial the instrument's capacities, testing its entire range. Set against the 'self-contained' character of the ritornello,[22] this trial is made ever more celebratory, entirely fitting, in other words, for the local occasion. And the otherwise inexplicable way in which the cadenza 'blurs almost entirely the sense of key'[23] also makes good local sense, displaying the instrument from the full gamut of harmonic perspectives.

In sum, one can imagine how Bach took advantage, in this case, of an emerging rhetorical strategy (the solo concerto), gave it a new twist (as a keyboard concerto) that was charged with a frisson (that unruly keyboard!) in a way that was wholly appropriate and meaningful as an occasioning device under the local conditions of musical culture at Cöthen. The form that emerged from these local circumstances, practices and resources was eventually bequeathed as a 'work' that could be read (by variously located readers) as historically significant (for example, McClary's reading). To provide a reading, however, is to engage in situated meaning-making. It is also a very different activity from the gathering of information about the local environment of production, distribution and reception/use.

In short, as the music sociologist Antoine Hennion has observed, by merely reading musical works we risk providing just one more in 'a long line of Bach interpretations'.[24] (Indeed, music criticism can be understood as involved in the *performance* of meaning.[25]) By contrast, we need to consider works from a range of perspectives including: cultural trends (new rhetorics, values, devices, discourses); large-scale events (including natural disasters, political change, economic developments); features of the worlds[26] in which music is made (conventions, technology, support personnel, funding, performance practices, reputation, distribution structures); local events (occasions, situations, news, local history,

24 Tia DeNora

events); and reception (time after time as the meaning of works is recursively established and modified, in their own time and later, by musicians, critics, scholars, listeners, patrons and others). In short, the question of 'how' musical meaning is possible needs to focus on the complexity of situated meaning production and the status of this production as a form of interpretative 'work',[27] that is as culture creation. Such an approach has affinities with the study of the everyday and with ethnography of history and cultural experience.

Case study two: occupational structure and local Enlightenment culture in Mozart's Vienna

During the eighteenth century concert life was transformed across Europe. This transformation involved a shift from private to public funding for music. In Vienna and the German-speaking lands, the old Hauskapelle (house ensemble) was abandoned and musicians increasingly had to build careers in a nascent freelance economy.[28] This inevitably involved compiling an income from teaching and touring, private commissions and private concertizing in the salons, and from benefit concerts. The new system meant that reputation took on heightened salience – to live, and to have enough work, a musician had to become known. As Moore has observed, this shift towards a 'star system' worked well for some musicians, some of the time.[29] However, it was antithetical to most musicians, most of the time.

For a while, during the 1780s, the system worked well for Mozart. In 1784, describing a series of highly successful subscription concerts, he wrote exuberantly to his father: 'The first concert ... went off very well. The hall was overflowing; and the new concerto [possibly K. 449] I played won extraordinary applause. Everywhere I go I hear praises of that concert.'[30]

Next to opera, the piano concerto was one of 'the two worlds in which Mozart was supremely predominant' during these, his 'golden years'.[31] Between 1782 and December 1786, Mozart introduced a total of fifteen concertos to the Viennese public, nearly all of which he premièred himself. This was his heyday for the piano concerto (he subsequently introduced only two more between 1787 and 1791).

This choice was first of all pragmatic. Johann Schönfeld's *Jahrbuch*[32] lists 167 virtuoso and amateur performers. Of these, seventy (41 per cent) were keyboard players. During the 1780s the keyboard was a 'hot' instrument: it was undergoing technological development as keyboard artists increasingly used it as a means for display. (During the 1760s and 1770s the most popular instruments for concerto treatment were the violin and flute.[33]) It was also an instrument of conspicuous consumption (expensive and like a piece of furniture) and, related to this, an aristocratic instrument. To distinguish oneself as a keyboard virtuoso was simultaneously to enhance one's chance of recruiting wealthy pupils. In addition, one can find signs of a growing trend towards musical display all over Europe during these years. As Morrow has observed, concertos were the 'central showcase' within which musicians' talents could be displayed.[34] 'For Beethoven as for J. C. Bach, Mozart and Clementi before him and Hummel, Moscheles, and Liszt after him', writes Leon Plantinga, 'the concerto was mainly a personal vehicle for the composer-virtuoso's performances, a means for displaying new musical ideas of which a central feature was his own distinctive style of playing'.[35]

In Josephinian Vienna, c.1784, the 'new musical ideas' elaborated in the concerto genre resonated with new, 'enlightened' ideas and practices – liberalism, toleration, the suppression of aristocratic powers (via a refusal to rule through the Hungarian and Bohemian Diets),[36] the lifting of censorship and, to some degree, economic resurgence. All of these ideas were forcefully promulgated by writers such as Josef Sonnenfels and his notion of the 'mittleren Klassen', whose desires and aspirations could, with care, be aligned with the needs of the state. In short, it is in Mozart's Vienna that we can observe a prime example of what has been termed the emergence of the public sphere.[37]

Central to the Enlightenment notion of the public sphere was the idea that individual will could be brought into convergence with (be constructed as) public opinion, via various forms of discussion and cultural persuasion. It is during this period, throughout Europe, that social thinkers (Locke and Rousseau, for example) began to concern themselves with the concept of moral, as opposed to political, law. Echoing Rousseau, Sonnenfels wrote: 'the most important aim is to ensure the uniting of the individual with the general good ... through which the individual citizen is bonded to society as a whole, bringing the understanding of the honourable citizen to enlightenment, and at the same time ensuring that his own desires are met'.[38]

It is at this time that the arts, in particular those art forms that depicted action and experience over time (as opposed to the static arts of painting and sculpture), took on a new social function, the moulding not so much of public opinion, but of two other Enlightenment inventions, subjectivity and the self. As George Eliot came to put it, some time later and in reference to a fictional character, 'Hetty had never read a novel: how then could she find a shape for her expectations?'[39] In the late eighteenth century numerous fictional and non-fictional pamphlets were produced and circulated, in which the individual's role was modelled. Similarly, in the dramatic arts, and, perhaps most kinaesthetically, in opera, social relations were performed for widening audiences, and for some of these less literate audiences, the performing arts would have been the primary contact with the new imagery – models – of agency and social being. This imagery was Rousseauian; it depicted an individual who, via his desires and passions, could be bound to the needs and structures of the whole.

One of Mozart's most significant contributions to the history of the concerto was his conceptualization of the relationship between soloist and orchestra. From 1784 onwards technical difficulties increase, enhancing the drama of the form. Also at this time the orchestra comes to be used in a wider variety of ways than hitherto, as Simon P. Keefe has observed, sometimes in dialogue with the soloist, via individual instruments and collectively.[40]

Thus the concerto – the form of figure–ground, solo–tutti – was a highly charged form, one that was produced and received as an object lesson in new forms of agency. '[I]t is not fanciful', Till observes, 'to hear in Mozart's piano concertos a representation of this dynamic relationship; a progressive dialogue between the individual expressive voice of the soloist and the wider "community" of the orchestra, the former distinguished from the latter, yet frequently drawing from the same fountainhead of ideas, and both ultimately uniting in joyous unanimity'.[41]

As Keefe has observed, the concerto was much more than a metaphor, whether for Mozart's audiences or for the readings provided by today's music analysts and critics. Understood in the context of dramatic theory as circulating in Mozart's Vienna, Mozart's concertos can be seen to provide templates against which knowledge about social relations could be produced.[42] They carried (or may be explored as having carried), in other words, intellectual significance for their recipients:

> Following every stage in the process of relational change in each movement
> would have been a highly demanding exercise for a contemporary listener;
> Mozart's concertos would certainly have provided a prime example of the
> kind of instrumental music that, according to Adam Smith, can 'occupy, and
> as it were fill up completely the whole capacity of the mind so as to leave no
> part of its attention vacant for thinking of anything else'. By engaging the
> listener in a challenging intellectual pursuit, Mozart offered him or her an
> excellent vehicle for learning about cooperation (or, more precisely, the quest
> for cooperation), a value deeply cherished in the age of Enlightenment.
> Mozart's concertos thus fulfilled the single most important requirement for
> all late-eighteenth century music and drama: the general instruction of the
> listener-spectator.[43]

In other words, music was not merely 'about' an abstract correlation between sonic structure and social structure. Rather, as we have seen in the case of Brandenburg No. 5 above, we risk, in Hennion's and Fauquet's words, providing yet another 'in a long line'[44] of interpretations if we confine our analytical attention to 'readings' of music's social significance. By contrast, a more nuanced understanding of music's connections to social structure and social action can be achieved by situating that analysis in the context of the music's contemporary contexts of production, distribution and consumption. Considering the interaction between musical practice and other cultural practices of the time and place is part of this project as is the often-overlooked topic of music's material practice. These topics are considered in the next case study.

Case study three: gendering the piano concerto

At a time when all music was performed live, musical performance was always, and at least implicitly, a visually dramatic event, one that inevitably involved bodily procedures, strictures about comportment and, at times, choreography. To speak of these matters is to deconstruct the technical neutrality of musical performance, and to recognize by contrast how musical performance may itself provide significant factors in the overall understanding of works and their perceived meanings. Here, much more than mere phrasing is at stake. More significantly, it is the performance *of* performance that is at issue. Music may, for example, make demands upon the body. It may be used by performers, as implicitly described above, for embodied display. In these respects, music performance is dramaturgical: the practices of performing may delineate various meanings.[45]

Circa 1800, there was probably no realm within musical performance as charged with social meaning as the keyboard. The piano in late eighteenth- and early nineteenth-century Vienna was at the heart of debates over aesthetic practice, a site at which new and often-competing aesthetics were deployed and defended, at times through the overt medium of the 'piano duel'.[46]

Enter Beethoven and the piano performing body. Using the Concert Calendars in Morrow's study of Viennese musical life as a database,[47] we can determine that between 1793 and 1810 – during which time Beethoven was perhaps the most frequently performed composer for fortepiano in Vienna – his works were performed most often by men: 79 per cent of performances of *all* his piano works were performed by men and 21 per cent by women; and 84 per cent of his concertos by men, 16 per cent by women. This contrasts dramatically with the proportion of male performances of Mozart: 26 per cent of all his piano works were given by men and 74 per cent by women; and 27 per cent of his concertos performed by men during the years 1787–1810 and 73 per cent by women.

Between 1803 and 1810 the number of performances of Beethoven's concertos was increasing. The number of performers who played his concertos (particularly after he retreated from performing them himself as his hearing failed) was also growing. And yet, there would appear to be no extant evidence of a female performance of a Beethoven concerto in Vienna after 1806 and before 1810, a time during which men increasingly took up his works. (Once a concerto was published, Beethoven tended not to perform it again himself.) Never before had women and men been divided within the piano repertory in this way, at a time when women continued to be active (Josepha Auernhammer, Frauline Kurzbeck, Baroness Ertmann, Countess Anna Marie Erdody and others were all featured on the concert stage at this time). Indeed, women would appear to have given as many and sometimes more performances of piano concertos than men during these years.

Why then, this segregation? Elsewhere I have suggested, tentatively, that Beethoven's music made new demands upon the piano performing body in terms of how it was to be performed – it required a more visceral keyboard approach, and more demonstrative physical action (the choreography associated with this action was sometimes lampooned as the century progressed).[48] For women, bodily composure was doubly important because of the risk not only of transgressing one's social status, but also one's femininity and propriety. Speaking of the oboe, for example, John Essex described it in 1722 as, 'too Manlike ... [looking] indecent in a Woman's Mouth'.[49]

Thus, the physicality demanded by Beethoven's music was incompatible with late eighteenth-century piano technology. It was also in opposition to strictures about appropriate feminine comportment – whether at the piano or elsewhere. But it was linked to the ways in which Beethoven cast himself within the form. As Plantinga notes: 'In his concertos, Beethoven typically cast himself as a leader; the concerto was for him mainly a youthful preoccupation intimately bound up with his prowess and ambition as a public pianist'.[50]

In short, and delineated through the material-practical realm of piano performance, Beethoven's concertos introduced a new (visceral and heroic) role for the soloist and also provided an exemplar of a new type of individual and his (sic) relation to the social whole. Beethoven's concertos provided a vocabulary of gestures and a compendium of movement styles associated with powerful individualism and with struggle. In this respect he pioneered strategies later exploited by Liszt, Chopin and

Paganini. As Charles Rosen observes, describing the athletics of double-octave effects:

> The true invention of this kind of octave display – or at least, the first
> appearance of a long and relentlessly fortissimo page of unison octaves in
> both hands – is to be found in the opening movement of Beethoven's Emperor
> Concerto. It marks a revolution in keyboard sonority. . . . It is initially with the
> generation of composers that followed Beethoven that the performer must
> experience physical pain with such octaves, starting with Liszt.[51]

Speaking of how music in the nineteenth century came to involve a 'look' as well as sonority, Richard Leppert has suggested that, 'more than ever before, performers' bodies, in the act of realizing music, also helped to transliterate musical sound into musical meaning by means of the sight – and sometimes spectacle – of their gestures, facial expressions and general physicality'.[52]

Is it possible to explore more specifically the kind of meaning that the material performance of Beethoven concertos helped to delineate? It is worth pausing here to reconsider Kant and the ways in which his notion of the sublime came to be linked to instrumental music in general, and to Beethoven in particular during the early nineteenth century. As Christine Battersby tells us, Kant's conception both of the sublime and of the genius was gendered, something clarified only in his less central texts. As Kant put it: 'Strivings and surmounted difficulties arouse admiration and belong to the sublime. . . . Laborious learning or painful pondering, even if a woman should greatly succeed in it, destroy the merits that are proper to her sex.'[53]

As it was elaborated in and through musical performance practices, the Beethoven imago came to be associated with a visual imagery. It also resonated with new ideas about the connections between appearance and social capacity and with configurations of social agency. At the same time, not everyone could occupy the new socio-musical spaces that the Beethoven imago implied. This is to say that the form of pianistic display that came to be associated with heroism, and with the ability to resist nature, was not only a masculine attribute but also one associated with a particular kind of male performer. This imagery was consequential for then-emerging conceptions of gender and sexual difference, for masculinity as well as femininity.

This gender divide widened over the course of the nineteenth century and throughout Europe as musical practice provided object lessons in gender-linked modes of agency. As Katharine Ellis has described it, during the nineteenth century musical life was increasingly characterized by, 'a stereotypically feminine world of decorative and sweetly plaintive expression, contrasting with the gigantic outbursts of Beethoven or the dazzling virtuosity of Liszt and Thalberg'.[54] The new forms of musical display, and the agencies they implied, not only excluded women from the heart of the musical canon; they also celebrated a currency of bodily capital (appearance, physique, comportment and temperament) that was not equally available to all men. Indeed it is during these years and shortly later that the discourse of piano playing begins to engage in gender stereotyping, Kalkbrenner's music, for example, being described as requiring 'muscular power' (and thus essentially better suited to male performers) as opposed to the 'grace' required for the performance of Chopin's works.

Ellis observes, with regard to mid-nineteenth-century France, that female pianists were, 'caught in a web of conflicting ideas concerning the relative value of particular keyboard repertoires that were themselves gendered, either explicitly or implicitly'.[55] (Parisian critics during this period were concerned not only with repertory, but also with the use of the body, with feminine 'attitudes' at the keyboard and with what was considered to be the 'appropriate' level of acting in performance.) From the perspective of French observers, the chief problem with women on the concert stage *c*.1844–5 (a time in which there was an influx of female performers) was that the vision of a woman at the keyboard, engaging in showmanship and physical power, was in direct conflict with Parisian mores concerning feminine conduct (mores reinforced by the Napoleonic Code of 1804 but stretching back to Rousseau's 'Lettre à M. D'Alembert'). No woman was to make, as Ellis observes, 'a spectacle of herself'[56] and it was for this reason that women came to be associated with the 'sweeter' and more delicate music of earlier times.

In short, women came to be marginalized in relation to the canon as a result of Beethoven's incorporation into his concertos (as well as into his other piano works) of particular types of bodies and bodily habits. As the century waned, and musical discourse (and musical technology) further reinforced these notions, it is possible to see the gender segregation of musical life being institutionalized through discourse and performance practice. The concerto, *c*.1803–10, played a significant role in this process.

The late nineteenth century and beyond – future directions for socio-musical research

As a culturally 'live' or 'hot' form, the heyday of the concerto occurred during the nineteenth century. Over half of the concertos performed in Vienna between 1800 and 1810 were performed by musicians who were not their composers.[57] By the early twentieth century, the concerto was an institution of musical life, more a performer genre than a composer-performer genre, and the soloist–orchestra relationship has been explored in a wide variety of manners. Concerto strategies have ranged from emphasis on the whole orchestra, allowing each section a turn for display, to conflict between soloist and group, to forms that play with audiences' pre-conceptions of the solo-instrument's properties and also with conventions about a concerto's length.[58] The form has also been appropriated for comic effect, as in Kleinsinger's *Tubby the Tuba*, where a stereotypically 'clumsy' instrument is featured as soloist (in turn helping to illuminate the ways in which instruments and their musical assignment itself reproduces social stereotypes),[59] in the antics of Victor Borge and in pieces such as Leroy Anderson's *Typewriter Concerto*. At the same time, preference for flamboyant and dramatic solo forms has been cited as a marker of social standing, at least in Paris.[60]

Within music sociology directions for future research would include the following interrelated topics: performance practice, in particular how soloists employ various performing strategies as part of their on-going professional identity construction, and also for the production of other forms of identity – gender identity, class, race and age (and including attention to embodied conduct as described above and also decisions concerning phrasing, tempo, instrumentation);[61] solo competitions and the production of musical judgement; cinematic depictions of concerto performance, rehearsal or composition; listening practices and consumption patterns; further analysis of musical-critical discourse; and, finally, the ways in which the concerto may come to be 'active' in extra-musical realms, how it may be drawn into interaction with other cultural practices and thereby come to provide resources for knowledge·production.[62]

Notes

1 Christopher Small, *Musicking: The Meanings of Performing and Listening* (Hanover and London, 1988). For a similar perspective, see also Howard S. Becker, *Art Worlds* (Berkeley and London, 1982).
2 Tia DeNora, *After Adorno: Rethinking Music Sociology* (Cambridge, 2003) and 'Musical Practice and Social Structure: a Toolkit', in Eric Clarke and Nicholas Cook (eds.), *Empirical Musicology* (Oxford, 2004), pp. 35–56.
3 Christoph Wolff, 'Instrumental Music', in Wolff *et al.*, *The New Grove Bach Family* (London, 1980), p. 156.
4 *Ibid.*, p. 157.
5 Susan McClary, 'The Blasphemy of Talking Politics During Bach Year', in Richard Leppert and McClary (eds.), *Music and Society: the Politics of Composition, Performance and Reception* (Cambridge, 1987), pp. 13–62.
6 *Ibid.*, p. 19.
7 *Ibid.*, pp. 22, 23.
8 *Ibid.*, p. 24.
9 *Ibid.*, p. 32.
10 *Ibid.*, p. 28.
11 *Ibid.*, p. 26.
12 *Ibid.*, p. 24.
13 *Ibid.*, p. 21.
14 Iris Murdoch, *The Good Apprentice* (London, 1985), p. 150.
15 DeNora, *After Adorno*, p. 40 and pp. 35–58 *passim*.
16 On the concept of 'do-ability', see Joan Fujimura, 'The Molecular Biological Bandwagon in Cancer Research: Where Social Worlds Meet', *Social Problems*, 35 (1988), pp. 261–83. For pragmatic perspectives on music-making, see Becker, *Art Worlds*, and Richard A. Peterson (ed.), *The Production of Culture* (Los Angeles, 1978).
17 Anthony King, *The Structure of Social Theory* (London, 2004).
18 Hans T. David and Arthur Mendel (eds.), *The Bach Reader: a Life of Johann Sebastian Bach in Letters and Documents* (London, 1966), pp. 71–5.
19 Richard D. P. Jones, 'The Keyboard Works: Bach as Teacher and Virtuoso', in John Butt (ed.), *The Cambridge Companion to Bach* (Cambridge, 1997), p. 142.
20 Wolff, 'Instrumental Music', p. 157; Malcolm Boyd, *Bach: the Brandenburg Concertos* (Cambridge, 1993), p. 16.
21 McClary, 'Talking Politics', p. 21, note 24.
22 *Ibid.*, p. 26.
23 *Ibid.*, p. 36.
24 Antoine Hennion and Joel Marie Fauquet, 'Authority as Performance: the Love of Bach in

Nineteenth-Century France', *Poetics*, 29 (2001), pp. 75–88, at p. 78.
25 See Tia DeNora, *Music in Everyday Life* (Cambridge, 2000), Chapter 2; Henry Kingsbury, 'Sociological Factors in Musicological Poetics', *Ethnomusicology*, 35 (1991), pp. 195–219; and Antoine Hennion, 'Baroque and Rock: Music, Mediators and Musical Taste', *Poetics*, 24 (1997), pp. 415–25.
26 Becker, *Art Worlds*.
27 Tia DeNora, 'How is Extra-Musical Meaning Possible? Music as a Place and Space for "Work"', *Sociological Theory*, 4 (1986), pp. 84–94.
28 See Tia DeNora, *Beethoven and the Construction of Genius: Musical Politics in Vienna, 1792–1803* (Berkeley and London, 1995), pp. 37–59. See also John A. Rice, *Empress Marie Therese and Music at the Viennese Court, 1792–1807* (Cambridge, 2003).
29 See Julia V. Moore, 'Beethoven and Musical Economics' (Ph.D. thesis, University of Illinois, Urbana-Champaign, 1987) and Norbert Elias, *Mozart: Portrait of a Genius* (Cambridge, 1993).
30 Emily Anderson (ed. and trans.), *The Letters of Mozart and His Family* (3rd edition, London, 1985), p. 872.
31 H. C. Robbins Landon, *Mozart: the Golden Years* (London, 1989), p. 140.
32 Kathrine Talbot (trans.), 'A Yearbook of the Music of Vienna and Prague, 1796 (by Johann Ferdinand von Schönfeld)', in Elaine Sisman (ed.), *Haydn and His World* (Princeton, 1997), pp. 289–331.
33 Cliff Eisen, 'The Classical Period', in 'Concerto', *NG Revised*, vol. 6, p. 247.
34 Mary Sue Morrow, *Concert Life in Haydn's Vienna* (New York, 1989), p. 158.
35 Leon Plantinga, *Beethoven's Concertos: History, Style, Performance* (New York, 1999), p. 4.
36 Nicholas Till, *Mozart and the Enlightenment* (London, 1992), p. 88.
37 See Jürgen Habermas, *The Structural Transformation of the Public Sphere: an Inquiry into a Category of Bourgeois Society*, trans. T. Burger with F. Lawrence (Cambridge, 1989) and Richard Sennett, *The Fall of Public Man* (London, 1977).
38 Till, *Mozart*, p. 92.
39 Quoted in Simon Frith, 'Afterthoughts', in Frith and A. Goodwin (eds.), *On Record: Rock, Pop and the Written Word* (London, 1990), p. 424.
40 See Simon P. Keefe, *Mozart's Piano Concertos: Dramatic Dialogue in the Age of Enlightenment* (Woodbridge and Rochester,

264   Tia DeNora

NY, 2001) and 'Dramatic Dialogue in Mozart's
Viennese Piano Concertos: a Study of
Competition and Cooperation in Three First
Movements', *MQ*, 83 (1999), pp. 169–204.
41 Till, *Mozart*, p. 177.
42 On this point see DeNora, *After Adorno*,
pp. 59–82, and Lucy Green, *Music, Gender,
Education* (Cambridge, 1997).
43 Keefe, 'Dramatic Dialogue', p. 197.
44 Quoted above, Hennion and Fauquet,
'Authority as Performance', p. 78.
45 See Green, *Music, Gender, Education.*
46 DeNora, *Beethoven*, pp. 147–69.
47 Morrow, *Concert Life.*
48 Tia DeNora, 'Music into Action:
Performing Gender on the Viennese Concert
Stage, 1790–1810', *Poetics*, 30 (2002),
pp. 19–33, and 'Embodiment and
Opportunity: Performing Gender in
Beethoven's Vienna', in William Weber (ed.),
*The Musician as Entrepreneur and
Opportunist, 1600–1900* (Bloomington, IN,
forthcoming).
49 Quoted in Richard Leppert, *The Sight of
Sound* (Berkeley and London, 1993), p. 67.
50 Plantinga, *Beethoven's Concertos*, p. 4.
51 Charles Rosen, *Piano Notes* (New York,
2002), p. 5.
52 Richard Leppert, 'Cultural Contradiction,
Idolatry, and the Piano Virtuoso: Franz Liszt',
in James Parakilas *et al., Piano Roles: Three
Hundred Years of Life with the Piano* (New
Haven, 1999), p. 255.
53 Quoted in Christine Battersby, *Gender and
Genius* (London, 1989), pp. 76–7.
54 Katharine Ellis, 'Female Pianists and Their

Male Critics in Nineteenth-Century Paris',
JAMS, 50 (1997), pp. 353–85, at p. 364.
55 *Ibid.*, p. 355.
56 *Ibid.*, p. 361.
57 Morrow, *Concert Life*, p. 159.
58 For example, the lyrical focus in Joe
Duddell's twenty-minute concerto for
percussion, *Ruby* (2002–3).
59 See Susan O'Neill, 'Gender and Music', in
David Hargreaves and Adrian North (eds.),
The Social Psychology of Music (Oxford, 1997),
pp. 46–66, and Nicola Dibben, 'Gender
Identity and Music', in Raymond Macdonald,
David Hargreaves and Dorothy Miell (eds.),
Musical Identities (Oxford, 2002), pp. 117–33.
60 Pierre Bourdieu, *Distinction: a Social
Critique of the Judgement of Taste* (Cambridge,
1984). See also Richard A. Peterson and Albert
Simkus, 'How Musical Tastes Mark
Occupational Status Groups', in Michele
Lamont and Marcel Fournier (eds.),
Cultivating Differences (Chicago, 1992),
pp. 152–68.
61 Lisa McCormick, 'Musical Performance as
Social Performance', in Ron Eyerman (ed.),
New Directions in Arts Sociology (Herndon,
VA, forthcoming). See also Jane W. Davidson,
'The Solo Performer's Identity' in Macdonald,
Hargreaves and Miell (eds.), *Musical
Identities*, pp. 97–116, and Hennion, 'Baroque
and Rock'.
62 See Keefe, 'Dramatic Dialogue', and Tia
DeNora, 'The Biology Lessons of Opera Buffa',
in Mary Hunter and James Webster (eds.),
Opera Buffa in Mozart's Vienna (Cambridge,
1997), pp. 146–64.

CHAPTER 8

Music as Agency in Beethoven's Vienna

THE MUSIC ITSELF?

Musicologists often complain that sociologists consider everything
except music itself. They have a point. The body of literature that is
sociology of music consists mainly of work on music's social shaping
and work devoted to music's role as a signifier of social status and
belonging. Very little has dealt with music's role in social ordering.

Posed as part of the growing counter to this trend, this chapter
deals with the question of how music is a medium for agency. By
agency, I mean capacities, modes, and opportunities for action, produced and distributed across individuals that afford preconditions,
pretexts, and media for social performance. I use a particular case
study of musical life—the reception and performance (at the piano)
of Beethoven in early nineteenth-century Vienna—to develop two
main themes. The first of these is that music, in conjunction with the
frames applied to it, is a medium for modeling role relationships in
and/or outside the musical realm. The second, related theme is that
the practical, situated, and material performance of music further
specifies music's discursive properties. As McCormick (this volume)
observes, performance is an all-too-neglected topic in music sociology.

Yet, the focus on music-as-practice (and music-as-performed) highlights the nonverbal, embodied, and otherwise tacit ways in which music may come to be understood as modeling, mediating, or otherwise registering social relations and sensibilities. Performance also illuminates the inevitable incompleteness of musical texts (notations), which, in conjunction with performance practices and performance occasions, come to be understood instead as "scripts"—that is, as implying choreography of, as Cook (2003) observes, "a series of real-time, social interactions between players; a series of mutual acts of listening and communal gestures that enact a particular vision of human society" (206).

Various scholars are now at work on this more symmetrical equation of music society. New modes of enquiry have pursued questions concerning music and the body, music, "health" and well-being, music and conflict resolution, music, place, space and identity, and music's real-time performance. These investigations have, in recent years, been posed and elaborated with some potentially powerful consequences for sociological theories of agency, for the understanding of mind-body issues, and for the better appreciation of the role of the aesthetic in social ordering (Eyerman and Jamieson 1998; Hennion 2001; Juslin and Sloboda 2001; Macdonald, Hargreaves, and Miell 2002; Clayton, Herbert, and Middleton 2003; DeNora 2000; 2003; Ruud 2002; Pavlicevic and Ansdell 2004; Clarke and Cook 2004).

Most of this work has, perhaps naturally, given its empirical and ethnographic nature, dealt with music in relation to current social life. Yet there is no reason why a "how to do things with music" focus may not be applied equally to historical topics; indeed, if we are to comprehend how and why our current musical conventions took shape and provide ordering materials in the ways that they do, we need to consider their histories. With this aim in mind, I turn now to a historical case study, one that, from somewhat different perspectives, I have considered on previous occasions (e.g., DeNora 1995). I will consider the question of how Beethoven and his music, in and through its production, reception, and performance, can be understood to have modeled new modes of agency in and beyond the musical world of Vienna in 1790–1810.

A NEW INTERIORITY? BEETHOVEN AND THE SELF IN MODERN SOCIETY

In a discussion of Liszt, Richard Leppert (1999) has written:

> For the first time in Western history, the cultural pecking order of the arts was rearranged so that music, formerly judged lesser

than the textual and visual arts, was considered pre-eminent. Music was the sonorous sign of inner life, and inner life was the sign of the bourgeois subject, the much heralded, newly invented, and highly idealized "individual." The European gold standard of the sonorous inner life was quickly and generally established as Beethoven. (253)

There is richness here for music sociology: Music, and in particular the conglomeration of Beethoven and his music, Leppert suggests, provided a point of reference through which the modern idea of the individual and of inner life were developed during the nineteenth century.

This theme has received attention from other music scholars, too, most notably Scott Burnham in his 1995 book *Beethoven Hero.* There, Burnham identifies features of Beethoven's rhetorical compositional style that, he suggests, provided the linchpin around which new images and conventions of various kinds in music came to coalesce—the concept of the "heroic" in music (and the musician as hero), the idea of the powerful and autonomous artist, the notion of the musician as engaged in moral struggle, the idea of music as a quest.

Burnham describes how Beethoven and his music came to be conceived as the "Beethoven Hero," within which Beethoven himself became "the embodiment of music" (xvi), the artist-as-hero who "liberated" music as Burnham puts it, "from the stays of eighteenth-century convention" (xvi). The Beethoven hero notion extends well beyond the works Beethoven composed in his so-called heroic style of about 1803–1809; it refers much more broadly to the new ideas of social and psychic agency that Beethoven and his music came to exemplify. These ideas were propounded and elaborated by generations of later composers, from Schumann, who speaks of what he terms Beethoven's "virile power," to Wagner, who wrote on the one hundredth anniversary of Beethoven's birth (1870) of how Beethoven had created music and new purposes of music fundamentally different from his predecessors. If Leppert and Burnham are correct, we should be able to trace this imagery as it was constructed in and around Beethoven's music and to consider how his music came to be constituted as a cultural "work space" (DeNora 1986) through which new conceptions of agency were elaborated.

We may explore this issue from many complementary angles. In what follows I deal with two. The first consists of a focus on discourse. I suggest that the development of the imagery of the Beethoven hero was primed by philosophical and literary critical discussions (Kant's notion of the sublime and Schiller's idea of sentimental art), that these discussions were then extended in musical critical discourse, and, finally, that the notions developed in musical critical discourse were then applied to Beethoven in ways that simultaneously modified both those notions and conceptions of Beethoven and his music. If this argument sounds convoluted, it is because it revolves around the reflexive constitution of, as I have described in earlier work (DeNora 1995), Beethoven and the categories through which he was perceived. Where what I have to say diverges from my earlier work on Beethoven is that I hope to demonstrate how philosophical ideas and their implications for the imagery of agency were recast through discussions of Beethoven's music as opportunities, stances, and postures of action.

The second angle deals with how the discourses associated with Beethoven came to be embodied and thus further specified and elaborated via that embodiment, in and through the performance of Beethoven's works, viewed in context of the culture of performance more widely conceived. In this respect, the topics covered may be read as interacting and exemplifying some of the points made elsewhere in this volume, in particular, McCormick's schematic conception of "music as social performance."

DISCURSIVE DEPICTIONS OF THE BEETHOVEN HERO

The Discourse of "Inner Life" Transposed from Letters to Tones

The idea of "inner life" and its external manifestation as individual agency took shape initially during the 1790s in philosophy, through Kant's notion of the sublime. As elaborated in the *Critique of Judgement* (1790) (for excerpts relevant to music, see translations in le Huray and Day 1981), Kant's notion possessed two important dimensions.

On the one hand, the sublime was mathematical, abstract, and linked to the infinite in its incomprehensibility. On the other hand, the sublime was dynamic; it was a *mental* (indeed, emotional) state, inspired by fear, in particular the fear instilled by natural phenomena (Kant offers examples such as volcanoes and thunder). And it was in and through this dynamic state that self-awareness, according to Kant, was constituted. The apprehension of sublime phenomena, he said, "allows us to discover in ourselves a capacity of resistance.... So sublimity is contained, not in any natural object, but in our mind and spirit, in so far as we can become aware of being superior to nature in ourselves, and thereby to nature outside of ourselves as well" (quoted in Webster 1997:59).

It is here that we see the germ of something new, typically hailed as the Enlightenment notion of human supremacy over nature and with it the idea of the self-reflexive agent. The Kantian sublime provided a vehicle through which the self-conscious and self-empowering individual could be elaborated. The apprehension of the sublime, in other words, led to self-awareness; it posed a relationship between nature (objective, external forces) and the subjective experience of nature (e.g., fear), and, through that experience, *freedom,* understood as the capacity for intervening and so resisting nature.[1]

This idea of "inner life" and its connection to a new and empowered form of agency was developed as an aesthetic theory by Friedrich Schiller in his 1795 discussion of "naive" versus "sentimental" art. There, Schiller posed a distinction between poetry that describes objects and the natural world from which it is not alienated (naive poetry) and poetry about the impressions objects make on the poet and thus, about the realm of the subjective ("inner life"). During the years between roughly 1801 and 1810, these notions were introduced to musical discourse, as other scholars have already shown (Webster 1997; Senner 1999).

In an article first published in 1801 and reissued more widely in 1805 in the *Berlinische Musikalische Zeitung,* the critic C. F. Michaelis described how music could depict the sublime and so arouse the feeling of awe associated with sublimity or how it could depict the subjective experience of feeling in the presence of the sublime:

> Music can either seek to arouse the feeling of sublimity through an inner structure that is independent of any emotional expression, or portray the state of mind aroused by such a feeling. In the first case the music can objectively be called sublime, like untamed nature, which arouses sublime emotions; in the second case, the music portrays what is pathetically sublime. The former resembles epic poetry; the latter lyric poetry. (translated and quoted in Webster 1997:62)

Here we see an early version of the notion that music could not only function programmatically, depicting natural phenomena, but that it could also provide analogues of subjective experience in the face of those phenomena—feelings of terror, awe, and longing, for example.

This idea was given further impetus in the same issue of the *Berlinische Muskalische Zeitung* in a second essay (by an author listed only as C. F. [Michaelis's first initials were C. F.—could it have been he?]). The writer says, "The composer can represent the subjective:

the expression of sensations and emotions, affects and passions.... This kind [of music] one can call lyrical. It is the expression of feeling, full of dominating subjectivity. It is not just beautiful, it is also moving" (quoted in Senner 1999:32).

How, then, was the musical sublime configured? In his essay, Michaelis points to musical devices such as

> long, majestic, weighty, or solemn notes ... long pauses holding up the progress of the melodic line, or which impede the shaping of a melody ... too much diversity, as when innumerable impressions succeed one another too rapidly and the mind is too abruptly hurled into the thundering torrent of sounds, or when ... themes are developed together in so complex a manner that the imagination cannot easily and calmly integrate the diverse ideas into a coherent whole without strain. (quoted in Webster 1997:62–63)

How, then, did these discussions square with Beethoven and his music? Thanks to work by Robin Wallace (1986) and William Senner (1999), it is possible to trace this development by reviewing the ways in which Beethoven's work was discussed and how the terms of that discussion modulated over time. These issues become clear if we focus on Beethoven's reception in the pages of the Leipzig *Allgemeine Musicalische Zeitung* (AMZ), the first journal to review Beethoven's work (it carried a review of early Beethoven works in its first issue in 1798) and the one in which his works were most systematically reviewed.

Reconfiguring Beethoven/Reconfiguring Critical Discourse

Beethoven fared poorly in the earliest issues of the AMZ. He is described, for example, in 1799 as, piling "one thought wildly upon another, and, in a rather bizarre manner, to group them in such as way that not infrequently an obscure artificiality or an artificial obscurity is produced" (Wallace 1986:8, describing the Piano Sonatas op. 10).[2] By 1802, however, after a barbed letter to the editor from Beethoven, in which he threatened to withhold his works from the journal's parent company, a music publisher, should his treatment at the hands of the reviewers not improve ("advise your critics to exercise more care and good sense"), Beethoven is viewed in a more favorable, albeit still preromantic, light in a review of the Violin Sonatas op. 23 and 24: "The original, fiery, and intrepid spirit of this composer, which even in his early works could not escape the attention of astute observers, but which did not always find the most cordial reception, probably because it sometimes sprang forth in a manner that was ungracious, impetuous, dismal and opaque … is now becoming ever clearer" (quoted in Wallace 1986:9).

This discursive process moved from initial hostility to Beethoven, to a slightly begrudging recognition of his "original" talent, to, eventually, depictions of the composer as hero and of the psychological intensity associated with the confrontation of the sublime. In this respect, the transposition of Kant's sublime into musical terms provided a useful resource with which to rehabilitate Beethoven. As Senner (1999) has so astutely observed, "in spite of Kant's intent to promote the public use of reason and his exclusion of music from his philosophy, his advocacy of the aesthetics of productive imagination and the autonomy of art provided the foundation for a view of art that Beethoven's contemporaries could use to attack his Enlightenment opponents" (15).

Accordingly, we see reference to the sublime and its musical construction taking shape in the pages of AMZ between roughly 1801 (the initial publication of Michaelis's essay) and 1805 when, in a review of the C-minor Piano Concerto no. 3, a critic wrote:

> The ever-growing intensity over 32 measures [achieved by drawing out the harmonic progress] … grips the listener irresistibly Beethoven produces a similar effect in the places where, traversing one or more octaves, usually in chromatic scales, he arrives again at the minor 7th or 9th with which the main theme begins, without, however, letting the listener come to rest, but holding him in tension until the theme is stated in its entirety. (Wallace 1986:15)

We begin to see here some of the ways in which Beethoven's music came to be seen as "holding" the listener in train to a new and psychologically charged psychoacoustical landscape, one in which restlessness, suspense, and shock had come to replace melodic and harmonic flow. As one contemporary, the composer Johann Wenzel Tomashek, put it upon hearing Beethoven improvise, "Not infrequently, the unsuspecting listener is jolted violently out of his state of joyful transports" (quoted in Landon 1970:104). Through the ways in which this "violent jolting" was paired with textual descriptions of its meaning, new habits of musical response, associated with new modes of psychic energy and resolve, were posed as opportunities for experience.

By 1810, the critical discourse of romanticism is fully unfurled in Beethoven's honor, illustrated most notably in E. T. A. Hoffmann's famous AMZ review of the Fifth Symphony. There, the idea of "inner life," musically configured, had fully arrived, proffered as the

cornerstone of a new, "romantic" aesthetic of autonomous art and
defined, above all, by "interminable longing" and, tellingly, by the idea
of being able to triumph over ("resist") nature. Hoffman associated
romanticism most closely with the medium of instrumental music,[3]
which he saw as "scorning every aid, every admixture of another art,
[it] expresses the pure essence of this particular art alone" (Senner
1999: 17). Of Beethoven, he wrote, "Beethoven sets in motion the
machinery of awe, of fear, of pain" (quoted in Burnham 2000:275).
And:

> Now Beethoven's instrumental music opens to us the realm of
> the colossal and the immeasurable. Glowing beams of light shoot
> through the deep night of this realm and we perceive shadows
> surging back and forth, closer and closer around us, destroying
> everything in us except the pain of that endless longing in which
> each joy that had risen in jubilant tones sinks back and perishes;
> and it is in this pain ... which seeks to break our breast with the
> chords of all the passions that we live on and become enchanted
> visionaries. (Wallace 1986:21)

Music's Actors—Implied Personae

In the space of little more than a decade, between 1799 and 1810, the
German-language critical discourse aligned the idea of the sublime
and Beethoven's music in ways that constituted a sea change in musical life. This change was characterized by two key features. First, as
music's subject matter shifted to the unfathomable, the tumultuous,
the terrifying and, adjacent to this, music was increasingly understood
as able to depict "inner life"—fear, awe, yearning, and resistance,
music modeled the ideas of psychological interiority, individualism,
and the capacity to resist and strive (freedom).

Second, insofar as music came to be seen as providing the best
medium for depicting the sublime, the musician—Beethoven—came
to be modeled also in new ways, as a heroic, and therefore high-status,
actor. It is here that we begin to glimpse the ways that the romantic
aesthetic came to be linked to social exclusion, widening gulf between
serious and popular taste and between artist and society, a point
recognized early on by Schiller himself when he speaks in his 1795
essay of how the sentimental artist is inevitably alienated from the
general public by virtue of his attempts to access the infinite (Senner
1999:15).

Similarly, Burnham (2000) describes how Hoffmann "helped
create a situation rare in music history: the little understood works

of a still living composer were accepted on faith as masterpieces of organic conception and sublime revelation, each held together by a deep and mysterious continuity which, in Hoffmann's words, 'speaks only from spirit to spirit'" (275–76). The new musical materials were (and this is a critical point) *simultaneously* both by-products of and resources for two forms of agency understood as capacity for action: (1) Beethoven's composition of *himself* as a new type of agent with new forms of entitlement and opportunity (a role that Beethoven assumed in an exclusive manner) and (2) the emergence of the critic as a high(er) status intermediary between composer and public.

On the first of these new roles, Beethoven was undoubtedly active in the process of producing himself as a new type of creative agent, one able to conjure forth in music "the colossal and the immeasurable" (quoted in Wallace 1986:21), whose grappling with tumultuous musical issues on an epic scale was able to prove himself as a musical "master." Such a being came to be treated as one who could command attention, one to whom devotion (in the form of silent respectful listening) was due (on changes in the culture of listening, see DeNora 1995; Johnson 1995). "I do not play for such swine," Beethoven notoriously exclaimed in 1802 (Thayer 1967:307), when one of his salon performances was met with less than rapt attention, and in so doing he marked the moment when the balance of authority between patron and musician had begun to shift—again with Beethoven as the linchpin—in favor of the latter.

In short, the Beethoven hero was an extraordinary individual, a "prince of music" as he once described himself to his patron, Prince Lichnowsky. As such, the role Beethoven assumed as a musician and a "master" of music, provided a model for a second, more generalized (and more aspirational) form of agency, the exemplary self, possessed of an ability to, in Kant's terms, "become aware of being superior to nature in ourselves, and thereby to nature outside of ourselves as well" (Webster 1997:59) ().

In sum, music, particularly instrumental music, provided the medium par excellence for the representation of the sublime, and, related to this, it represented "inner" experience. In this sense, Beethoven's musical innovations can be understood to have provided new resources for the configuration of subjective experience; they modeled that experience through the temporal medium of tones. Related to music's new role, new forms of social and psychic agency were also modeled, for both musicians and listeners. Through the ways in which the musician (Beethoven) could be seen to "grapple" with musical material, he became heroic, and, by channeling his listeners' energies, he was simultaneously repositioned in relation to his listeners over whom he came to be seen as having power, through the ways he could command and hold attention, and evoke terror and awe.

FROM DISCOURSE TO PRACTICE

So far, I have dealt with musical experience framed through the pairing of philosophical notions, musical forms, and musical-critical texts. I have yet to consider how Beethoven's music was also made meaningful in and through practical performance—my second aim in this chapter. It is here that questions about how the mediating role of performance as situated activity and as, in this volume, McCormick terms "social performance" is constitutive in its own right of the cultural structures that provide resources for and thereby mediate action.

How and to what extent is it possible to explore these forms of agency as they came to be *enacted* in the milieu of Beethoven's Vienna? And to what extent did the enactment of this agency further elaborate these possibilities and their meanings—how, for example, was the Beethoven imago further specified in and through the how, who, what, when, and where of musical performance practice? I suggest there is much to learn in this regard by moving beyond the level of the cultural analysis of musical texts and their social meanings to consider how these texts came to be performed. Accordingly, in the next section I examine Beethoven's instrumental music as it was performed between 1792 and 1810.

Musical Bodies

At a time when all music was performed live, musical performance was always, and at least implicitly, a visually dramatic event, one that inevitably involved bodily procedures, strictures about comportment, and, at times, choreography. To speak of these matters is to deconstruct the technical neutrality of musical performance and to recognize, by contrast, how musical performance may itself provide significant factors in the overall understanding of works and their perceived meanings. Here, I mean much more than mere phrasing. I mean the performance of performance, the ways in which that music may make demands on the body and how music may be used by performers for embodied display. In these respects, music performance is dramaturgical: the practices of performing may delineate various meanings.

Circa 1800, there was probably no realm within musical performance as charged with social meaning as the keyboard. The piano in late eighteenth- and early nineteenth-century Vienna was at the heart of debates over aesthetic practice, a site at which new and often-competing aesthetics were deployed and defended, at times through the overt medium of the "piano duel" (DeNora 1995:chap. 7). In what ways, then, did the demands made by Beethoven's piano works on the piano-performing body serve to highlight the keyboard artist as a particular type of actor? How, in other words, were the models provided by Beethoven's music further delineated in and through the embodied and visual display associated with their performance? For example, how did musical performance further specify notions about heroic action—more specifically, the embodied lineaments of that action? Who came to be cast as Beethovenian performers? And, equally relevant, who did not? For not all musicians, it would appear, were equally entitled to take up the opportunities for musical action offered by Beethoven's works.

"The Ladies Do Not Wish to Play"

In 1796, Frau Bernard described in her diary how her piano teacher, Andreas Streicher, introduced her to Beethoven's recently published Sonatas op. 2: "One day Streicher put some things by Beethoven in front of [me]; they were the piano sonatas opus 2 which had just appeared at Artaria's [c. 1796]. He told [me] that *there are some new things in them which the ladies do not wish to play* because they are incomprehensible and too difficult, would [I] like to learn them?" (Landon 1976–80:IV:67, emphasis added).

I have described elsewhere (DeNora 2004) how Streicher was probably correct in his assessment that the "ladies did not wish to play" Beethoven. Between 1793 and 1810—at which time Beethoven was perhaps the most frequently performed composer for fortepiano in Vienna—Beethoven's works were performed most often by men: 79 percent of performances of *all* his piano works were performed by men and 21 percent by women, and 84 percent of his concertos by men. Put the other way round, only 16 percent of Beethoven's concerto's were performed by women. This percentage contrasts dramatically with the proportion of male performances of Mozart: 26 percent of *all* his piano works were given by men and 74 percent by women; 27 percent of his concertos were performed by men during 1787–1810 and 73 percent by women.[4]

Between 1803 and 1810, the number of performances of Beethoven's concertos was increasing. Also growing were the number of performers apart from Beethoven who played his concertos (particularly after he retreated from performing them himself as his hearing failed). Yet women continued to be active (Josepha Auernhammer,

Frauline Kurzbeck, Baroness Ertmann, Countess Anna Marie Erdody, and others were all featured on the concert stage during these years). Indeed, women would appear to have given as many and sometimes more performances of piano concertos than men did. However, there is no extant evidence of a female performance of a Beethoven concerto after 1806, a time during which men increasingly took up his works. Once a concerto was published, Beethoven tended not to perform it again himself, and, as his hearing worsened, he entrusted the performance of his works to others. Never before had women and men been divided within the piano repertory in this way.[5]

In other work (DeNora 2004), I have considered why women seem to have been so conspicuously absent from performing what were, arguably, the most prestigious works in the keyboard repertory at a time when they continued to play the concertos of other composers. I have suggested that this gender segregation in the repertory marked the beginning of the women's exclusion from the heart of the musical canon and from the emerging notion of "serious" music during these years.[6]

I have also suggested that it was physical and performative features required and implied by Beethoven's works, and the ways that these features clashed with conventions and mores concerning pianistic display that made the highly public performance of Beethoven (exacerbated by the figure/ground nature of concertos) difficult for women. To understand this issue, it is necessary to contextualize it in terms of who played which instrument, circa 1790.

In the 1780s and 1790s, the keyboard was the predominant instrument for quasi-professional musicians and for aristocratic musical amateurs. For the latter, the allure of the keyboard instrument lay in two features: First, it was an expensive instrument, one that was also physically conspicuous. Second, it permitted a display of embodiment, musically conceived, that was commensurate with, in the 1780s, aristocratic ideals of comportment and bodily display, ideals outlined in 1796 by Frau Bernard's teacher, Andreus Streicher, in his *Handbook for Piano Care and Good Musicianship*. Streicher described the ideal piano-performing body as unobtrusive, self-effacing, one in which all traces of physical and technical effort were suppressed. Just as, in the contemporary phrase of the 1780s, music should "flow like oil" (i.e., tones equally matched so as to create a smooth surface—the analogy was matched pearls, the jewel most worn by Vienna's aristocrats), so, too, Streicher tells us that the good pianist plays in a manner such that "no one is even aware of the artistry."

This quiet body was a vehicle for the display of aristocratic composure and, as such, was commensurate with the favored dance forms of aristocrats during these years—the minuet, for example. Circa 1796 in Vienna, to be an active, overtly physical, musical body was considered lower status—aristocrats simply did not play the types of instruments that called for puffing or puffed cheeks or that involved spittle.

For women, this type of bodily composure was doubly important. To engage in too overtly physical a form of musical display compromised social status but, additionally, femininity and propriety. Thus, circa 1796, the confluence of aristocratic and gender ideologies applied to music rendered male and female bodies at the keyboard equally equipped and equally matched.

It is in this context that we need to consider Beethoven's music in terms of the demands it makes on the pianist's body. Beethoven's music, particularly the devices it employs to represent the sublime (thundering chords, double octaves, sudden and surprising motifs), reinscribes the performing body in terms of its display in ways that brings the pianist's body into sharp visual relief, made most apparent in the concerto genre, when the soloist's body is featured in front of an orchestral backdrop. The embodied techniques featured in Beethoven's music supplanted the aristocratic body with something new, a more dashing, visceral, and energetic body. Beethoven's music can, in other words, be understood to have renegotiated the aesthetics of the body, in ways that downgraded aristocratic values and replaced them with the materiality of visibility of the productive and active musical body.

The mannerisms and gestures associated with Beethoven's music are precisely those that Streicher denigrates in his discussion of the "bad" pianist (or "keyboard strangler"), the player

> of whom it is reputed, "he plays extraordinarily such as you have never heard before." ... Through the movement of his body, arms and hands, he seemingly wants to make us understand how difficult is the work he has undertaken. He carries on in a fiery manner and treats his instrument like a man who, bent on revenge, has his arch-enemy in his hands and, with cruel relish, wants to torture him slowly to death.... He pounds so hard that suddenly the maltreated strings go out of tune, several fly in the direction of bystanders who hurriedly move back in order to protect their eyes.... But why ... does the player have such an obstinate instrument that it will only obey his fingers and not his gesticulations? ... His playing resembles a script which has been smeared before the ink is dried. (quoted in Jones 1999:4, emphasis Streicher's)

As the period-instrument maker and piano historian Margaret Hood (1986) has observed, "Some of the mannerisms [Streicher] ridiculed characterized Beethoven's aggressive and dramatic style of playing" (I:4). Streicher's manual was published in 1796, on the cusp of Beethoven's rising fame. Indeed, it is in the same year that Beethoven initiated his campaign for piano-technological change. He wrote to Streicher from his concert tour in Pressburg, to thank Streicher for the loan of an instrument while on tour (see DeNora 1995:176), "I received the day before yesterday your fortepiano, which is really an excellent instrument.... It is far too good for me ... because it robs me of the freedom to produce my own tone." And again, later in the same year: "The pianoforte is still the least studied and developed of all instruments.... I hope that the time will come when the harp and the pianoforte will be treated as two entirely different instruments." Hood speculates that it was perhaps because of the shifting tide of musical fashion, particularly Beethoven's rapidly rising star, that Streicher's pamphlet was only briefly in circulation.

Beethoven's Bodies

In terms how it is to be performed, Beethoven's music made new demands on the piano-performing body—it required a more visceral keyboard approach and more demonstrative physical action (the choreography associated with this action was even lampooned as the century progressed). These characteristics were not compatible with late eighteenth-century piano technology, and they were in opposition to strictures about appropriate feminine comportment—whether at the piano or elsewhere.

At least in part, the new pianist inscribed in Beethoven's music was Beethoven himself. Observations from his contemporaries suggest his pianistic style was strenuous (DeNora 1995:chaps. 6, 7, and 8). The Beethoven biographer A. W. Thayer has speculated that this visceral approach may have been the result of "all the hardness and heaviness of manipulation caused by his devotion to the organ" (Thayer 1967: I:160) (an instrument that, during the 1780s when Beethoven was active in Bonn as court organist, required a degree of strength far greater than that required by the fortepiano).

At the same time, the body configured in Beethoven's works and in the performance of his works was not reducible to Beethoven's body. True, Beethoven may be understood to have inscribed his body into his music. But so, too, his music came to provide the standard against which his embodied traits then came to be perceived and hailed as insignia of his (and subsequent musicians') genius.

It is here that we see most clearly the reflexive relationship between Beethoven's visceral piano style and the image of the Beethoven hero. The mutual referencing of these two things in turn illustrated the new image of the individual in terms of its opportunities for embodied—and symbolically embodied—action. "Full of vitality, a picture of strength," said Ignaz Seyfried, circa 1820 (quoted in Wegeler and Ries 1987:14) of Beethoven. He became known for his sudden and unpredictable and impulsive behavior—his "raptus," as he and his circle termed it (the tendency to shift impulsively to a preoccupation when overtaken by an idea or inspiration) and his short temper. These characteristics—Beethoven's dynamism—came to be seen as further evidence of his exceptional identity and abilities, his genius.

The musical depiction of "inner life" and its outer correlate of heroic action can be understood to have been delineated not only through musical material but, simultaneously, through the physical practices of its performance that gave rise to a visual imagery of heroic action, musically configured. And it is here that we start to see how music, in and through its performance/enactment, provides object lessons in how to be an agent. In this case, it provided a vocabulary of gestures and a compendium of movement styles associated with powerful individualism. Speaking of how music in the nineteenth century came to involve a "look" as well as sonority, Richard Leppert (1999) observes that, "more than ever before, performers' bodies, in the act of realizing music, also helped to transliterate musical sound into musical meaning by means of the sight—and sometimes spectacle—of their gestures, facial expressions and general physicality" (255; see also Leppert 1993).

During these years in Vienna, similar images were being forged and developed in the scientific and pseudoscientific cultures of physiognomy and Mesmerism (Lavater, the father of physiognomy, continued to promote Mesmer's ideas long after Mesmer himself was forced to leave Vienna, after a scandal involving one of his patients, the pianist Maria Theresa Paradis). There, it is possible to see the gendered notions of capacity for the sublime, heroism, and the rapt or captive audience also being developed and resonating with musical culture. As in music, the notion that special qualities of individuals were locatable in the physical and/or psychological traits of that individual was a concept that inevitably cut across more democratic ideas of talent and meritocracy.

CONCLUSION

As it came to be elaborated in and through musical performance practices, the Beethoven imago was associated with an imagery initially

118   *Tia DeNora*

forged in philosophy and aesthetics, and elaborated via bodily performance. That imagery and its musical enactment in turn forged new
ideas about the connections between appearance and social capacity,
with configurations of social agency. The opportunities to inhabit
these configurations were differentially distributed along gendered
lines in ways that were consequential for then-emerging conceptions
of gender and sexual difference, for masculinity as well as femininity. Further research on performance occasions, revisions to scores in
anticipation of those occasions, and reports of performance practices
(and their social distribution) will further enrich our understanding of
how performance—in this case in the Vienna of Beethoven— helped
sketch or script possibilities for social relation and action.[7]

This gender divide widened over the course of the nineteenth
century and throughout Europe. Music, in and through its practice,
provided object lessons in gender-linked modes of agency. The new
forms of musical display, and the agencies they implied, not only
excluded women from the heart of the musical canon; they also celebrated a currency of bodily capital (appearance, physique, comportment, and temperament) that was differentially distributed to men.
The "freedom" to strive, it would appear, was not readily available to
all as, increasingly in music, appearance mattered.

NOTES

1. We see Beethoven employing this discourse of resistance, indeed
dramatizing himself as a kind of sublime actor on numerous occasions in his
letters. For example, in the famous letter of November 16, 1801, in which
Beethoven speaks to his friend Franz Wegeler, he describes how "I will seize
Fate by the throat; it shall certainly not bend and crush me completely....
I am no longer suited to the quiet life" (Anderson 1961:68 as quoted in
Downs 1970:586).

2. Compare this to Michaelis's description of the musical corollaries
of the sublime, quoted earlier and initially published in 1801 ("too much
diversity, as when innumerable impressions succeed one another too rapidly").

3. "[Music] is the most romantic of all the arts—one might say, the
only purely Romantic art" (quoted in Senner 1999:17). The essay appeared in
the preeminent music journal of the day, the Leipzig *Allgemeine Musikalische
Zeitung*.

4. The four female performances of Beethoven concertos are given over
a one-year period, between 1801 and 1802 (three by Josepha Auernhammer
and one by a Miss Stummer, about whom nothing else is known—perhaps
she visited Vienna only briefly) and one performance in 1806.

5. Of course, Mozart wrote some of his concertos for his own performance, whereas he wrote others for his female students, but during these
years, the women who performed Mozart concertos were not by any means
restricted in terms of their access to Mozart's works.

6. For discussions of the gendered character of the musical canon in
the nineteenth century and beyond, see Ellis (1997), Citron (1993), Mc-
Clary (1991), Solie (1993).

7. Ongoing work at Exeter is examining these issues through a collaboration between myself and a musicologist, Timothy Jones, who is a
specialist in, among other things, the study of Mozart's concerto autograph
scores.

Bibliography

Burnham, Scott. 1995. *Beethoven Hero.* Princeton, N.J.: Princeton University Press.
————. 2000. "The Four Ages of Beethoven: Musicians (and a Few Oth-
ers) on Beethoven." In *The Cambridge Companion to Beethoven,* ed. G.
Stanley. Cambridge: Cambridge University Press.
Citron, Marcia 1993. *Gender and the Musical Canon.* Cambridge: Cambridge
University Press.
Clarke, E., and N. Cook. 2004. *Empirical Musicology: Aims, Methods, Pros-
pects.* Oxford: Oxford University Press.
Clayton, M., T. Herbert, and R. Middleton, eds. 2003. *The Cultural Study
of Music: A Critical Introduction.* London: Routledge.
Cook, Nicholas. 2003. "Music as Performance." In *The Cultural Study of
Music: A Critical* Introduction, ed. Martin Clayton, Trevor Herbert,
and Richard Middleton. New York: Routledge.
DeNora, Tia. 1986. "How Is Extra-musical Meaning Possible? Music as a
Place and Space for 'Work.'" *Sociological Theory* 84, no. 1: 84–94.
————. 1995. *Beethoven and the Construction of Genius: Musical Politics in
Vienna, 1792–1803.* Berkeley: University of California Press.
————. 2000. *Music in Everyday Life.* Cambridge: Cambridge University
Press.
————. 2003. *After Adorno: Rethinking Music Sociology.* Cambridge: Cambridge University Press.
————. 2004. "Embodiment and Opportunity: Bodily Capital, Gender and
Reputation in Beethoven's Vienna." In *The Musician as Entrepreneur,*
ed. W. Weber. Bloomington: Indiana University Press.
Downs, Philip. 1970. "Beethoven's 'New Way' and the Eroica." *Musical
Quarterly* 56: 585–604.
Ellis, Katherine. 1997. "Female Pianists and Their Male Critics in Nine-
teenth-Century Paris." *Journal of the American Musicological Society*
50: 353–85.
Eyerman, Ron, and Andrew Jamison. 1998. *Music and Social Movements:
Mobilizing Traditions in the Twentieth Century.* Cambridge: Cambridge
University Press.

119a *Bibliography*

Hennion, A. 2001. "Music Lovers: Taste as Performance." *Theory, Culture & Society* 18, no. 5: 1–22.

Hood, Margaret. 1986. "Nannette Streicher and Her Pianos." *Continuo* (May): 2–5 and (June): 2–7.

Johnson, James. 1995. *Listening in Paris.* Berkeley: University of California Press.

Jones, Timothy. 1999. *Beethoven: The "Moonlight" and Other Sonatas Op. 27 and Op. 31.* Cambridge: Cambridge University Press.

Juslin, P., and J. Sloboda, eds. 2001. *Music and Emotion: Theory and Research.* Oxford: Oxford University Press.

Landon, H. C. Robbins. 1970. *Beethoven: A Documentary Study.* New York: Macmillan.

————. 1976–80. *Haydn: Chronicle and Works* (5 vols.). Bloomington: Indiana University Press.

Le Huray, Peter, and James Day. 1981. *Music and Aesthetics in the Eighteenth and Early-Nineteenth Centuries.* Cambridge: Cambridge University Press.

Leppert, R. 1993. *The Sight of Sound: Music, Representation, and the History of the Body.* Berkeley: University of California Press.

————. 1999. "Cultural Contradiction, Idolatry, and the Piano Virtuoso: Franz Liszt." In *Piano Roles: Three Hundred Years of Life with the Piano,* ed. J. Parakilas. New Haven, Conn.: Yale University Press.

Macdonald, R., D. Hargreaves, and D. Miell, eds. 2002. *Musical Identities.* Oxford: Oxford University Press.

McClary, Susan. 1991. *Feminine Endings.* Minneapolis: University of Minnesota Press.

Pavlicevic, M., and G. Ansdell, eds. 2004. *Community Music Therapy.* London: Kingsley.

Ruud, Even. 2002. "Music as Cultural Immogen—Three Narratives on the Use of Music as a Technology of Health." In *Research in and for Higher Music Education,* ed. I. M. Hanken et al. Festschrift for Harald Jørgensen. Oslo: Norwegian Academy of Music.

Senner, Wayne M. 1999. *The Critical Reception of Beethoven's Compositions by His German Contemporaries, Vol. I.* Lincoln: University of Nebraska Press.

Solie, Ruth, ed. 1993. *Musicology and Difference.* Berkeley: University of California Press.

Thayer, Alexander Wheelock. 1967. *Thayer's Life of Beethoven,* 2 vols., rev. and ed. by Elliott Forbes. Princeton, N.J.: Princeton University Press.

Wallace, Robin. 1986. *Beethoven's Critics.* Cambridge: Cambridge University Press.

Webster, James. 1997. "The Creation, Haydn's Late Vocal Music, and the Musical Sublime." In *Haydn and His World,* ed. E. Sisman. Princeton, N.J.: Princeton University Press.

Wegeler, F., and F. Ries. 1987. "Biographical Notes." *Beethoven Reconsidered,* trans. F. Noonan. Arlington, Va.: Great Ocean Publishers.

CHAPTER 9

The Pebble in the Pond: Musicing, Therapy, Community

Prelude: Constructivism and Music Therapy

Along with many sociologists, my position is constructivist. This means beginning with the premise that the facts and features of human social existence, even those that we take to be natural and immutable, are by contrast formed in and through human cultural, social, and material-technical practices. And, like many sociologists, I apply constructivism equally to so-called "soft" matters such as identity and personality and to "harder" things such as quantum physics. This view understands the realm of natural facts, to the extent they become known and experienced, as the result of institutional practices and procedures (shared ways of orienting to, perceiving, classifying, and representing data), further complicated at times by knowledge-based controversies and campaigns (Barnes 1985; Latour & Woolgar 1986; Knorr-Cetina 1999; and a small portion of my own work, DeNora 1996).

To make this assertion is by no means to debunk science or to undercut the value/applicability of scientific findings. Rather, it is to understand knowledge production and the perception of reality (and 'nature') as social endeavours, to entertain the possibility that "things may be otherwise." Later in this essay I will try to clarify this point with examples from relational theories in the sociology of health and illness. First though, I want to connect the constructivist perspective to socio-musical studies.

My own research has explored music's dynamic role as resource for social ordering and self-regulation—a medium for the construction

TIA DENORA is Professor of Sociology of Music at Exeter University. She is author of *Beethoven and the Construction of Genius* (California 1995/Fayard 1998), *Music in Everyday Life* (Cambridge 2000), and *After Adorno: Rethinking Music Sociology* (Cambridge 2003). Her current work focuses on music, science and embodied culture in Beethoven's Vienna and she is preparing background research for a study of conceptual and evaluative issues in and around the area of mind, body, agency, and environment. Contact: Department of Sociology and Philosophy, SHiPSS, University of Exeter, Amory Building, Rennes Drive, Exeter EX4 4RJ. Telephone: +1392-263280. Email: tdenora@exeter.ac.uk

TIA DENORA

of knowledge, mood, emotion, embodied capacity, memory, and interaction-style (DeNora 2000). I have developed this work through specific case studies of musical use and deployment and through an empirical programme based upon the concept of the musical event (DeNora 2003), by which I mean specified temporal periods of actual musical engagement linked to specified transformative outcomes. As I see it, music is an often-unacknowledged part of our environmentally distributed toolkit for reality construction. Musical features, for example, may be transferred to, transposed onto, or referred to seemingly extra-musical matters, as when music's perceived structural properties serve as a template for thinking about other (extra-musical) things. Investigating the question of how music is involved in this process helps, I think, to highlight the non-verbal, embodied, and aesthetic features of social ordering activity as an on-going practice; it helps to show how music may afford agency, action, and concerted activity.

It is from within this set of contexts (constructivist, music sociological with a focus on everyday musical practices) that my own interest in music therapy has taken shape. And it is this set of contexts that I bring to the following discussion of *Community Music Therapy*, a landmark volume in music therapy's growing connections to research and practice in community music, the sociology and anthropology of music in daily life, and studies of informal musical learning.

Music Therapies – A Widening Terrain?

As several commentators on the history of music therapy's occupational status have observed (Ansdell 2002), the site of music therapy has shifted over the decades. In part, this change has been linked to a search for professional standing in relation to health and caring professions more widely. Initially, during the 1960s, 1970s, and before, in music therapy's early and pioneering

phase, a great deal of work was conducted outside the music room. But because the boundaries of the site were permeable, music therapy's status as a profession was also unclear. During the 1980s and 1990s, and partly in response to music therapy's perceived "low status," music therapists began to develop what has since emerged as the conventional bounded site of a therapy setting— the music room—and with this, the private client-therapist relationship, and medical and psychoanalytic models of illness and cure. Through this boundary work, music therapy assumed heightened status as a profession. The specification of a sequestered, specifically therapeutic site for music therapy was, in other words, occupationally enabling—it permitted music therapy to emerge with a clear identity and professional mission.

In recent years, however, the boundaries are again becoming blurred, and once again music therapy is being extended beyond the music room. Key proponents of this shift, such as Brynjulf Stige, have described it as one in favour of context, an orientation toward practices in or overlapping with the social environment, understood as a range of institutions and everyday life settings. As Even Ruud puts it, in the book's forward:

> For many years, music therapy seemed less preoccupied with larger social forces or cultural contexts. Music therapists insisted upon the boundaries between their discipline and others, such as music education, community music practices or alternative healing medicines. (p. 11)[1]

Delightfully, there is little concern in the pages that follow with the maintenance of boundaries. Instead, and the editors make this clear at the outset, community music therapy is described as, "a different thing for different people in different places...you will not find authoritative definitions in this book...What you will find is a wide and colourful range of examples, alongside stimulating thinking, discussion and speculation – with a little

---

[1] When direct reference to page and chapters numbers are given, the reference is to Pavlicevic & Ansdell's *Community Music Therapy.*

TIA DENORA

added provocation and challenge" (p. 17). Dip into these pages and you will find a healthy mixture of approaches and disciplines, from neurology, to creative music therapy, to the social psychology of music—naturally, perhaps, given my own background in music sociology, I was delighted to see signs of this interdisciplinary cooperation.

Rainbow principles aside, however, the volume may well spark discussion and debate, allusions to which the editors anticipate in their introduction, aptly entitled, 'the ripple effect' (following the metaphor of a pebble dropped into a pond). For to propose a shift from what, in Chapter 12 Dorit Amir terms "individualized music therapy" (i.e., "therapy with very clear boundaries between inside and outside, between 'therapy life' and 'community life'" [p. 249]) to cultural and contextual issues, is to propose some realignments, even if only implicitly (aptly summarised by Anna Maratos in Chapter 6, "Whatever Next?"). Of what then, might these implications consist?

Community Music Therapy – Dissolving Distinctions?

First, there is the dual question of what we mean by music, and what we mean by community. In Chapter 3, Gary Ansdell deals with theoretical perspectives on these issues, pulling together themes from New Musicology, the sociology of modernity and the self, anthropology, psychology, cognitive science, and music therapy. Music, Ansdell suggests, should be understood in connection to the environments where it is perceived, produced, and used as a medium of social relation, as "musicing" (Here Ansdell employs David Elliott's (1995) use of the term, akin to Small's (1998) "musicking"). Continuing this line of thought, Ansdell develops the notion of music "as ecology" by which he means, as he put it in his 1997 article, "a balance of interlinking forms and processes in context" (p. 74). Music's role may then be understood as part of the climate through which community as "achieved experience" (p. 82) and identity as "a socially

constructed mode within culture" (p. 82) are facilitated within particular times and spaces.

These conceptions are in turn associated with further implications for music therapy, its role and its future—in particular for the range of roles, conceived in the plural, a music therapist may be required to assume. Community music therapy's aim to establish a symmetrical, dialogic relationship between therapist and client(s), and its call for dialogue and heightened reflexivity on the part of all participants in a music therapeutic event implies redistributions of authority between those participants. This theme is discussed by Simon Procter, in his chapter, "Playing Politics: Community Music Therapy and the Therapeutic Redistribution of Musical Capital for Mental Health."

Working with a non-medical community resource centre for people with experience of mental illness in London, Procter describes how, as he puts it, the ethos of "community" "actively promotes a model of well-being which recognises…the contributions of each individual within the communal." This recognition, Procter continues, redefines the role of the therapist who becomes "someone with particular skills and training who is employed to deploy these in whatever way is most appropriate for the particular people I am working with" (p. 219).

As Procter's term "particular" implies, community music therapy takes a client-centred focus, adopting a 'whatever works' methodological stance and grounded in the local, as Leslie Bunt describes in his chapter on Bristol's *MusicSpace* (pp. 269-80). This focus in turn may imply a social redistribution of expertise—who, for example, knows best a client's needs? In this sense, community music therapy's methodology overlaps with principles of ethnographic practice in the social sciences (Hammersley & Atkinson 2000), the aim of which is to understand how members of a setting make sense of the world, their lay knowledge and local classification practices. In particular, it chimes with key principles in the specialist area known as Participatory Design (Suchman 1987; Ehn 1993; Jordan & Henderson 1995; Tudhope, Beynon-Davies & Mackay 2000). These principles,

TIA DENORA

typically applied to technology assessment and design, include: (1) respecting users regardless of status and recognizing their lay-expertise (indeed learning *from* users), (2) understanding their skill in its own terms, from the point of view of their situated values, and (3) seeking to improve users' ability to use a 'technology' through consultative dialogue. Viewed from the perspective of Participatory Design, community music therapy may be understood as seeking to access and use local knowledge so as to engage in participatory action research, deploying music for various uses—from diversion and entertainment to more ostensibly 'transformative' ends, such as helping to make an ambience habitable, or providing resources with which differences may be resolved.

Quite obviously the parallel between Participatory Design and Community Music Therapy is imperfect since not all music therapy users/clients come to therapy equipped to engage in practical dialogue about their "needs." Nonetheless, there is always a degree of involvement and therefore degrees of scope for fine grained attention to client-centred perspectives. In both realms of activity, one need not be overly directive, overly formulaic or prescriptive in assessing client needs; to the contrary, "good" therapist/systems designers of any kind will attempt to find ways of eliciting the particular situation, atmosphere, and requirements of a client or client group.

Inevitably, this tuning in to the meaning systems of others further blurs the distinctions between insider/outsider, and client/therapist, dissolving them into the flow of on-going, situated activity. Therapy, in short, becomes less distinct from what actors do in the course of their daily lives (which incidentally reminds us of how we are all empowered to do and be able to do the work of maintaining the individual and collective fabric as a routine part of our daily lives in and through the ways we use culture). Such dissolution can, as Procter goes on to explain, be invigorating for the therapist: "I lose some authority and status, but gain freedom and opportunity" (p. 219) – freedom, for example, to be with those actors, to act with them inside the

collective musical frame. This is by no means to suggest that the trained music therapist is or should be deemed dispensable. Rather, it implies that those skills may be usefully deployed when set firmly in context of whatever the local happens to be; the music therapist becomes, more than ever, perhaps, akin to a midwife—supportive, being with, having been through similar situations many times over, *but* prepared to take immediate and effective action should an emergency arise, and—equally importantly—knowing how to recognise signs of a potential or impending emergency. In Brynjulf Stige's (2002) sense, this is a shift from "therapy" to, "health musicking," defined by Procter as the promotion of relational health and well-being, is a move that partially aligns music therapy, community arts, and health promotion. This topic is developed by Harriet Powell in Chapter 8.

Occasioning Agency, Occasioning Health

A key feature in relation to both well-being and health is the creation and maintenance of an environment in which expressive and coordinated action and expectation of continuity can be sustained, in Antonovsky's (1987) and Giddens' (1999) sense, one where 'ontological security' is fostered. Jane Davidson takes up this theme in her chapter, "What can the Social Psychology of Music Offer Community Music Therapy?" Drawing on a series of empirical studies—her own and others—Davidson surveys music's role as a bonding device early in the life course, and describes the social-psychological benefits associated with participatory music making, such as self-expression and relief of anxiety.

These themes are illustrated in an institutional context by Trygve Aasgaard in Chapter 7 ("A Pied Piper among White Coats and Infusion Pumps"). Is he, Aasgaard reflects, an "entertainer... or a 'serious' therapist" (p. 149)? Making music in a hospital, while accompanying children undergoing treatment for cancer as they move and are moved from one space to another (e.g., for bone transplants), and as they await, accept,

TIA DENORA

or recover from treatments, Aasgaard's sonic and physical 'accompaniment' helps make the strange familiar, gives it meaning, and provides continuity across otherwise discontinuous medical spaces.

Equally importantly, Aasgaard's "Pied Piper"-like activities allow these children to simply have fun, be normal, have time out from their "sick roles." We have, at least in the West, too few customs for depicting and validating the experience of serious illness outside of the medical frame. We also have a paucity of practices for keeping life-threatening illness connected to "normal" life: as scholars such as Kathy Charmaz (1991) have described, the experience of chronic and life-threatening illness is often accompanied by circumstances that lead to the loss of self. Musical activity in the hospital—not therapy per se, but rather musical opportunities for belonging, for making connections between patients and between patients, their families, medics and carers —provides means, motives, and opportunities for being together, having 'fun' and, in settings where one may be severed from physical strength, from most of one's resources for self expression, for remaining human, for remaining part of 'a community'. Aasgaard points to the very subtle sets of skills by which this therapy (or its "clown" [p. 154]) operates:

> It is almost as though music therapy's ability to *divert* the children from boredom and various problems is more appreciated, or noticed, than its ability to connect severely ill young patients, and their families, to normal, healthy activities, or, simply, to living life. (p. 153)

Under the guise of this just-clowning-around (or diversion), however, much may be achieved. For one thing, under guise of frivolity, potential participants in 'music therapy' are activated, and may take the initiative to help structure what will become the musical event. Children, parents, nurses or teachers will approach the "entertainer" with, "a favourite instrument, or a song that might be included" (p. 156). Or a parent may tell of a child's 'outside' interest in music. In all of these

endeavours, there is an emphasis on 'whatever works', i.e., a co-determination of what is required, therapeutically speaking, and a willingness to adopt an ad hoc approach (again, in the manner of the midwife). Through this pragmatic and flexible approach, transformations of many kinds may be effected, including transformations of the very settings and institutions within which community music therapy activities occur.

Interdisciplinary Potential

Coming to this work as a sociologist of everyday musical practice and its connections to such matters as the care of self and the aesthetic bases of interaction, I found these on-going developments in community music therapy extremely exciting. Scratch their surface and you touch the bedrock of some of the largest and most interdisciplinary topics going in scholarly and scientific enquiry, for example, the issue of embodied and emotional agency.

I and other scholars (Bull 2000; Sloboda & O'Neill 2001; Hennion 2001) have described how music may be seen to provide non-verbal resources for action stances and styles, and cues to actors about types of social setting. Actors use music both to modify and enhance mood and they may unconsciously shift mood under musical conditions. In observing these processes, it is possible to see cultural repertoires "in action," by which I mean that actors can be seen to orient to musical conditions in ways that set the tone for, or "anchor," patterns of action and bodily conduct such as style, tension, and emotional stance, all of which are made known to and experienced by self and others, and often in mutually referential ways. In this respect, the study of musically-composed action deepens ideas and concepts currently being discussed in cultural sociology, in particular, the question of how culture, "creates a situation of action" (Swidler 2001, p. 83). For cultural sociologists, moment-to-moment mutual orientations, configured musically as "therapy" sessions, highlight music's on-going parameters as resources and opportunities for expressive action

TIA DENORA

in real time and over time as stylistic habits and as opportunities for coordination and mutual entrainment. In this sense, music therapy illuminates the too-often ignored and too-little theorised tacit bases of action and subjectivity—the aesthetic, expressive, and emotional dimensions which serve as the matrix of more overtly conscious and deliberate linguistic modes of interaction. Music therapy also highlights how even the body's so-called "natural" features—physiology, strength, arousal, coordination, energy, skills—are more accurately understood as socially, culturally, and technically constructed (Williams 2002; Newton 2003; Williams 2003; Freund, McGuire & Podhurst 2004).

For example, in my earlier research on aerobic exercise (DeNora 2000) I suggested that music may provide prosthetic devices or media of bodily enhancement and extension. With carefully chosen music, aerobics participants were able jump higher, coordinate better, and retain stamina longer than they could without music. Indeed, so powerful was music at masking fatigue, that improperly used it could lead to injury. So too, there are tapes, CDs, and MP3 files especially designed for the medically-oriented recalibration of bodies, for aligning bodily processes with patterns that help to inculcate deeply embodied habits over time. In both aerobics and guided meditation, this recalibration is achieved through informal learning and bodily practice. In both cases, moreover, it is by no means merely bodily; it is also corporeal-social orientation. It involves, that is, an orientation to and preparedness for action in the external world, and for some types of action not others (hence the warnings not to drive operate machinery after using a blood pressure CD and the ritual cool-down phase of aerobics sessions – in the former, one is too relaxed to drive, in the latter, too aroused for driving activity).

In short, "our" bodies, "their" processes—physiology, the sensation of pain, capacity—can be understood to be and be amenable to being musically composed and thus, bodies' states and conditions may not be as "natural" (and thus as unalterable) as we might think. (I will return to this topic below.) In my view, music therapy's long-

standing uses of music for precisely these social-embodied realignments has enormous potential to illuminate our understanding of the connections between body, mind, and cultural practice and this should be the subject of further theoretical and conceptual work. In short, music therapy, as a topic, is capable of teaching sociologists a great deal about the non-cognitive bases of social ordering and social agency and of the supposedly 'natural' body.

Music as Haven and Work-space

Music therapists of all kinds have shown us how music has the power to mask social differences, to cohere otherwise disparate individuals and groups, and, in cases where individuals may not be able to use linguistic modes of communication, to provide alternative channels for myriad forms of being-together-in-time. Once we consider music as a resource for being together, or, in Even Ruud's 1997 words (quoted on p. 253), a medium that can be "used and experienced in a way which positions people in relation to time and place, other persons or transcendental values," it becomes obvious that yet another conventional (and otherwise obdurate) boundary is dissolved, namely, the walls of clinics, hospitals and hospices. These walls need not confine community music therapy's work which may be extended, as Oksana Zharinova-Sanderson, Dorit Amir, and Mercédès Pavlicevic describe in, respectively, Chapters 11, 12, and 1, to the body-politic, in the guise of non-governmental organizations (Chapter 1) and environments where immigrants and refuges are involved in negotiating biography, past values, and customs in new cultural contexts (Chapters 11, 12).

Zharinova-Sanderson's chapter, which deals with the *Behandlungszentrum fuer Folteropfer* (The Centre for the Treatment of Torture Victims), describes music therapy as it was initially introduced as a complement to verbal therapies. Music provided a way for clients to be expressive without the intervention of linguistic translation. Via a case study, Zharinova-Sanderson describes how a framework for therapy took shape, and how

TIA DENORA

music therapy helped foster ways of transcending linguistic and other cultural barriers. Under extreme circumstances whereby trust in others has been severely eroded by violent abuse, Zharinova-Sanderson describes how music, as it unfolds over time (and time and time again) may serve as a symbolic medium in which trust is rekindled and healing facilitated. Conceived in this manner, music can provide a virtual safe haven, a place or cultural work space in which social relations may be built and rebuilt, and represented in sounds, in sound structures and their associated meanings, and in the social and embodied relations of sound's production. To take the next step, as did the client described by Zharinova-Sanderson, of *performing* music for others, is to engage in activity that has the potential to reaffirm one's identity (e.g., one's roots, as, in the case described, Kurdish) and thus to present one's self to a new audience-community, to join and be accepted into that community musically mediated. It is also equally important to enrich that community with new and different ways of musicing. Here, and in an enabling sense, the medium is the message: music making under these circumstances conjoins healing, well-being, and health with collective representation, the spiritual, and, as Brynjulf Stige describes in his chapter on "Culture, Care and Welfare", healing rituals (p. 100), i.e., public or semi-public events involving not only "therapist" and "client" but larger groups of community (p. 93 – Stige references some of the excellent historical work that has been devoted to this topic by Gouk [2000] and Horden [2000]). It bears observing that such 'rituals' need not involve the features we typically associate with the word *ritual* (institutional formality, dedicated paraphernalia, costumes, dedicated celebrants or settings); they may seem mundane – 'performing rites' in Simon Frith's sense, a simple singing or even listening together or virtually, a quiet comfort in, for example, the repetition of a long-loved song, the making together of newly learned music as a symbolically new and shared social terrain.

I would like to think that the issues community music therapy highlights form part of a continuum of musicing in daily life, a continuum that extends

as well to music's role in so-called extra-musical matters and events, such as the importance of pace, timing, volume, melody, and rhythm in face-to-face communication and the rhythms of interaction. Community music therapy thus challenges our understanding of what "therapy" looks like, reconfiguring it in, among other things, the guise of ordinary interaction, and repositioning it here, there, and everywhere, that is not only within the purview of a therapeutic session. In this sense it helps us to recognise that there is a continuum of therapeutic intervention, and that it may not always be easy to say, after the fact, what was and was not "therapeutic."

Along these lines, it is also worth considering the various levels on which music and the musical may be noted, perceived or otherwise enter our consciousness and this last issue is linked to another music and community health matter—music's use within public and corporate spaces. (Adorno [1976] wrote, in somewhat evaluative terms, on the topic of listening modes, but see also musicologist Ola Stockfelt [1997] on subliminal listening, and composer Brian Eno's [1975/2005] *Discrete Music*.)

What are Music's Effects and How To Assess Them?

Thinking about community music therapy and its connection to public health/well-being in the broadest sense undoubtedly complicates the question of how to assess and measure music's therapeutic effects. In my view, this complication is productive, since it reengages discussion about our too-often tacit understandings of what therapeutic "success" looks like, perhaps also enriching medical conceptions of effectiveness. For example, whether as an adjunct or alternative to medical care, music therapy of any kind reintroduces cultural and social dimensions to the often-exclusively pathological discourses of medical and psychiatric evaluation, shifting the centre of gravity from 'cure' to something more performative and situated—an emphasis on the creation of situated moments of transcendence

TIA DENORA

and togetherness. Over time, these moments provide new contexts for action and interpretation, described by David Stewart, in Chapter 14, "Transformational Contexts in Music Therapy." Shared music making, Stewart suggests, can "reshape and transform the relationships between self, illness, and health" (p. 290).

To the extent that such musicing involves selection (this tone, not that one, now, not then, what I/you/we do) it provides materials that can, at any time, be read as a kind of oracle in the quest for meaning—who am I, who are we, then, now, in future, what is our mood and how is it changing? What is conflict, suffering, what is resolution, and many other things (see DeNora 2003, Chapter 3)? This is but one respect in which music may (virtually) transfigure otherwise seemingly pre-given states or conditions by transposing them into sound. To the extent that music is being-together-in-time, as Alfred Schutz so eloquently described (Schutz 1964), over time music's transfiguration of states and conditions gains validation, becomes a social achievement and a referent for how collective action elsewhere might proceed. In this respect, musicing may ultimately lead to critical consciousness of 'what else' might be transformed (the radical promise often attributed to music and its potential as a medium of subversion and/or social change). For example, we may find in music various resources that may be used to cope with, resist, accept, or redefine some condition or situation, whether it be physical or mental pain, displacement, distrust, loss, or death's soon or eventual certainty.

Relational Health – Socially Constructed Health – Healthy Cultures?

These last points overlap with issues currently being debated more widely within the sociology of health and illness and its discussion of health and illness as *relational*, that is, as taking shape in relation to social, institutional, technological, legal, linguistic and aesthetic practices and assumptions, even at the deepest levels of physiological conditions and 'impairments',

ability and disability. In a series of recent reflections on the classification and lived reality of physical mobility, for example, the sociologist Peter Freund (2001) has described how the meanings and implications associated with an inability to walk with ease, or to walk at all is, while undeniably real in the physical sense, also made manifest and naturalised as a social reality (and thus diminished or augmented) in relation to a range of socially constructed systems – the built environment, transport, wheelchair and prosthetic technology, policy, and aesthetics. So, too, several scholars have described how, under some patterns of livelihood, it is possible for a 'disability' to become invisible or irrelevant – as with the case of the New England island, Martha's Vineyard, where sign-language was the community's first language and where 'disability' takes on a 'now you see/experience it, now you don't' character, highly relevant on the mainland, but irrelevant on the island, thanks to alternative communicative channels which minimise the difference between those who can hear and those who cannot (Groce 1988).

Here we see the mind/body issues discussed earlier re-specified in terms of a conception of health, disability, well-being, capacity, and embodiment as distributed entities. By this I mean that relational conceptions of health and illness highlight the reality of physical/mental states and well-being as taking their *experiential* significance from their location in wider systems of meanings, materials, and practices. That is to say that their meanings reside in the practices and cultural media available for registering their reality. For example, the experience of pain may be altered or over-ridden by subsuming it into a larger structure, whether that structure masks pain (think of Oliver Sacks (1984) musicing down a mountain with an injured leg) or transfigures pain/ anguish through narrative (Aldridge 2003). In all of these examples, we see how the extent of a disability or an illness may be reconfigured in relation to practices, materials, beliefs, and values.

As the various contributors to *Community Music Therapy* observe, music's ties to 'healing' and to social bonding extend back through the millennia; modern forms of music therapy are but

TIA DENORA

one version of folk healing practices from around the world. As a music sociologist, I found this book exceptionally helpful in highlighting some of the very fruitful intersections between music therapy and other areas of socio-musical research —music sociology (my own field), social psychology of music, music geography, 'new' musicology, ethnomusicology, and music's role in developing relational theories of embodiment, ability and well-being. The various perspectives, practices and projects described in this volume compel our attention to music's dynamic possibilities and transformative potential in relation to social care, and to music therapy of all kinds, as strategies for healing, yes, but equally importantly, as knowledge-based interventions in our attempt to understand (construct) social and cultural bases of being—health, identity, and opportunities for agency broadly conceived—that involve sympathy, and that, in the most inclusive sense pragmatically possible, enhance life.

References

Adorno, Theodor W (1976). *Introduction to the Sociology of Music* (trans. E B. Ashton). New York: Continuum.

Aldridge, David (2003). Music therapy and spirituality; A transcendental understanding of suffering [online]. *Music Therapy Today*. Retrieved February 20, from: http://musictherapyworld.net

Ansdell, Gary (1997). Musical Elaborations. What Has the New Musicology to Say to Music Therapy? *British Journal of Music Therapy, Vol. 11,* no. 2, pp. 36-44.

Ansdell, Gary (2002). Community Music Therapy and the Winds of Change [online]. *Voices: A World Forum for Music Therapy.* Retrieved April 20, 2005, from: http://www.voices.no/mainissues/Voices2(2)ansdell.html#tilbake1

Antonovsky, Aron (1987). *Unravelling the Mystery of Health.* San Francisco: Jossey-Bass

Barnes, Barry (1985). *About Science.* Oxford: Blackwells.

Bull, Michael (2000). *Sounding out the City.* Oxford: Berg.

Charmaz, Kathy (1991). *Good Days, Bad Days: The Self and Chronic Illness in Time.* New Brunswick, New Jersey: Rutgers University Press.

DeNora, Tia (1996). From Physiology to Feminism: Reconfiguring Body, Gender and Expertise. *International Sociology, Vol 11,* no. 3, pp.359-83.

DeNora, Tia (2000). *Music in Everyday Life.* Cambridge: Cambridge University Press.

DeNora, Tia (2003). *After Adorno: Rethinking Music Sociology.* Cambridge: Cambridge University Press.

Ehn, Pelle (1993). Scandinavian Design: On Participation and Skill. In: Schuler, D. & Namioka, A. (Eds.). *Participatory Design: Principles and Practices* (pp. 41-77). Mahwah, NJ: Lawrence Erlbaum Associates.

Elliott, David (1995). *Music Matters.* Oxford: Oxford University Press.

Eno, Brian (1975). *Discrete Music. Liner Notes* [online]. Retrieved April 11 2005, from: http://music.hyperreal.org/artists/brian_eno/discreet-txt.html

Freund, Peter (2001). Bodies, Disability and Spaces: The Social Model and Disabling Spatial Organisations. *Disability & Society, Vol 16,* no. 5, pp. 689-706.

Freund, P., McGuire, M. & Podhurst, L. (2003). *Health, Illness and the Social Body: A Critical Sociology* (4th edition). London: Pearson Educational.

Frith, Simon. 1996. *Performing Rites: Evaluating Popular Music.* Oxford: Oxford University Press.

Giddens, Anthony (1999). *Modernity and Self Identity.* Cambridge: Polity.

Gouk, Penelope (Ed.) (2000). *Musical Healing in Cultural Contexts.* Aldershot, UK: Ashgate Publishing Company.

Groce, Nora (1988). *Everyone Here Spoke Sign Language: Hereditary Deafness on Marthas Vineyard.* Cambridge, MA: Harvard University Press.

Hammersley, Martin & Paul Atkinson (2000). *Ethnography: Principles and Practice.*

TIA DENORA

London: Routledge.

Hennion, Antoine (2001). Music Lovers: Taste as Performance. *Theory, Culture and Society, Vol 18*, no. 5, pp. 1-22.

Horden, P. (2000). *Music as Medicine: The History of Music Therapy since Antiquity.* Aldershot: Ashgate.

Jordan, B. and A. Henderson (1995). Interaction Analysis: Foundations and Practice. *Journal of the Learning Sciences, Vol. 4*, no. 1, pp. 30-103.

Knorr-Cetina, Karin (1999). *Epistemic Cultures: How Science Makes Knowledge.* Cambridge, MA: Harvard University Press.

Latour, Bruno & Steve Woolgar (1986). *Laboratory Life: The Construction of Scientific Facts.* Princeton: Princeton University Press.

Newton, Tim (2003). Truly Embodied Sociology: Marrying the Social and the Biological? *Sociological Review, Vol 51,* no. x, pp.20-42.

Pavlicevic, Mercédès & Gary Ansdell (Eds.) (2004). *Community Music Therapy.* London: Jessica Kingsley Publishers.

Sachs, Oliver. (1984). *A Leg to Stand on.* London: Duckworth.

Schutz, Alfred (1964). Making Music Together. In: *Collected Papers,* Vol. 2. The Hague: Martinus Nijhoff

Sloboda, John & Susan O'Neill. (2001). Emotion in Everyday Listening to Music. In: Juslin, P. & Sloboda, J. (Eds.). *Music and Emotion: Theory and Research.* Oxford: Oxford University Press.

Small, Christopher (1998). *Musicking.* Hanover, NH: Wesleyan University Press.

Stige, Brynjulf (2002). *Culture-Centred Music Therapy.* Gilsum, NH: Barcelona Publishers.

Stockfelt, Ola (1997). Adequate modes of listening (trans. Anahid Kassabian & Leo G Svendsen). In: Schwarz, D., Kassabian, A. & Siegel, L. (Eds.). *Keeping Score: Music Disciplinarity, Culture* (pp. 129-146). Charlottesville: University Press of Virginia.

Suchman, Lucy (1987). *Plans and Situated Actions: The Problem of Human-Machine Communication.* Cambridge: Cambridge University Press.

Swidler, A. (2001). What Anchors Cultural Practices? In: Schatzki, T., Knorr Cetina, K. & von Savigny, E. (Eds.). *The Practice Turn in Social Theory* (pp. 74-92). London: Routledge.

Tudhope, Douglas, Beynon-Davies, P. & Mackay, H. (2000). Prototyping Praxis: Constructing Computer Systems and Building Belief. *Human-Computer Interaction, Vol. 15*, pp. 353-83.

Williams, Simon (2002). Corporeal Reflections on the Biological: Reductionism, Constructionism and Beyond? In: Bendelow, G., Carpenter, M., Vautier, C. & Williams, S. J. (Eds.). *Gender, Health and Healing: The Public/Private Divide.* London: Routledge.

Williams, Simon (2003). Marrying the Social and the Biological? A Rejoinder to Newton. *Sociological Review, Vol 51,* no. X, pp. 550-561.

CHAPTER 10

HEALTH AND MUSIC IN EVERYDAY LIFE
– a theory of practice

Denne artikel er baseret på især to undersøgelser foretaget af medlemmer af Kunst-sociologi-gruppen ved Exeter University (UK). Undersøgelsernes fokus er almindelige menneskers anvendelse af musik ('lay-musicking') [Begrebet 'musicering' (musicking) refererer til C. Small m.fl.s tolkning af 'musik' som en interpersonlig aktivitet mere end et objekt]. Data fra undersøgelserne bruges som afsæt for udvikling af en teori om musikkens psyko-kulturelle rolle og funktioner som et kommunikations- og regulerings-medie, og som et redskab til at skabe mening i dagliglivets specifikke, tidslige kontekster. Der trækkes forbindelser mellem de processer, der kan observeres i 'læg-musicering', og musikterapeutisk teori og praksis, og dette sker på en måde, der understreger, hvad musiksociologien kan lære af musikterapien og af lægfolks musicering inden for sundhedsområdet.

1. Introduction

This article is organized around two key tasks. The first is to outline the importance of everyday musical activity – musicking as Small (1998) termed it – in relation to health and well-being and to lodge that discussion in context of the growing body of work devoted to music's role as a health resource or 'technology of health' in daily life (Ruud 1997; 2002; DeNora 2000; Batt-Rawden 2006a; 2006b; in press; Brown and Theorell 2006). The second is to conceptualize 'health' and 'illness' as environmentally-mediated and environmentally-sponsored performance. In what follows, the second task will be developed first, and the theoretical concepts this task provides will be used to conduct the first task. Overall, the argument, briefly stated, is that a constructivist perspective focused on everyday musicking, set in context of a broader understanding of health as socially produced in daily activity and within the various enclaves of daily experience, highlights music's importance as a resource of health management outside of, but arguably facilitated by, music therapeutic and/or quasi-therapeutic practice.

Tia DeNora. PhD. Professor of Sociology of Music and Director of Research, Sociology/Philosophy, University of Exeter.

272   *Tia DeNora*

2. Health as performed

Within constructivist perspectives, health and illness are conceptualized as social facts, that is, their reality takes shape in ways that stand outside of individuals and is made known through the varied ways in which health is conceptualized, assessed, performed and perceived in social life. Health, in other words, is 'known' according to socially recognized indicators of ability, capacity, and condition as these are demonstrated by actors to self and others in varying modes of interaction (Mehan et al 1986; Goffman 1961; Radley 1984).

This is to say that health is performed in social settings and in relation to performance conventions and materials. For example, in some countries today, when we visit a health professional – for a medical check-up, let us say – we submit ourselves to a battery of tests (blood pressure, heart rate, cholesterol, and so on). We then receive an assessment (like a report card) of how 'healthy' we are in relation to established measures. Our 'bad' cholesterol is low, our blood pressure 'perfect', our short-term memory is failing, we are experiencing 'mild depression'. When we repeatedly 'pass' or 'fail' the tests designed to ascertain these things, we are deemed, by medical practitioners, to be healthy or ill. Health, in other words, is indicated by the passing of some tests or trials that accord with cultural conceptions of what it *means* to be healthy. When we have achieved a good 'report card' time and time again, we accumulate an identity – we are 'healthy'. Health, in other words, is health-status. We are apportioned degrees of this status according to how we repeatedly perform in the various trials and tests that are set for health-assessment. (It bears noting that there will be many other tests, some in existence, some only imagined, some we probably could never imagine, that will be conducted. The omissions are equally interesting to the social study of medical science.)

Crucial here is that health measurements are *meaningful* to those they describe. That is to say that the social act of, for example, making reports, prognoses and the offering of treatment interventions may itself recontextualize our perception of our physical being. These recontextualizations are in effect new meanings and new beliefs, and recent research has suggested that these 'placebo effects' may be linked to actual physiological changes in ways that highlight the power of belief, suggestibility and associated 'mind-body' interactions (Zubieta, et al 2005). Certain beliefs may, in other words, provide active ingredients of future health-status, and they may facilitate or hinder future health-performances, including those that can be assessed physiologically.

To take some simple examples: individuals may experience a 'lift' after being told that their health has improved or that a medicine will help them: they may, from that moment and for some interval of time, feel more 'positive', experience greater energy, and/or greater motivation to continue with some form of health-regime. Conversely, they may feel despondent on receipt of 'bad news' and so be more likely to adopt the 'sick role'. Alternatively, the cognitive 'certainly' associated with an official diagnosis, may bring relief, especially if they have lived with undefined illness for some time, even when the diagnosis is itself 'bad news' (Hilbert 1986). In all of these examples, recognized health-statuses have (potential) recursive power; they are part of an in-put loop in health-performance insofar as they may structure capacity for healing and recovery, and the phenomenological experience of 'symptoms', including pain, both phantom and transcended. This theme, which will be developed below, is critical to the investigation of culture's role and its mechanisms in the construction of health and illness. It is vital to any consideration of music as an everyday health technology. First, however, it is necessary to expand the notion of health performance under development here.

Medical technologies of health assessment are only one way that health is registered and made known to self and other. There are others more mundane. We may 'know' our current health status by how we are 'able' to perform various tasks, even mundane tasks such as being able to climb stairs, hold a job (or a particular type of job), or feed ourselves, for example. All of these 'performances' show us (to ourselves and others) as able. They are demonstrative of health-status.

Reconceptualizing health in social, behavioural and dramaturgical terms (as health-status, health performance and health practices) illuminates health as an achieved, constructed, condition, socially situated in time and space. This reconceptualization points in turn to the question of health-pragmatics, that is to the practices by which 'health' is attained and maintained through various socio-technical and cultural actions. And this focus on pragmatic action in turn illuminates the question of resources: what does it take to produce repeated 'passings' as healthy, however these are registered. (For related theoretical literature on the pragmatics of performance in other contexts, see Chambliss 1990; DeNora 1991 and Garfinkel 1968). How, in other words, can we develop a grounded theory of health pragmatics? The next section of this article (part two of task one) considers each of these interlinked forms of resources in turn, so as to develop grounded, pragmatic theory of health-status as it is produced between rather than within individuals and between individuals, material culture and norms.

3. Health as relational and socially distributed opportunities for performance

We often think, in commonsense terms, that our criteria of health (how we register it, as described above) are not culturally and historically specific and are not produced in the here-and-now of everyday occasions, time after time. When we operate in this way, we fall prey to a fallacy; we conceptualize 'health' as a simple 'matching' exercise, where instance is mapped on to category (e.g., a case of mumps, hysteria, lunacy, too much bile). This fallacy prevents us from recognizing how our categories of health are (a) not immutable, as some of the examples just stated highlight, but rather, historically specific and (b) not neutral and pre-given 'containers' but formative of our perception (recognition) and self-perception of health and illness. In other words, categories (of health/illness) provide a grid for perception, both prospectively and retrospectively (Mehan et al 1986); they call our attention selectively to some things while suppressing our sense of other things and they suggest arrangements, hierarchies and connections between things. Our criteria and categories of health and illness, in short, take shape within cultural meaning systems and different systems produce cognitive schemes of health and illness. These schemes both structure and are structured by institutionalized patterns of recognizing and dealing with instances of categories of health/illness. These schemes and patterns are what make forms of health and illness manifest as aspects of social reality. In these ways, health – its psychological and physical characteristics – is a collective and emergent matter, socially constructed. To speak of health as 'constructed' is not to deny the apparent reality of physical states (e.g., the spots we recognise as 'measles' or, the ability to complete particular tasks) but to recognize that their consequences are socially and technologically mediated.

For example, consider the health-status of being physically mobile. Mobility is a relational state and a meaningful state; it is not 'merely' a property of individuals but rather emerges from a series of practices and interactions with the built environment. This interaction – between humans and objects and between humans and categories of meanings – will augment or diminish ability/disability according to how the built environment is organized (Freund 2001). If curbs are converted into sloping surfaces, if traffic lights allow for longer crossing times at the 'walk' or 'green man' [sic] signs (or the aural signal that tells visually impaired people that it is safe to cross a road), if we do away with stairs, then the difference between wheelchair users and walkers is of less consequence. If, by contrast we raise curb height to three feet, we have not only created a barrier between those who are able to walk and those who aren't, we may also create a barrier between those who are able to climb and those who cannot. So too, technologies and normative assumptions about what counts as 'speaking' may determine who is or is not communicatively disabled. Nora Groce's study (2006) of how hearing impairment was, for all practical purposes, inconsequential in 19th-century Martha's Vineyard is a case in point. Because the material practices of work did not require spoken interaction and because, in her titular phrase, 'everyone here spoke sign language' the social impact of physical conditions, such as not being able to hear, was greatly diminished. This is to say that the social impact of physical and/or mental 'symptoms', as measured in and through a range of performances through which one passes as healthy or ill (not being able to hear or walk, not being able to rouse oneself to 'get on' with the playing of a social role, not being able to 'fight' a life-threatening tumour) is the *experiential* realm. It is this realm where health and illness matter and where they are lived as day-to-day 'realities'.

In both these cases (mobility; hearing impairment), social action is the realm where normative frames are routinely plied in ways that produce the identity of illness/health, that align features of our bodies, minds and their capacities with categories of meaning such as 'seriously ill', 'learning disabled', physically disabled' and so forth. These categories become 'real' (i.e., socially significant as types of health and illness) as they pass through the various social channels devoted to their recognition. In what ways, then, may actors seek to modify and/or stabilize normative frameworks and environments and thus, their health-status as known and experienced by themselves and/or others? And, to state the core topic of this article, how may music, in particular everyday musical activity, be understood as a technology through which this modification (simultaneously of self and environment) is achieved? The second half of this article seeks to answer these questions by considering three examples that highlight the importance of music in the mundane project of health-performance. In a nutshell, how can music in everyday life provide resources for health as everyday experience? To what extent are musical resources similar to the material and organizational resources so far discussed and to what extent are they different? Finally, to what extent does considering this question enrich current conceptions of the aetiology and management of health? In the next section, the theoretical groundwork for this investigation is clarified through the concepts of affordance and appropriation are introduced so as to provide the foundation for a theory of music as a technology of health.

4. Affordance and appropriation

If the performance of health-status is a relational, emergent and collective activity, one that takes shape with reference to environmental properties and normative procedures, how, then, should we understand the relationship between properties and procedures on the one hand, and health performances on the other hand? In what follows, the concepts of affordance and appropriation are presented in order to develop the theory of music as a health resource that will be presented in part two.

The concept of affordance, originally introduced by J. J. Gibson (1958), highlights the constitutive role of environment in action, perception and consciousness (Gibson 1958 [for discussions of the affordance concept in music studies see DeNora 2000; Clarke 2005]). Objects, materials and conventional patterns of doing things may lend themselves to some things and may make other things more difficult. Simply illustrated, a spherical object may be easier to roll than a cube, loamy (versus clay) soil may make it easier to grow root vegetables. The absence of curbs and stairs affords wheelchair mobility, their presence, the cognitive recognition of significant 'difference' between able bodied and dis-abled [sic], the unimportance of using speech for communication within a culture affords the apparent unreality of difference between people's capacity to hear.

But how do affordances come to afford? Objects do not »cause« actions or the ways to which they are oriented. They do, though, present structuring properties that enable and or constrain action, and through their access and use. Indeed, an object's or material's affordances may actually 'lead' individuals or groups to do things that they might not have intended, wished or thought about doing – simply because they *can* be done. This is to say that the opportunities that objects provide are made manifest through action. It is how we engage with objects that action is structured by those objects. In other words, clay soil does not 'cause' an absence of carrots; gardeners and farmers make that 'cause'. However, the presence of clay soil may provide an important factor that provides a condition of action: it is taken into account by farmers when they decide what crops to plant (whether as a conscious strategy [e.g., 'it will be too difficult to harvest carrots and they will not grow so well in this soil'] or as semi-conscious and embodied decision [e.g., the memory of the back-breaking work of pulling the crop up last time]. So too, slanted walk-ways, as opposed to steps and curbs, may afford mobility and the ubiquity of sign language may afford communicative inclusion and thus diminish the perception of 'disability'. In all of these examples, affordances are produced through an interaction between people, interpretations and decisions and the use of materials. Affordances are are the product of practices of appropriation, achieved in and through practical action and how to locate affordances may have to be learned . We are afforded help (or hindrance) from the objects around us, but simultaneously, we constitute those objects' affordances just as they constitute us and what we may afford – our capacities (and incapacities). This reciprocal and emergent feature of affordances highlights the role of human resourcefulness in their discovery.

We are now in a position to consider music's mechanisms of operation in daily life and its role as a medium that may afford health. Music's role as a health technology depends, in other words, on how it is appropriated and on what it affords through this process. In what follows, examples from two studies (both completed at or in connection with the Exeter Arts Sociology Group) will be used to develop a theory of music's role as a 'technology of self' (DeNora 1999; 2000) and a technology of health promotion and self-care study (Batt-Rawden and Tellnes 2005; Batt-Rawden and DeNora 2005; Batt-Rawden, DeNora and Ruud 2005 Batt-Rawden and Aasgaard 2006; Batt-Rawden, 2006a; Batt-Rawden 2006b).

Tia DeNora   277

5. Music as a 'technology of the self'

In her work on music in everyday life, based on participant observation and in-depth interview data in the USA and UK, DeNora (1999; 2000; 2001) has described how music comes to afford a wide array of uses in the various processes of mundane self-care and self-regulation. These uses range from emotional regulation and modification (sometimes as part of 'emotional work', understood as the bodily cooperation with an image of how one should feel/appear as an emotional being [Hochschild 1982]), to music's role as a prosthetic technology of the body, to the ways in which music functions as a template or exemplar for cognitive processes and knowledge formation. In this section, examples of each of these tasks will be considered in turn.

Consider 'Becky', describing how she uses music as a resource for recalibrating herself emotionally, prior to taking part in an evening activity:

Becky: If I was feeling particularly like I wasn't really looking forward
           to where I was going, then I would have to put something really
           lively on to try and get me in the mood.
Q.   Where might you be going that you weren't really looking for-
           ward to?
Becky: Family gatherings [laughs]. Or some sort of meeting to do with
           the scouts, I tend to really not look forward to that. (Interview w.
           Becky, aged 26, UK)

Here, Becky describes how participation in social situations require certain emotional and embodied properties ('get me in the mood') that are features required of participants. To draw herself into the appropriate 'mood', she describes how she uses music as a tool of emotion management, in this case, to modify her current emotional state and heighten her mood. Music here is a resource that Becky uses so as to fulfill social responsibilities, to align her with what she perceives is required.

Over half of the fifty six interviewees (all women between the ages of 18 and 78), particularly those under forty, described how they functioned as 'DJs' to themselves, using music to configure and reconfigure mood, energy and social orientation:

> [If I'm going to] *sleep, sometimes I'll throw on a few tracks to wake me*
> *up, nice 'n slow and then I'll throw on something else. And then, some-*
> *times, you know, if I'm not really, not in that relaxed mood, I'm like you*
> *know, 'I don't wanna [sic] listen to that' and I'll throw something fast*
> *on, or something fast is playing and I'm like 'That's too chaotic for me*
> *right now, I have to put something slow on'* (Latoya, aged 19, USA)

The respondents were highly aware of the music that would best serve their various needs as they sought to retain control over self and to care for themselves in daily contexts. They described how they knew that certain music would have particular 'effects' on them (for example, conjure up certain memories, or 'soothe' them) and they described how they associated certain music with particular social or personal tasks (the music of Enya, for example, was, for one respondent, music associated with bath time, and never with other times). In all of these examples, the music's 'effects' – what it came to afford were linked to the ways in which musical materials (e.g., the languorous melodies of Enya's slow numbers), biographical and situated couplings (e.g., the respondent first encountered Enya's music in a floatation tank), and generic/stereotypes associations associated with types of people, scenes, situations, moods). In all cases it was an admixture of music, connotations and consumption/production practices – the musical 'event' (DeNora 2003) that produced music's effects on actors. It was never 'music itself', nor merely interpretations/responses overlaid on that music (on the importance of avoiding these dual positions, see Hennion forthcoming).

It is important to develop this point: music's affordances are found in and through active practices of listening or otherwise appropriating music. This is a point well underscored by many other researchers (Gomart and Hennion 1999; Hennion forthcoming; Greasley and Lamont (2006); Greasley in progress; Sloboda and O'Neill 2001; Batt-Rawden 2006a; 2006b; in press). Gomart and Hennion (1999), for example, have described the minute practices by which musical 'amateurs' or 'music lovers' construct the listening environment, the minute rituals through which the music's sacred or magical powers 'over' them are activated and in ways that are often then forgotten. As in DeNora (1999; 2000; 2001) they show how people, whether singly or in groups, draw together music and other materials in ways that provide mutual frames and that augment the ways in which those musics and materials seem 'fit' for the purpose. These practices of arrangement or, in Bruno Latour's term, assemblage (Latour 2005) are what empower music/materials in ways that come to have power over actors. Those actors are, in other words, colluding in their own subjection to musical/material 'control' (see DeNora 2000, Chapter 2 on this point). So, for example, when one respondent uses music so as to 'soothe' her, and to lower her stress levels before going out for the day, she not only chooses music that brings back comforting childhood memories of hearing her father play piano at bedtime (and he himself had chosen 'appropriately' soothing music for that hour some forty years earlier!), but she sets herself up in her living room, sitting in a rocking chair, 'nestled' as she puts it, between the stereo speakers. She does not, in other words, try to listen to this music for this purpose while engaging in some other busy or potentially stress-producing task, but is rather, active in crafting a specific type of musical event (DeNora 2003).

To varying extents, the forms of emotional modification discussed above also involve corporeal modification. The informants in DeNora's music in everyday life study described how they sought to tap music's properties so as to affect bodily capacities – energy levels and motivation for exercise, for example:

> *Let's say I'm doing the warm-up. You want quite catchy music because some of [the class] are just not in the mood and if you've just got the drumming noise then you think, 'Oh, what the hell's going on? But I do it to motivate people...Let's say I've had a load of people who aren't really up for it and I've chosen a tape that's like OK, you find them just lolling around...[whereas] when they're doing sit ups...you need a lot of teaching points [instructions] and you...need [music] for a beat not to motivate them...* (Sarah, aerobics teacher, UK).

Here, Sarah describes how careful music programming can enhance her aerobics students' motivation, and thus their bodily performance. In the fieldwork on aerobics, it became clear that music's role as a motivator and condition of bodily performance worked in ways that spoke directly to the body – for example, as contagious rhythm and as a structure capable of profiling bodily movement and as virtual reality, for example, providing the illusion of climbing, of covering ground or of gaining strength (DeNora 2000: 96-103). Music's role in the everyday world of physical labour further illustrates music's role as a prosthetic technology of the body, heightening and sustaining physical capacity, for example, when hoisting sails (shanties) or when weaving wool (DeNora 2000: 104-6).

Finally, music may help individuals to make knowledge, including self knowledge, and within this focus, to transcend difficult, stressful or extreme times and circumstances. It may also, adjacent to this task, facilitate narratives of self. For example, Lucy, one of the respondents in the music in everyday life study, can be seen here to elaborate her self-identity in relation to a musical structure, describing how she 'identifies' herself with the 'middle voices' in music:

> *I think that maybe that characterizes me in life, that I don't like being in the limelight, I like to..[pauses]...[be] part of a group. And, you know, pressing forward and doing my bit but not [pause]...seeing what needs doing and doing it but not being spotlighted and being 'out front' sort of thing* (DeNora 2000:69).

In their work on music's role in social movement activity, Eyerman and Jamieson (1998) have described how music functions as an exemplars, by which they mean, in a sense akin to Thomas Kuhn's (1970), 'paradigm-constituting entities that serve to realign ...thinking' (Eyerman and Jamieson

280   *Tia DeNora*

1998: 128). When musical materials provide the source of the exemplar, Eyerman and Jamieson, add, they not only have consequences for thinking, but are also consequential for living and feeling. In this brief example from one respondent, Lucy, we see music providing a metaphor that comes to structure or help to identify something extra-musical, namely, her personality – she is not someone to 'press forward' but rather, as she says in a later passage, someone who seeks to fill in the middle of things. In this way music provides a mirror, indeed, a kind of 'magic mirror' in which one may engage in problem solving and identity construction. The process was not dissimilar to that described by Bonde (2005) in a study of the Bonny Method of Guided Imagery and Music (BMGIM) and the development of imagery and narratives over time. In both the informal everyday life setting, and in GIM settings facilitated by music therapists, music can be seen to afford narrative construction through its connection (by participants themselves) to images, metaphors, scripts and narratives, and other cultural repertoires that promote rehabilitation, transcendence and general 'coping'.

In all of these examples above, focused on emotion regulation, body modification and narrative and cognitive development, we see music providing a self-stabilizing resource, one that is appropriated by respondents and used to achieve tasks that are linked to self-care and self-stability. While the link to health-status is only implicit in these examples, we can nonetheless see how music provides a typically tacit or unobserved resource for self-maintenance. This maintenance includes many aspects of self associated with mental health and mental strength, that is, with the ability to cope with adversity, stress-management, self-monitoring, and self-awareness. It is possible to see individuals here acting as lay-therapists to themselves and, sometimes (as when they deploy music to create ambience and scene) others. This skill is part of the lay methods by which actors take care of themselves, by which they foster continuous performances of self-stability and social competence. These skills are mostly sub-conscious, subsumed by other goals and tasks and deployed in response to the fluctuating, the local and the fleeting; they are not typically part of the skills that actors are aware of but rather they are operational skills (Batt-Rawden and DeNora 2005: 292). How, then, is it possible to see these skills being deployed in ways that are more overtly and explicitly linked to health? To explore this question, a recent study of music as a technology of health promotion for the chronically ill is now considered (Batt-Rawden 2006a; Batt-Rawden 2007; Batt-Rawden, DeNora and Ruud 2006; Batt-Rawden and DeNora 2005; Batt-Rawden 2006; Batt-Rawden and Tellnes 2005; Batt-Rawden and Aasgaard 2006). This study has developed the music 'as a technology of self' perspective via Even Ruud's focus on music as a 'health technology' by exploring musical activity explicitly in relation to self-therapy with an eye to policy recommendations for palliative care and, even more intriguingly, music's role – alongside more physical matters such as diet and exercise – as a means for health promotion

6. Music as a technology of health promotion in everyday life

Outside the realm of music therapy, and with some very notable exceptions (Gouk 2000; Ruud 1997; Stige 2003; DeNora 2000; Sloboda and O'Neill 2001; Pavlicevic and Ansdell 2004) music's role as an everyday health technology outside of the hospital and medical/therapeutic arena has been a little studied topic. Batt-Rawden's recent work has helped to remedy this gap. Her study, an action research investigation, focused on how individuals could reflect and learn how to use music as a health technology so as to diminish or divert attention from symptoms, promote healthy behaviours and generally reconnect with self-narratives and self-identities linked to health and health promotion. The project drew together a sample of 22 Norwegian participants[1] who were interviewed eight times over the course of a year. During this time, each participant was asked to contribute to the production of a series of CD compilations in which they shared, through the researcher as mediator, their musical loves, associations and memories. The point of the project was less to find out about 'how' they experienced music than to use this question as a springboard into a project of informal learning (Batt-Rawden and DeNora 2005), to help participants discover and rediscover how to use music as a 'technology of the self' (DeNora 1999) and thus also as a 'cultural immunogen' (Ruud, 2002).

A wide range of 'uses' emerged from Batt-Rawden's interview data. For example, the participants described how they used, and learned how to use, music to cope with a range of tasks, problems and symptoms – for example, as a substitute for sleeping tablets, as a motivational device to 'move' out of low moods or depression, as a model or exemplar of where they hoped to be, as a reminder of how they 'could' be or were when 'at my best', as a way of 'dealing with' various problems and sorrows and as a medium through which they could connect with others, and virtually to each other via the CDs and through the researcher. In relation to connection to others, it is also possible to see here how the study of individual musical practice, as a health promoting technology, connects with a wider focus on music in the community and community music therapy, for example as collective identities and musical strategies can be seen to emerge within particular musical-social spaces (Trythall 2006; Stige 2003; Pavlicevic and Ansdell 2004; Bergh forthcoming)

---

1 Participants in the study were between 34 and 65 years of age, nine men and 13 women, of different socio-economic status. These were people suffering or recovering from some form of chronic illness (muscular disease, neurological disease, cancer, anxiety or depression, chronic fatigue), all of whom had previous experience of active music making (though some had to curtail musical activity due to illness) – ten played or sang, the remaining twelve were involved in folk clubs, choirs, concert attendance and home-listening

282   *Tia DeNora*

Research participants also described how they used and/or learned to use music to modify the body, in particular to create relaxation, whether as part of preparation for sleep or as a way of 'forgetting' ones ills or as a way of redirecting attention away from distressing noises or thoughts. For example, Batt-Rawden describes how her research participants found, through music, new ways of solving practical problems that otherwise augmented their illness-status and did so in ways that allowed them the apparent reality of health. Central to this process was returning a sense of 'wholeness'. And at times the linking of music to other environmental affordances produced a (virtual? Or real?) sense of wellness, for example, here one participant describes how the combination of music and driving creates a feeling of freedom ('flying') and affords a space in which one is both in control and able to be expressive:

> *...when I fly away at high speed...it is lovely to listen to music. I feel I move in time and space and along with the music within me. I am singing in my car when I listen to my music...;* (Batt-Rawden 2006a:105).

From stage to stage, as the CDs were distributed and discussed, the participants were encouraged to think about and describe the role music played in their lives and life histories, and how, increasingly, they used it to promote their own health. The various stages in this process highlight how participants' came to produce *for themselves but with resources and models offered by the researcher* modes of conscious awareness of music's 'powers' and skills of musical use over the course of the year-long project phase. In the process, they learned also how to adjust themselves, their environments and habits in relation to this new form of consciousness and the new skills of 'health musicking'.[2]

It is important to note that it was not *music, per se*, that achieved the outcome of connecting, of social recovery and Batt-Rawden's focus on the ritual features of music and self-healing illuminate this point clearly. For music to 'work' occasions and situations that empower it (and its makers/recipients) need to be constituted; as with the work by DeNora, Gomart and Hennion, and Sloboda and O'Neill described earlier, music's affordances are created through the appropriation-work of users (the study participants) though it was greatly enabled by the facilitative work of the researcher and other participants who shared narratives, tips and pointers – all part of the informal learning of how to 'use' or appropriate music.[3] Participants

---

2   Begrebet kan oversættes med 'sundheds-musicering'. Vedr. oversættelsen af begrebet 'musicking' til 'musicering', se s. 30.
3   Again, this work was accomplished by participants themselves, albeit facilitated by, in this case, the researcher, who presented her own 'health-musicking' as a model to her research participants.

engaged in a process of informal learning about how to 'tell' about music's meaning and uses in their lives, thus creating for themselves (and for fellow participants) pointers and tips on how to use music so as to promote health and well-being, connection to others (specific and generalized) and self-empowerment, i.e., the ability to determine self-conditions, and also how to activate music such that it might 'work' in health-promoting or otherwise beneficial ways. And they referred to their musicking experiences in terms of 'high points', something to be valued, treasured. Batt-Rawden's work focused as well on the bridges participants made between music reception (listening) and music production (performing), and so illuminated the process of empowerment associated with active music listening. Learning how to use music as a platform for engaging in self-narrative and self-knowledge in turn motivated some participants to extend that learning and music activity to the realm of production, making their own musical resources. For example:

> *What I have gained through this project is to reinforce my belief that the strongest effect I gain from music is through playing and singing with other people, this synergy effect is like an encounter of love, it is so mysterious, just like somebody connects you to heaven, it is so strong this playing together, you know...* (Male, 53, recovered from depression)

and:

> *The situation of being isolated from the work situation is not very pleasant. Through this project I have been able to contribute a lot and that means a lot to me. It has been very inspiring and also a huge contrast to being 'unable to work'. It has been very important to me that I have been able to focus on my resources and the kind of resources I have through music...huge contrast to my feelings of weariness and tiredness. This project has actually made me make contact with a folk-music group in my community and now I am feeling so good. I have regained control and well-being in my life. It is great...* (Female, 52, recovered from depression and severe back-pain two months before final round of fieldwork).

Here, we see how participation in the very creation of those materials that are then recursively used as affordance structures for health may be a vital feature in the form of empowerment that is linked to health promotion – ontological security and self-identity maintenance (Aasgaard 2002; 2004; Rolvsjord 2004; 2006). To be able to create, that is, to generate materials that 'fit' one's situation, and to hear/perceive oneself actually producing the very media that stabilize that self (i.e., to be able to creatively alter one's sonic/aesthetic environment) is a powerful resource – and a means by which one can demonstrate health-status (here as the ability to negotiate the – aesthetic – environment), one's ability, as a maker of one's world and thus, an author of the world as it affects oneself. In that transcendent moment one is actively performing self-health and it is in these mundane instances, often fleeting, that it is possible to see music's value in everyday, real-time healthcare.

7. Conclusion

If 'health' is health-status, that is, a meaningful entity that is affected recursively by self-meaning and interpretation and by previous attributions of health-status, and if it is performed in connection with resources, then it is of vital importance to 'un-pack' health performance and to investigate its constituent practices and the props through which health-performances are afforded. If *music* provides an important form of resource that affords or supports health, then the study of health-promotion needs to consider how music features in everyday care of self and health-performance in mundane settings. In DeNora's study, music afforded various personal enhancement features as well as a medium with which to set the scene for social encounters. In Batt-Rawden's study, music not only afforded care of self – as featured in DeNora's work (2000; 2003) but also afforded social participation. Her research participants took delight in knowing they were (initially) virtually linked to each other through the researcher, through whom – and through their CD selections – they could communicate with each other (they agreed to meet in person at the project's end and some have remained in touch). Thus we see music providing social capital (Procter 2006; Putnam 2000), that is a medium of bonding which is itself a health resource. A focus on lay skill in music use, and on the craft of music therapists and affiliated health-music workers, as they assist individuals and groups to use music for self and community care is one way to create much needed 'bridgework' between the forms of musical activity that transpire in the treatment room, those that occur in community centres and those forms of everyday self-care that take place in a range of domestic and private settings where music can be seen to afford health-performances and health-statuses. By considering the often hidden lay-therapeutic functions music serves in everyday life, it is possible to return to music's use in hospital and therapeutic settings with new eyes, focusing on the role of the client/patient and what they bring to the music (therapeutic) event – their 'lay' craft. From there, it is also possible to see the craft of the music therapist or health-musician with new eyes as they seek to activate latent health-musicking skills in those with whom they work (Procter 2004; Trythall 2006). Everyday music practice is, in other words, a very rich seam for the study of human creativity and skill as applied to health performance and healing conduct.

REFERENCES

AASGAARD, T. (2004): A Pied Piper among White Coats and Infusion Pumps: Community Music Therapy in a Paediatric Hospital Setting. In Ansdell, G. & Pavlicevic, M. (eds.) (2004), *Community Music Therapy*. London and Philadelphia: Jessica Kingsley Publishers.

AASGAARD, T. (2002): *Song Creations by Children with Cancer – Process and Meaning*. Thesis submitted for the degree of Doctor of Philosophy, Institute of Music and Music Therapy, Aalborg University.

BATT-RAWDEN, K.B & DENORA, T. (2005): Music and Informal Learning in Everyday Life. *Music Education Research*, vol. 7, no. 3, pp. 289-304. London: Routledge.

BATT-RAWDEN, K.B. & TELLNES, G. (2005a): Nature-Culture-Health Activities as a Method of Rehabilitation; An Evaluation of Participants' Health, Quality of Life and Function. *International Journal of Rehabilitation Research,* vol. 28, no. 2.

BATT-RAWDEN, K.B & TELLNES, G. (2005b): Music and Health Promotion. A case study. In: Tellnes, Gunnar (Ed.). *Urbanization and Health. New challenges to Health Promotion and Prevention*. Oslo: Academic Press, UniPub.

BATT-RAWDEN, K.B. & DENORA, T. & RUUD, E.: (2005): Music Listening and Empowerment in Health Promotion; A study of the Role and Significance of Music in Everyday Life of the Long-term ill. *Nordic Journal of Music Therapy;* 14 (2): pp. 120-136.

BATT-RAWDEN & AASGAARD, T. (2006): Music a Key to Kingdom. *Electronic Journal of Sociology* . http://www.sociology.org/content/2006/tier1/batt-rawden.html: ISSN – 1198 3655 – pp. 1-21.

BATT-RAWDEN, K.B. (2006a): *Music and Health Promotion: The role and Significance of music and musicking in everyday life for the long term ill*. PhD Thesis, submitted. University of Exeter.

BATT-RAWDEN, K.B. (2006b): Music – a strategy to promote health in rehabilitation? An Evaluation of participation in a 'Music and Health Promotion project'. *International Journal of Rehabilitation Research,* vol. 29 (2), pp. 171-173.

BATT-RAWDEN, K.B. (in press): Music as a transfer of faith – towards recovery and healing. *Journal of Research in Nursing*.

BERGH, A. (Forthcoming):. Music and Conflict Resolution. *Music Scientif* .

BONDE, L.O. (2005): »Finding a New Place...« Metaphor and Narrative in One Cancer Survivor's BMGIM Therapy. *Nordic Journal of Music Therapy*, 14 (2), pp. 137-154.

BROWN, S. & T. THEORELL. (2006): The Social Uses of Background Music for Personal Enhancement. Pp 126-62 in S. Brown & U. Volgsten (Eds.*), Music and Manipulation: On the Social Uses and Social Control of Music*. New York and Oxford: Berghahn Books.

CHAMBLISS, D. (1989): The mundanity of excellence: an ethnographic report on Stratification and Olympic Swimmers. *Sociological Theory*, vol. 7 (1), pp. 70-86.

CHAMBLISS, D. (1992): Reply to DeNora's Comment. *Sociological Theory*, vol. 10 (1) pp. 103-5.

DENORA, T. (1991): Comment on Chambliss' Mundanity of Excellence. *Sociological Theory*, vol. 10 (1), pp. 99-102.

DENORA, T. (1999): Music as a Technology of the Self. *Poetics* 27, pp. 31-56.

DENORA, T. (2000): *Music in Everyday Life*. Cambridge: Cambridge University Press.

286   *Tia DeNora*

DENORA, T. (2001): Aesthetic agency and musical practice: new directions in the sociology of music and emotion. Pp. 161-80 in P. N. Juslin and J. A. Sloboda (eds) *Music and Emotion: Theory and Research*. Oxford: Oxford University Press.

EYERMAN, R. & A. JAMIESON. (1998): *Music and Social Movements*. Cambridge: Cambridge University Press.

FREUND, P. (2001): Bodies, Disability and Spaces: the social model and disabling spatial organisations. *Disability & Society*, vol. 16, no. 5, pp. 689-706.

GARFINKEL, H. (1968): *Studies in Ethnomethodology*. New York: Basic Books.

GIBSON, J.J. (1958): *The Senses Considered as Perceptual systems*. Boston: Houghton Mifflin.

GOFFMAN, E. (1961): *Asylums*. New York: Anchor Books.

GOMART, E. & HENNION, A. (1999): »A sociology of attachment: music amateurs, drug users,« in J. Law and J. Hassard (eds.), *Actor Network Theory and After*. Oxford and Malden, MA: Blackwells, 220–247.

GOUK, P (Ed.). (2000): *Musical Healing in Cultural Contexts*. Aldershot: Ashgate.

GROCE, N. (2006): *Everyone Here Spoke Sign Language*: Cambridge, MA: Harvard University Press.

GREASLEY, A.E. & LAMONT, A.M. (2006): Music preference in adulthood: why do we like the music we do? In *Proceedings of the 9th International Conference on Music Perception and Cognition*, (CD rom) (ed. M. Baroni, A. R. Addessi, R. Caterine & M. Costa). Bologna, Italy: University of Bologna.

HENNION, A. (Forthcoming): Those Things that Hold Us Together: Taste and Sociology. *Cultural Sociology*, vol. 1 (1): 97-114.

HILBERT, R. (1986): Anomie and the Moral Regulation of Reality: The Durkheimian Tradition in Modern Relief. *Sociological Theory* 1986, vol. 4, no. 1, pp. 1-19.

HOCHSCHILD, A. (1983): The Managed Heart: commercialization of human feeling. Berkeley, Los Angeles and London: University of California Press.

MEHAN, H., A.HERTWECK & J.L. MEIHLS. (1986): *Handicapping the Handicapped: Decision Making in Students' Educational Careers*. Stanford: Stanford University Press.

PAVLICEVIC, M. & G. ANSDELL (eds.) (2004): *Community Music Therapy.* London and Philadelphia: Jessica Kingsley Publishers.

PROCTER, S. (2004): Playing Politics: Community Music Therapy and the Therapeutic Redistribution of Musical Capital for Mental Health. In: Pavlicevic, Mercedes & Ansdell, Gary (Eds.). *Community Music Therapy*. London: Jessica Kingsley Publishers.

PROCTER, S. (2006): 'What are we playing at? Social capital and music therapy'. In Edwards, R.; Franklin, J. & Holland, J. (eds) *Assessing Social Capital: Concept, Policy and Practice*. Cambridge: Cambridge Scholars Press.

PUTNAM, R (2000): *Bowling Alone*. New York: Simon and Schuster.

RADLEY, A. (1984): The embodiment of social relations in coronary heart disease. *Social Science and Medicine* 19, pp. 1227-34.

ROLVSJORD, R, (2004): Therapy as Empowerment. Clinical and Political Implications of Empowerment Philosophy in Mental Health Practices of Music Therapy. *Nordic Journal of Music Therapy*, vol. 13, no. 2, pp. 99-112.

ROLVSJORD, R. (2006): Whose Power of music? A Discussion on Music and Power-Relations in Music Therapy. *British Journal of Music Therapy*.

RUUD, E. (1997):. Music and Quality of Life. *Nordic Journal of Music Therapy*. vol. 6 (2), pp. 86-91.

RUUD, E. (2002): Music as a Cultural Immunogen – Three Narratives on the Use of Music as a Technology of Health. In: Hanken et al. (Eds.). *Research in and for Higher Music Education. Festschrift for Harald Jørgensen*. Oslo: NMH-Publications: 2.

RUUD, E. (2004): Foreword: Reclaiming Music. In Pavlicevic, Mercédès and Ansdell, Gary (Eds.) (2004). *Community Music Therapy*. London and Philadelphia: Jessica Kingsley Publishers.

RUUD, E. (2005): Music: A salutogenic way to health promotion? . In Tellnes, G. (Eds.) *Urbanization and Health. New challenges to Health Promotion and Prevention*. Oslo: Academic Press, UniPub.

SLOBODA, J. & S. O'NEILL (2001): Emotions in Everyday Listening to Music. In P. Juslin & J. Sloboda, *Music and Emotion: Theory and Research*. Oxford: Oxford University Press.

SMALL, C. (1998): *Musicking: The Meanings of Performing and Listening*. Hanover: Wesleyan University Press.

STIGE, B. (2003): *Elaborations towards a Notion of Community Music Therapy*. Faculty of Arts, University of Oslo.

TRYTHALL, S. (2006): Live Music in Hospitals: A new 'alternative' therapy. *The Journal of the Royal Society for the Promotion of Health*; 126 (4): 113.

ZUBIETA, J.-K., J. BUELLER, L.R. JACKSON, D.J. SCOTT, Y. XU, R.A. KOEPPE, T.E. NICHOLS & C.S. STOHLER (2005): Placebo Effects Mediated by Endogenous Opioid Activity on μ-Opioid Receptors. *Journal of Neuroscience* 25: 7754-7762.

CHAPTER 11

Evidence and Effectiveness in Music Therapy

Problems, Power, Possibilities and Performances in Health Contexts (A Discussion Paper)

Editor's Note

This article and the responses which follow have their origins in papers presented at a music therapy research symposium entitled *Evidence-Based Practice and Music Therapy: A Further Perspective* held on 25th November 2005 at the Nordoff-Robbins Music Therapy Centre, London.

Abstract

Adopting a knowledge-based controversy perspective, this article considers critically the 'fit' or appropriateness of the so-called 'gold standard' of assessment – the Randomised Controlled Trial. It sets the growing dominance of this method within music therapy in the contexts of medical work and the changing social relations of medical expertise, the importance of local practice in music therapy (and healthcare more widely), and the politics of representation as they apply to medical modes of accounting and measurement. I then consider what is overlooked when experimental models are used as the prime mode of perceiving the music therapeutic process and suggest that they may not provide a good or appropriate way of observing, accounting for and assessing music therapy. I suggest that they are not amenable to the observation and documentation of temporal and local craft practices and that these practices provide the active ingredients of music therapy's effectiveness. I conclude that music therapy is poised to highlight the radical performative and social features of health status and that these features have far-reaching implications for our concepts of illness and the aetiology of illness and, most importantly, for the ways in which we conceptualise and implement therapeutic procedures of all kinds.

Introduction and Background

At one time the Fox and the Stork were on visiting terms and seemed very good friends. So the Fox invited the Stork to dinner, and for a joke put nothing before her but some soup in a very shallow dish. This the Fox could easily lap up, but the Stork could only wet the end of her long bill in it, and left the meal as hungry as when she began.

"I am sorry," said the Fox, "the soup is not to your liking."

"Pray do not apologise," said the Stork. "I hope you will return this visit, and come and dine with me soon."

So a day was appointed when the Fox should visit the Stork; but when they were seated at table all that was for their dinner was contained in a very long-necked jar with a narrow mouth, in which the Fox could not insert his snout, so all he could manage to do was to lick the inside of the jar.

"I will not apologise for the dinner," said the Stork: "One Bad Turn Deserves Another."

Aesop: *The Fox and the Crane*

Different technologies, including different technologies of measurement, have consequences for knowledge. When thinking about techniques for evaluating the effectiveness of health procedures, it is important to consider what might be wasted if we apportion data through inappropriate technologies of measurement and representation (beakers versus saucers and the wastage of soup in the case of Aesop's tale). This is certainly the case for music therapy, which is currently responding to demands related to Evidence Based Practice.

As Ansdell, Pavlicevic and Procter have observed (2004), music therapists are becoming increasingly anxious about the need to account for the effectiveness of what they do in a manner commensurate with the evidence-based movement in medical research. Titles of music therapy publications attest to this anxiety, as does the discourse used when discussing the 'challenge' posed by EBP or the 'need' to 'engage with' the 'demands being made' of music therapy to participate in providing evidence that backs up its claims. As Jane Edwards described it in 2002:

> ... EBM is increasing its hold as the dominant approach to determining service provision in hospitals and health administrations around the world. It has influenced perceptions of the value of all patient care 'outcomes' in medical contexts, not just with reference to services provided by doctors and physicians but also allied health and nursing services.
>
> (Edwards 2002: 29)

Inevitably, EBM (or EBP) discourse bears traces of the medical model and the predominance within medical research of certain notions of health and illness - pathology, an aetiology lodged in bio-psychological terms, and a conception of treatment as a specific and typically pharmacological or surgical intervention. As I will describe below, this medical framing of health and illness has by no means gone unchallenged by music therapists (e.g. Procter 2002; Rolvsjord 2004).

In regard to music therapy, EBP has different consequences for different constituencies – for the professional status of music therapists and for potential clients of music therapy. I suggest (following discussions by various music therapists who have examined EBP critically) that it would be no bad thing if music therapists were to think critically about the 'fit' or appropriateness of assessment methods and their purported hierarchy since the 'gold standard' of these methods, the randomised controlled trial (RCT), was designed for testing physical matter (and physiological reactions): how applicable is the RCT for music therapy, a mode of activity that is, essentially, a form of human cultural interaction (more than physical reaction)? In posing this question, I certainly do not mean to suggest that music therapists should, like Aesop's stork, seek some sort of revenge (even if they were in a position to do so!) against the 'scientists' who serve up data in (possibly) 'inappropriate' containers: it would be unreasonable to reject, unilaterally, the RCT protocol.

On the contrary, thinking critically about, on the one hand, the 'fit' between music therapeutic aims and craft techniques and, on the other hand, methods of evaluation, is a way of enhancing scientific understanding writ large, in relation to these (and wider healthcare) issues. Thus the EBP debate might be broadened to consider features of health, illness and 'treatment' that exceed narrow medical definitions of treatment and health procedure.

In what follows, I examine the topic of evidence-based demands in music therapy from a sociology of science perspective, one focused on knowledge-based controversy. My comments are arranged as themes, beginning with sociological issues that centre on medicine and moving towards music therapy, its craft and the potentially greater role music therapists might play in renegotiating evidentiary hierarchies.

Theme 1: Sociology of health occupations and the politics of knowledge formation

Occupational status, professionalisation, and de-professionalisation are three of sociology's classic themes. Of all the arenas in which these themes have been pursued, medicine has undoubtedly been one of the most frequently considered (Starr 1982; Friedson 1988). Linked to the politics of expertise and knowledge formation, social movements, economics and policy, this area is fascinating to students of conflict, power, and social change.

In the nineteenth and early twentieth centuries, medicine and doctors rose to prominence in the field of healthcare occupations, sidelining nurses, midwives and folk healers, a change that was both class and gender based (Witz 1992). In the last three decades we have witnessed the de-professionalisation of medicine, a shifting in the balance of power from the autonomous clinician (the chief consultant, for example, as 'God' in communicative settings (Atkinson 1995; Davis 1989) – see discussions of evidence hierarchies below) to the health manager. In Europe, the UK and the USA, in public and in private healthcare systems, this shift has been driven by health economics. And as with virtually every other area of production, it has pursued the concept of efficiency. Translated back into economics, that typically means spending less and getting more (producing a good, e.g. health/cure), and, in cases where healthcare is privatised, amassing profit.[1]

Partly a response to the very healthy values of transparency and accountability (linked to patient advocacy and to democratic modes of healthcare assessment), the movement, internationally understood,

---

[1] Music, a relatively inexpensive 'medical' technology, is interestingly placed in this regard.

is also part of a global shift in the politics of medical authority, a set of techniques that reconfigures authority at a collective (organisational and administrative) level and that diminishes the authority of particular clinicians. In this way, healthcare managers (e.g. hospital administrators) are empowered, via the technologies of risk assessment and their statistical batteries, to authorise doctors, who are authorised to administer particular treatments according to instrumentally rational codes of practice. This shift in power-relations is in classic sociological terms a shift in favour of bureaucratic authority.

Theme 2: The changing social structure of clinical expertise

When we speak of the need for 'evidence', and when we invoke, sometimes implicitly, criteria for the format such evidence should take, we are inevitably simultaneously configuring a world of knowledge relations, a 'who, what, when, where and how' of what to know and what to do to know. How knowledge is produced and communicated, its formats and modes of distribution are, in other words, never neutral. If there is currently a move in favour of, for example, randomised clinical trials, reliability and transparent procedure, this is in great part linked to the shift in power between medical and managerial personnel, to the rise, especially in the USA, of litigation, and to the desire, in the face of these trends, for global procedures of control, i.e. for regularised methods of treatment and administration of treatment. The drive towards regularisation and accountability (as produced by findings that can be abstracted and upheld as justification for particular ways of doing) is always a move that favours managerial sectors: it moves criteria of evaluation away from the valuing of individual expert (in this case clinical-practical) opinion and in favour of documentable evidence. This shift is neither intrinsically 'good' nor 'bad': its value still lies in its processes of implementation, its content and reception (for example, which recommended course of treatment?) by various constituencies.

In terms of clinical practice, the shift in the basis of medical authority has been linked to a dramatic growth over the past three decades of pharmaceutical treatments (marked by global distribution procedures, increasingly proactive sales representatives and marketing via, for example, the sponsorship of medical activities such as conferences and journals and the pharmaceutical sponsorship and sometimes 'capture' of self-help groups). This growth has been associated with the Evidence Based Practice movement and, within that, the rise of the RCT as the so-called 'gold standard' (see for example Wigram 1999, 2002; Edwards 2002, 2004; Ansdell, Pavlicevic and Procter 2004).

Cultural sociologists are often interested in the broad question of how culture changes. Within this, we question how culture may be pushed and pulled by individuals and groups so that it moves in particular directions. We often study processes of what we speak of as cultural entrepreneurship, following the ways that groups may seek to innovate in the realm of value and practice so as to institute new ways of doing, seeing and relating. Such activity often involves reconfiguring criteria of judgment, whether aesthetic, ethical or cognitive/scientific (indeed these are intertwined in practice). In changes that involve scientific culture or cultures of knowledge production, we often speak of these processes in terms of Knowledge Based Controversies, by which we mean disputes about facts (the utility, authority, and proper representation, procedures of discovering and relative importance of facts). How we determine what counts as knowledge, and as 'good' knowledge, provides the basis for social relations, not just the relations of individual actors, but the relationship and structure of social roles (for example, in relation to health care, who is more important: the doctor, the midwife or the priest?).

Theme 3: Local procedures, local controls

What, then, is at stake, in controversies about evidence, its production, reliability and validity? Most of my work has been in the area of music sociology, but I have maintained a long-standing interest in the area of the sociology of science and technology, historically conceived. My own area of interest here is lay expertise.

In the early 1990s, I conducted a research project concerned with the politics of expertise in the area of women's reproductive health. This was at a time when that field of healthcare was undergoing dramatic change in the face of new technologies such as IVF (DeNora 1996). I was interested in the topic for how it afforded a glimpse into power struggles within the medical and health sciences/practice at a time of change and I was interested in contestations over how best to configure knowledge. These struggles spoke directly to issues about the distribution and authority of what I understood as 'local' expertise. The project examined historical documents about Fertility Awareness methods and effectiveness[2] and data from in-depth interviews with women who used the method, one animal psychologist and fertility specialists in the USA and UK.[3]

[2] T DeNora, ESRC Project, 1991-1992, University of Wales, Cardiff: 'The construction of an alternative (cervical mucus) method of contraception, 1960-1992'. The documentary data included articles published between 1960-1992 in medical and scientific journals, newspapers, popular magazines, popular scientific texts and manuals about contraception, and government publications.

[3] The primary data was documentary. The interviews were supplementary, used to explore issues arising in the text

The project focused on the discourse strategies by which the method was configured in evaluative terms, the criteria according to which it was configured, and the implications of these for practice and for social relations (including sexual politics, the imagery of gender difference and the distinction and status of professional versus lay experts). It examined a specific and so-called 'alternative' method of contraception: the cervical mucus or 'fertility awareness' method. Of particular interest was the method's provision, via amateur practice, of 'alternative' depictions of the so-called 'facts' of female reproductive physiology and, related to this provision, the social relations involved in the production (recognition) of those 'facts' as facts about the status of the fertile female body (for example, how good were they? Could one bank on them for contraceptive purposes?)[4]

The reader might reasonably ask how this topic is relevant to music therapy. Beyond the obvious issue that both mucus contraception and music therapy to some extent exist on the margins of 'mainstream' medical practice, both also owe their effectiveness to the local ways in which they are practised – to local forms of expertise and to attention to local circumstances. I think the importance of the local opens up critical issues for music therapy's assessment in Evidence Based evaluative contexts and this theme will recur throughout the remainder of this article.

To begin: an exemplary RCT of music's ability to sedate children who are about to undergo EEG testing was conducted over four years (Loewy et al 2005). The children were divided into two groups. One group received a standard dose of 60mg to 1.5g of chloral hydrate. For the other group, a live music therapist, working one-to-one with each child, played music for/with that child, after consulting with each child's caregiver so as to identify music that was 'of kin to the subject's cultural realm' (p.3).

Loewy et al state that the therapist used standard music therapy techniques, such as singing familiar lullabies 'in accordance with the child's breathing rate'. Live music, in other words, was essential since (it is implied) the critical intervening feature of the music for sedation lay in its ability to entrain subjects' physical responses, and thus induce sleep. Recorded music was eschewed because 'at a predetermined tempo [it] would not provide for such entrainment procedures that are

instrumental to the work of a music therapist'[5]. The study concludes that music therapy was an effective means of inducing sleep. Only 1 out of 34 children in the music therapy group required complementary intervention after 30 minutes as compared to 12 of the 24 children in the chloral hydrate group. Moreover, sleep induced by music therapy would appear to be better suited to the needs of administering the EEG: 97.1% of the children exposed exclusively to music completed the EEG recording successfully, compared with 50% of those subjected exclusively to chloral hydrate.

Note here that, unlike chloral hydrate, music therapy required a local person (an actual music therapist) to do locally specific things (make music in accordance with the child's musical background and current physiological state) in real time (to respond to ongoing developments). As the authors put it:

… the music therapist is a part of the environment, playing soothing music that relates to the patient, caregiver, and staff needs, thereby attending to, and adjusting to the instant input and response of the immediate situation…Live music can…be shifted in the moment or entrained to match the breathing rate of a child's physiological response. Adapting the meter/tempo of music to match the breathing rate of a child's response can enhance the child's ability to relax.

(Loewy et al 2005: 324)

While these things can, in craft terms, undoubtedly be specified, they cannot be predetermined outside of and in advance of any specific set of local circumstances: that is, without local temporal data. By contrast, as with fertility awareness, there is, I would suggest, considerable local (devolved) 'skill', 'expertise', even 'science' at work here (in the sense that practice is dependent upon a range of skills, procedures and accumulated wisdom and its features may produce reliable effects, time after time). I would further suggest that the characteristic feature of local expertise is that it cannot be abstracted from its contexts of application. One cannot afford to ignore local matters in either of these areas of practice and for this reason, neither music therapy nor mucus contraception may be viewed as amenable to inevitably distal (i.e. abstract and globally administered) forms of managerial control.

Of course this study could be critiqued on the basis that the music therapy's reliability was too heavily dependent upon the skills of the particular music therapists – too dependent upon the local administration

---

[4] Used 'correctly' the 'failure rate' is 2% according to UK Family Planning Association Figures, see: http://www.fpa.org.uk/guide/contracep/natural.htm For US Food and Drug statistics, see: http://www.fda.gov/fdac/features/1997/conceptbl.html
I deliberately put these terms in quotes to call attention to their role as discursive figures.

[5] It is noted that there are important traditions in music therapy that do make use of recorded music, such as Guided Imagery in Music, and that Loewy et al are referring to their own tradition.

of procedures. (Pushing this, one can imagine an extreme critical response along the lines of, "to say 'music therapy' was administered is about as specific as saying 'drugs' were administered – we don't even know what we're testing!") This indeterminacy as to what is being tested tends to worry medical administrators: in pharmacological or surgical contexts, it may create vulnerability since it is more difficult to 'prove' that no procedure has been violated, for example, as fewer conditions of administration can be determined in advance.

By contrast, chloral hydrate is (or is presumed to be) 'inert': it needs merely to be administered in a prescribed dose. These 'benefits' associated with pharmacological instruments may persuade managers (threatened by law suits, competing for time, striving for greater efficiency) that despite the side effects associated with chloral hydrate (nausea, vomiting, motor imbalance, gastrointestinal effects, agitation and restlessness, local skin and mucosal lesions, toxicity, sedation difficulty, hyperactivity, mild respiratory depression, cardiac arrhythmia, hyperbilirubinemia) it is, nevertheless, 'better'.[6] Jane Edwards describes this type of dilemma in a nut shell:

A difficulty however, is that music therapy in practice does not simply consist of the administration of a consistent protocol, such as three minutes of one type of music followed by four minutes of another. At times, explaining this factor in service proposals or reports might be important in order to elucidate the seemingly idiosyncratic design and method of music therapy research findings to administrators.
(Edwards 2002: 31)

Theme 4: Science as artful accounting – when is a property 'stable' and when is it not?

Science and the reporting (construction) of scientific findings involves, inevitably, a kind of artful 'making'. Scholars such as sociologists and anthropologists of science who have spent time in laboratories and with 'hard' scientific research groups in areas such as astronomy, mathematics, the biosciences and physics and who, equally importantly, have collaborated with scientists about their practical activities and who have been trained at advanced level in the sciences in question, have described the processes of, for want of a

better term, allocation and accounting work that is absolutely necessary to the 'discovery' or, more accurately, production of 'findings' and the conduct of experiments and other observations that produce those findings (For a good sample of classic work see Knorr-Cetina & Mulkay 1983.)

By allocation work I mean something akin to the apportioning of data discussed at the start of this article via Aesop: the ways in which features of a phenomenon are contained or made available for consumption as (and ranked as) facts. This process of apportioning, containing or allocation involves a range of perceptual and representational practices, sometimes ones that are not verbally or even consciously acknowledged and that organise phenomena into their associated accounts.

For example, what is and is not important to know about a given phenomenon? What can be 'explained away' as noise, artefact or trivial? These issues often determine whether or not something is even discovered or brought to light as a finding. Scientific activity 'translates' nature, events and happenings into other representational media. For example, summary statistics, graphs, charts, abstractions and other renditions of phenomena, such as diagrams, drawings or slides, within narrative accounts are representational media: they abstract phenomena. These media are not neutral containers; they pre-structure what about phenomena can be seen, reported and conveyed. The point is that, mediated by institutional procedures (how we test, how we look, the tools we use), theory-laden perception (we perceive with a bias towards convention) and procedures of reporting, scientific findings translate phenomena into what are sometimes called institutional facts – ways of representing phenomena that are structured by constraints of science or other knowledge-making worlds. Inevitably, some features of phenomena in their 'raw' state are allocated, in this scientific accounting, to the column of 'hidden figures' or 'things we can afford to ignore'. The interesting point for sociologists of science (at least for those sufficiently conversant in the technical features of scientific activity) is: could it have been otherwise and how and why did X or Y come to be allocated as background information (and implicitly something that may be ignored)? For here is the nub of what makes a knowledge-based controversy and one that leads us back to the root of the English word translation, better understood as traduction, or 'traduced', 'betrayal'.

In the example of a music therapy RCT discussed above (Loewy et al 2005), we can see similar allocation processes at work. First, imagine that this study might be criticised for the fact that, as Edwards has discussed (2002), music therapeutic application is not usually 'consistently' applied across all subjects. (I have rehearsed this imaginary hostile response above.)

[6]In addition, there are various organisational constraints, such as the need to schedule medical procedures. Chloral hydrate may be more generally reliable as a way of sedating a child (though this is not what Loewy et al observed!), but one associated with side effects. Music therapy's 'success' here is embedded in its local implementation and a child's conscious or subconscious reactions to musical stimuli. But since its effectiveness is dependent upon the interaction of many complex factors locally in time/place, music therapy may not be as amenable a means of sedation to organisational needs.

Of course, this was one of the key points that the authors suggested made music so effective! The whole point was that music therapy works best when its application is locally determined and in real time! Beyond this, though, might the music therapist counter that, in the interests of symmetry, the same criticism might be applicable to both the music therapy variable and to the chloral hydrate variable? For example, are we quite sure that the 'same' drug was administered to all recipients? Most probably, and in keeping with the protocol, the same dose (in mgs) of the same chemical was administered. But virtually all of us know that drugs interact with individual body chemistry and metabolism in varying ways, not to mention local conditions and psycho-cultural factors (in other words, age or weight are not precise enough as controls for dosage) – all of this is glossed and sidelined as 'side-effects' or not noticed, allocated as 'background'.

Secondly, and relatedly, what do we mean by 'sleep': isn't sleep a qualitative phenomenon? Indeed, both of these factors could turn out to be important if we were to unpack the study and consider, more specifically, the differences within experimental categories and groups as well as between them. For example, one of Loewy et al's findings was that those children allocated to the music therapy treatment group proceeded successfully through the EEG test more frequently than those who were given chloral hydrate.

In short, when we unpack experimental procedure we open, to mix metaphors, a can of worms. Many of the stable items and assumptions are de-stabilised: even something as apparently simple and clear cut as how long it takes to get someone to go to sleep. (Imagine if we were dealing with something more complex, such as forms of co-ordination, pain perception or, more complex still, sense of well-being!) And when we step, as it were, inside the black box of experimental procedure, we find that music therapy may be able to take on an empowered theoretical role, as an equal partner in medical dialogue. When it is depicted within the framework of outcomes and variables, music therapy's visage is simplified: when, by contrast, it is portrayed according to frameworks that allow it to engage with and help to determine appropriate criteria for 'testing' health procedures, we can begin to see how music and musical procedures are not mere handmaidens of medical ones. We are also granted a quite different understanding of health, illness, effectiveness and ineffectiveness and it is to these themes that the rest of my discussion is oriented.

Theme 5: Double Blind, or Triple Blind to Music Therapy?

Various music therapy scholars have discussed evidentiary hierarchies. For example, Wigram (2002)

describes an eight stage structure, from most to least prestigious:

1. Systematic review
2. Review
3. Randomised controlled trials (RCTs)
4. Case control studies
5. Case series
6. Case reports/case studies
7. Qualitative studies
8. Expert opinion
   (cited in Ansdell, Pavlicevic & Procter 2004: 15)

Similarly, Edwards (2002) draws upon the Australian National Health and Medical Research Council, itself having adopted the US Preventive Services Task Force levels as follows:

Level 1
Evidence obtained from a systematic review of all randomised control trials (i.e. what has appeared in the music therapy literature as 'meta-analysis' for example in Furman 1988).

Level 2
Evidence obtained from at least one properly designed randomised control trial.

Level 3
This refers to three levels but basically includes all studies that have used comparative method but are not 'properly designed' randomised control trials.

Level 4
Evidence obtained from case series, either post-test or pre-test and post-test.
(Edwards 2002: 29)

My sense of music therapy's response to the 'demands' for Evidence Based Practice is that so far, if anything, it has been too willing to bow to presumptions about evidence hierarchies such as these summarised by Wigram; Ansdell, Pavlicevic and Procter; and Edwards (all of whom have articulated robust responses to EBP). In part I suspect this is because music therapy, as an 'allied health discipline', is still somewhat nervous about its own professional standing and about its continued welcome in medical and mental health settings.

But just how well suited is music therapy to the RCT format – at least at this stage of the game? Bunt and Pavlicevic (2001) have described the importance of, as Ansdell aptly puts it, the 'music between' (Ansdell 1995) client and therapist, and the dynamic, emergent emotion thereby produced, as the kernel of music therapy and its craft (2001:197). These interactive features are precisely those that are often excluded and/or derided by proponents of the RCT (see Rolvsjord, Gold and Stige 2005 on how to combine the 'problem orientation' of the RCT with the 'resource-orientation' of cultural and context based music therapy).

Why then should music therapists necessarily accept this hierarchy of evidentiary levels or, alternatively, how might music therapists reconfigure the contours and parameters within a level – effecting change in how we think about such things as 'treatment variables', 'control' and other features of RCTs, in general and in terms of specific RCT designs? To what extent 'must' music therapy be contorted to fit the valued paradigmatic practices of medical science? If this contortion is like trying to fit a square peg into a round hole, and if the peg of music therapy has to be trimmed to fit that hole, what type of material will be severed from music therapy's process in order to make it fit the parameters and representational discourses of variables, test procedures and outcomes (and the systematic review of these procedures)? What, in other words, is traduced or allocated to the category of residual, problematic or unimportant? On the other hand, when are RCTs and other so-called 'higher' forms of evidence appropriate, and when might they be of especial value?

In the remaining sections of this paper I address the first of these questions by considering music therapy as a specific form of practice – with specific skills and linked to or fostering specific resources and social relationships (e.g., between patients/clients, their families and those who, in one way or another care for or treat them). I suggest that an important step in thinking about appropriate criteria and methods of evaluation for music therapy (i.e. how is music therapy different from pharmacological therapy?) is to attempt to open our eyes to aspects of health, healing and treatment processes that are otherwise allocated to the territory of 'unimportant' or, worse, for all practical purposes, never seen at all. What then, are some of the things that the RCT as a way of looking at music therapy misses and how can we use these things to think about proactive strategies in the politics of representing what counts as 'good' evidence?

Theme 6: The Goldilocks effect?

Goldilocks was sleepy, so she thought she would lie down and have a little nap. First she got upon the **GREAT BIG BED,** but it was just as hard as the **GREAT BIG CHAIR** had been; so she jumped off and tried the **MIDDLING-SIZED BED,** but it was so soft

that she sank right down into the feather cushions and was nearly smothered.

"I will try the **TEENY TINY BED",** she said, and so she did, and it was so comfortable that she soon fell fast asleep.

(Traditional fairytale)

As in the story of Goldilocks, whether something is effective (not too peppery, too salty, too big, small, hard or soft in this case) has much to do with how it measures up (or down) to the requirements of those who wish to use it – her, his or their size and shape, tastes and perceptual schema. And just as medical research has been concerned with evidence-based standards of effectiveness, so too EBM has promoted procedures for collecting and analysing data connected to the predominant type of material it wishes to test – drugs.

Fair enough, perhaps: an RCT is concerned with testing quantifiable outcomes of consistently applied stimuli. It is easy to see why such an assessment procedure is, as Goldilocks said of the porridge, 'just right' for testing drugs: drugs are highly literal, pre-programmed things; they are administered in precision-controlled manners and in precise doses; they have no judgement, consciousness or agency of their own; they can, in other words, not adjust themselves to emerging conditions. This is to say that 'interactions' between drug and patient, such as an allergic reaction to penicillin, are, assuming the drug contained what it should have contained, due to how it was received by the body of the patient; the interaction was all one-sided.[7] This is why drugs are tested by RCT; they are a therapeutic aid designed for administration (once prescribed) in a mechanical manner ('take as directed'). Thus, the RCT conditions of testing drugs suit the ways drugs have been designed to be used in medical settings.

But how well does the RCT 'fit' music therapy as a diverse set of practices and a complex set of skills, stimuli and interactions? As various writers in music therapy have noted, music, especially when administered by a live music therapist, is a very different type of therapeutic aid (indeed it may be disputed whether it is a 'therapeutic aid' or rather a way of relating). For one thing, a music therapist, unlike a pill, is, like the patient, a human being: she/he is intelligent; has been trained, has perception, judgement, and skill; moreover, she/he exercises these attributes in real time, in response to emerging situations.

---

[7] But who says that this is the case? And is it? Some would argue that its identity may only really be known through the multifarious ways in which it combines with various individual bodies thus revealing those things that are allocated as – merely – its possible and – reading the labels of the drug - numerous 'side effects' (Latour 2005).

Music therapy might be considered to be rather like Goldilocks: arriving on the scene and hoping to be invited to sit down at the table and share in some soup. In fact, unlike Goldilocks, many music therapists have actually been invited to sit at the clinical table in recent years, as the various collaborations between medical clinicians and music therapists in the research literature attest (see Aldridge *et al* 2005). But, to switch back to Aesop's fable of the Fox and the Crane, what have been the technologies with which music therapy has been required to sup? If we think of music therapy as it comes to be 'translated' (traduced?) into RCT technologies of perception/representation, what knowledge (potential facts and alternative modes of knowing – the soup!) is wasted? What cannot, in the tall beaker (as opposed to the shallow saucer) of 'scientific' protocol, be appropriated or known?

Music therapists are much better equipped to answer this question than I am. What follows are issues that have struck me in my experience of music therapy thus far. They are issues about how it might be possible to stop wasting so much of the data that might otherwise be nourishing to music therapy's 'scientific' credibility, a wastage that could be stopped if it were not felt that it had to be poured into containers where, at the end of the RCT so much is (perhaps needlessly) thrown away. I present these comments to highlight the importance of our categories of data representation and measurement containers to the 'construction' of 'scientific' facts: facts which, to all practical purposes, we come to recognise as effective and real.

Theme 7: Too long or too short versus 'just right': temporality in the treatment/healing process

RCTs are concerned with outcomes (pain abatement, sleep inducement, regulation of body rhythms, mood modification, somatic co-ordination or skill acquisition) and they therefore sideline what happens in time. Yet clearly the size of a chosen time interval can heighten or suppress the 'effectiveness' of phenomena. Consider the relatively trivial 'illness' of a minor headache. If we are testing the effects of an analgesic, and we determine the test interval to consist of a six-hour period (and if most headaches disappear on their own by then), we are most likely to show a greater effectiveness rate for the analgesic. Conversely, if the headaches remain and are merely masked by the pain reliever, then we would need to choose a time interval of shorter duration so as to capture the 'relief' factor (for in six hours the pain will be 'still there' and the temporary relief may have passed unnoticed).

So too, definitions of efficacy in music therapy embed tacit notions of the temporal structure of outcomes, and in ways that construct what will and will not be admissible as data. For example, to return to the study by Loewy *et al*, one might want to consider the longer durée implicated in music therapy versus other treatment forms (as alluded to in the discussion of the disadvantages of chloral hydrate – the need to keep patients who have received chloral hydrate under observation): to stretch the temporal envelope, extending it beyond the administration and completion of the EEG. To do so is, inevitably, to become involved in the politics of health-representation, to enter into the renegotiation of clinical criteria 'for whom' (Procter 2004a).

Alternatively, one might wish to consider a far more dramatically curtailed temporal window of treatment/treatment administration – the window of instants, moments, or fleeting phases. Considering the 'treatment' phase in terms of these micro-units – and their role in some 'longer' temporal process – may highlight the importance of the client's phenomenological experience in and of music therapy. (I would argue that a similar approach might be applied to the subjective experience of pharmacological therapies too: a topic that, to my knowledge, has been largely ignored.) For example, remaining with the overtly 'medical' and physiological topic of pain, consider the management of more severe pain or strong discomfort. In such a case, the use of analgesic medications may be associated with mental side effects that a client wishes to avoid, whereas music therapy may provide ways of redefining pain, reallocating it within spiritual narratives where it is transcended (Aldridge 2003). As with any form of transcendence, changes in meanings may be both fleeting and/or achieved in 'moments'. These moments may, however, be put to good effect. They may be used as building blocks to more connected phases of 'healing' and of the experience, over time, of well-being, even in the face of extreme illness/pain/suffering. In this respect they may provide the resources that become 'turning points', 'first steps' and so on.

An example of this from music therapy practice is an extract contained in a paper on the modulation of affect (Ansdell & Procter 2004) in which a client is led through a series of musical moments away from a violent outburst and towards co-operative, interactive musicing. In the context of music in everyday life, I have seen examples of these matters in my own work (DeNora 2003). For example, in organisational settings (e.g., a retail outlet) a fragment of a song may 'capture' a consumer such that her previous plans and orientation are abandoned and she is drawn in more firmly to desiring and engaging with goods and materials in the retail ecology.

In a more ecological, but still medical frame, I am thinking of on-going work by Gary Ansdell that I have observed in the field. I have watched in admiration as Ansdell contains, opens up, suggests and underpins communal music making in a mental health facility. So too, in her research on concerts in hospital and hospice settings, Susan Trythall describes how highly skilled musicians (not music therapists) find ways of holding attention, crafting time so as to create 'key moments' and to make spaces between these moments so that they may achieve their role of drawing together group attention, thus establishing a sense of 'group' to be perceived by and commented upon by the group – this is collective identity construction via key moments (see Trythall 2006; Batt-Rawden, Trythall and DeNora in press).

Still in the ecological frame, Trygve Aasgaard has considered the phenomenology of time from a pragmatic angle focused on how to make time last, as it were ('how long does a moment last?': Aasgaard 2002). He shows how such moments may be prolonged through the cultivation of expectancy (p. 205) and the practices through which such expectancy might be encouraged and sustained (which of course is a way of holding a particular focus/orientation, one that mitigates against ill-being):

It is astonishing that any person in a physical condition as poor as described above, is at all able to be eagerly waiting for song activities to come. I interpret this behaviour as examples of sick children – temporarily leaving their roles of being passive and suffering patients – and becoming committed…

(Aasgaard 2002: 204; see also Aasgaard 2004).

These micro moments of in-process transcendence, mood realignment, pleasure, and captivation may never be registered if at the end of a session we ask a patient to rate their pain on a scale of 1-10 (for they will no doubt respond based on the present moment of interrogation) or if, at the end, we evaluate only outcomes.[8] And yet, within the full time span during which music therapy occurs (an hour, days, months), the standard deviation of subjective orientation (pain perception, mood shift, pleasure, enthusiasm) may have been high. Within a larger time interval we need to learn how to appreciate heterogeneity of real world experience (the RCT erases this heterogeneity – see Rogers (2000) on the importance here of qualitative studies) and to appreciate that even a moment (perhaps

ten seconds?) of transcendence or change may be 'worth', as Americans say, 'a million dollars'. The value of time is not in its quantity: thus we need to find appropriate measures for the timeframes that do matter – to clients, patients and users, for example.

When we consider the matter of behavioural phenomena in music therapy (for example in the field of mental health), time frames and activities in time become more crucial yet, pointing the way back towards the importance of case studies and qualitative data, at least as the starting point for subsequent quantification. For example, in Ridder's research on elderly people with dementia (2002, 2004), 'memory' or overall behavioural tendencies may not change (following the client over time and outside/after therapy, perhaps in conjunction with interviewing their families/carers, seems to be an under-explored area), but behaviours within the music therapy sessions may be visibly altered. Clients may demonstrate physical signs of calm and somatic organisation dramatically different from when no music is happening and thus gain valued respite and reconnection with, among other things, their former selves. This is a critical issue in music therapy, one very poorly addressed by the RCT protocol and vital to any understanding of how our identities emerge against aesthetic and other resource materials that are available as the grounds for identity production and maintenance (see Magee 2001).

* * *

In his poem 'Ignorance', Philip Larkin speaks of how it is:

Strange to be ignorant of the way things work:
Their skill at finding what they need,
Their sense of shape, and punctual spread of seed,
And willingness to change;
Yes, it is strange,

Even to wear such knowledge - for our flesh
Surrounds us with its own decisions –

(Larkin 1964)

Larkin goes on to speak of how our ignorance is such that, despite these decisions of the flesh, we waste our time on 'imprecisions', such that when we come to die we are surprised, having 'no idea why' such a state of affairs could have occurred.

Larkin's poetry is known for its virtually congenital form of pessimism. It is possible, however, to raise our consciousness, to be less ignorant or, rather, to tap the latent intelligences we all possess about our health and our social relation to health and illness, thus enabling us to engage in more overt strategies of, broadly conceived, health promotion. This leads to the final

---

[8] In my retail example, neither of the two consumers so 'hooked' made a purchase and yet they came much closer to making a purchase than they had elsewhere under observation over a one hour period.

theme I want to present here: the craft of music therapy – both the craft of the music therapist (the general craft or lore of music therapy as it is taught, researched and practised and the particular real time skills of individual music therapists) and the crafts of his/her clients. This theme will lead to my concluding points on health as performance.

Theme 8: Craft – the music therapist's and the client's

The music therapist (conceived here broadly as someone who facilitates music [live or recorded] in relation to the healing, health and well-being of another individual or a group) is not a pill but rather a human being, someone standing by and in some way helping the client(s), patient(s) or user(s) to achieve some aim – a state of mind, emotion or body, a new skill, or merely a social connection – which some set of individuals (we need to ask which ones and why – see Procter 2004a) has identified as a desirable outcome for some individual(s) (again, which ones and why?). To study master craftspersons at work and to compare case-by-case what can be done with and without that craft is surely one very good way of further codifying music therapy's often tacit body of knowledge/skill, perhaps in ways that, further along, will lend themselves to more appropriate RCT designs for music therapy.

A focus on the music therapist's craft as the active ingredient in music therapeutic effectiveness leads to the symmetrical concern with what the client does. Music therapy is social action. It is meaningful activity over time, even if it involves only a therapist playing for a client or listening to pre-recorded music. How the client responds and the activities she/he brings to the music therapeutic situation are as much a part of music therapy's 'effects' as what music therapists contribute and this point is surely well-recognised in music therapy discourse.

RCTs, with their focus on outcomes, relegate these features to the background. Yet it is here that we may understand the actual mechanisms of how music may or may not work. Indeed, this activity is part of what in the terminology of the RCT would be described as the 'treatment variable', part of what it takes to produce an 'effective' result, however 'effectiveness' is defined.[9] Clients/users, in any realm, employ an often wide range of skills and practices to help make something work. These practices are often invisible, learned and conveyed informally, and discovered by accident. They are nowadays often traceable via web-based discussion lists where they fall under the heading of 'self-help'. Studies of lay music use have highlighted many of the ways in which users mobilise musical resources for self-

care, healing and health promotion and new models of music therapeutic practice have also been developed to illuminate clients' appropriations of musical affordances, especially in areas such as mental health (Rolvsjord 2004; Rolvsjord, Gold and Stige 2005; Procter 2002) and, recently, conflict resolution (Bergh in press). How to attend to music, anticipate key musical moments (such as emotional highs), select or selectively listen to the musical stimulation that one 'needs' (c.f. Larkin's poem above) or 'craves', how to explain music's processes of operation to one's self, how to breathe with music, to recognise and co-operate bodily with emotional modification or physical entrainment, to envision and engage in guided imagery or associated creative activities such as drawing or creative writing (Bonde 2005), to interact and craft one's own musical utterances in response to those of the therapist or musical group, and to be reflexive about one's responses to questionnaires and surveys seeking to measure one's responses to music (Bonde 2005) – all of these activities constitute the client's/user's/listener's skill, informally conceived. Their exploration might also shed some light on what is typically glossed as the placebo effect, one of the greatest natural resources within health care and intrinsically linked to the power of mind in relation to matter and the self-perception of physical, bodily phenomena.

If we are to understand the mechanisms of music's effects, then, it is important to develop a symmetrical focus on both the music therapist's and the client's craft in health promotion/healing activity and this focus on process is a vital component of valuing music therapy's role as an effective modality in health care. We need, in my view, more theories of these small things: how, for example, a patient / client / user latches on to a 'useful' musical resource, how they learn (and can be informally encouraged) to craft narratives of self that enhance the effectiveness of the healing agent, musical or otherwise. Clearly, participatory designs may further this process of enquiry (Batt-Rawden 2006; Batt-Rawden & DeNora 2005; Rolvsjord 2004; Procter 2002, 2004b).[10]

---

[9]In a sense, music therapy is 'behind' drug therapy in terms of evaluation, since, unlike in the pharmacological arena, there is no corresponding phase of 'development' where underlying mechanisms [e.g., drug chemistry and the properties of chemical interaction and chemical reception] are explored. This focus on basic mechanisms might allow music therapy to take a step back so as to take two steps forward – by amassing a research base of its 'basic science'. Perhaps exploratory and qualitative research are more important for music therapy than for pharmacology, at least at this stage?

[10]I should note that this is my general bias regarding all forms of data collection and analysis. For a programmatic statement of the sense-making procedures of social scientific 'subjects', see Cicourel (1973).

Conclusion: Health as Performance; Health Ecologies

Within sociology of the body and sociology of health and illness, recent work has highlighted how the conditions we take to be attributes of health and illness can be very usefully understood to arise in response to what social, material and cultural environments afford and in relation to one's ability, capacity and opportunities for action, understood as the ability to appropriate resources, symbolic and material. I have written about these issues in relation to music therapy before, speaking of relational conceptions of health and illness. This work overlaps with themes within music therapy that highlight health as an ecological and performed phenomenon.

These conceptualise health/illness as taking their experiential significance from their location in wider systems of meanings, materials and practices. That is to say that their meanings reside in the practices and cultural media available for registering their reality. For example, the experience of pain may be altered or over-ridden by subsuming it into a larger structure, whether that structure masks pain or transfigures pain/anguish through narrative (Aldridge 2003). In all of these examples, we see how the extent of a disability or an illness may be reconfigured in relation to practices, materials, beliefs and values. For example, the sociologist Peter Freund (2001) has described how the meanings and implications associated with an inability to walk with ease, or to walk at all, are, whilst undeniably real in the physical sense, also made manifest and naturalised as a social reality (and thus diminished or augmented) in relation to a range of socially constructed systems – the built environment, transport, wheelchair and prosthetic technology, policy, and aesthetics. Several scholars have described how, under some patterns of livelihood, it is possible for a 'disability' to become invisible or irrelevant – as with the case of the New England island Martha's Vineyard where sign-language was the community's first language and where 'disability' took on a 'now you see/ experience it, now you don't' character, highly relevant on the mainland, but irrelevant on the island, thanks to alternative communicative channels which minimised the difference between those who could hear and those who could not (Groce 1988).

Other sociologists, particularly those with advanced training in biology (e.g. Birke 2003) have described how even the material body may be understood to take shape in interaction with culture – with technologies, physical and material practices, customs and mores such that, over generational time, and even over biographical time, it is often impossible to extricate 'nature' from 'culture'.

The point is obvious: physical health as well as mental health is culturally constituted and this thought is shared, I would suggest, by music therapists who, because they are 'with' clients locally and in real time, have fine-grained understandings of the temporal and social vicissitudes of health and health statuses. If this is the case, then music therapy's role and importance is by no means complementary. Indeed, music therapy provides a radical challenge to assumptions about 'illness' and its aetiology and a powerful alternative to the symptom/treatment conception of health and illness. Perhaps, as the base of large-scale randomised clinical trials of music therapy expands and manages to demonstrate that, even when tailored to fit the containers of medical evaluation, music can be demonstrated to be effective (e.g. Talwar *et al* 2006), music therapy will emerge as an equal partner in the search for health-based knowledge. Perhaps, moreover, as it gains equality and a place at the table, it will increasingly be able to help determine the shape and format of appropriate technologies by which to measure, contain and apportion what is delivered as 'medical' knowledge.

Acknowledgement

I would like to thank all participants at the original symposium for stimulating comments. I would especially like to thank Gary Ansdell, Mercédès Pavlicevic and Simon Procter for the instructive talks we have had on these issues over the past year, and Sophia Acord for discussions about Evidence Based Research in the field of Education. I also want to thank Tony Wigram and Gary Ansdell for their thoughtful responses to this paper which they initially presented at the Symposium, and which follow here.

Tia DeNora is Professor of Sociology of Music at Exeter University. She has research interests in music in everyday life, cultural theory and, most recently, music therapy's craft and its role in debates about evidence. Her books include Music in Everyday Life (2000) and After Adorno: Rethinking Music Sociology (2003).

References

Aasgaard, T. (2002) *Song Creations by Children with Cancer – Process and Meaning*. PhD Thesis, Institute of Music and Music Therapy, Aalborg University, Denmark

Aasgaard, T. (2004) 'A Pied Piper among white coats and infusion pumps'. In M. Pavlicevic and G. Ansdell (eds) *Community Music Therapy*. London: Jessica Kingsley Publishers

Aldridge, D. (2003) 'Music therapy and spirituality: a transcendental understanding of suffering'. *Music Therapy Today* February 2003. Available online at www.musictherapyworld.net

Aldridge, D.; Schmid, W.; Kaeder, M.; Schmidt, C. & Ostermann, T. (2005) 'Functionality or aesthetics? A pilot study in the treatment of multiple sclerosis patients'. *Complimentary Therapies in Medicine* 13: 25-33

Ansdell, G. (1995) *Music for Life.* London: Jessica Kingsley Publishers

Ansdell, G.; Pavlicevic, M. & Procter, S. (2004) Presenting the Evidence: *A Guide for Music Therapists Responding to the Demands of Clinical Effectiveness and Evidence-Based Practice.* London: Nordoff-Robbins Music Therapy Centre

Ansdell, G. & Procter, S. (2004) 'Music therapy and the creative modulation of affect: an interdisciplinary inquiry'. Paper given at "Music, Emotion, Action": A National Research Seminar in Musicology. Department of Music and Theatre, University of Oslo, Norway, 23rd October 2004

Atkinson, P. (1995) *Medical Talk and Medical Work.* London: Sage

Batt-Rawden, K.; Trythall, S. & DeNora, T. (in press) 'Health musicking as cultural inclusion'. In J. Edwards (ed.) *Music and Health.* Cambridge: Cambridge Scholars Press

Batt-Rawden, K. (2006) 'Music - a strategy to promote health in rehabilitation? An evaluation of participation in a music and health promotion project'. *International Journal of Rehabilitation Research* 29(2): 171-173

Batt-Rawden, K. & DeNora, T. (2005) 'Music and informal learning in everyday life'. *Journal of Music Education Research* 7(3): 289-304

Bergh, A. (in press) 'Music as a resource for conflict transformation'. *Musicae Scientifiae*

Birke, L. (2003) 'Shaping biology: feminism and the idea of 'the biological''. In S. Williams, L. Birke & G. Bendelow (eds.) *Debating Biology.* London: Routledge

Bonde, L.O. (2005) 'Finding a new place. Metaphor and narrative in one cancer survivor's BMGIM therapy'. *Nordic Journal of Music Therapy* 14(2): 137-154

Bunt, L. & Pavlicevic, M. (2001) 'Music and emotion: perspectives from music therapy." In P. Juslin and J. Sloboda (eds) *Music and Emotion* Oxford: Oxford University Press

Cicourel, A.V. (1973) Cognitive Sociology: *Language and Meaning in Social Interaction.* Harmondsworth: Penguin

Davis, K. (1988) *Power Under the Microscope: Toward a Grounded Theory of Gender Relations in Medical Encounters.* Dordrecht: Foris Publications

DeNora, T. (1996) 'From physiology to feminism. Reconfiguring body, gender and expertise in natural fertility control'. *International Sociology* 11(3): 359-383

DeNora, T. (2003) After Adorno: *Rethinking Music Sociology.* Cambridge: Cambridge University Press

Edwards, J. (2004) 'Can music therapy in medical contexts ever be evidence-based?' *Music Therapy Today* 5(4). Available online at www.musictherapyworld.net

Edwards, J. (2002) 'Using the Evidence Based Medicine framework to support music therapy posts in health care settings'. *British Journal of Music Therapy* 16(1): 29-34

Freund, P. (2001) 'Bodies, disability and spaces: the social model and disabling spatial organisations'. *Disability & Society* 16(5): 689-706

Friedson, E. (1988) *Profession of Medicine: A Study of the Sociology of Applied Knowledge.* Chicago: University of Chicago Press

Furman, C. (ed.) (1988) *Effectiveness of Music Therapy Procedures: Documentation of Research and Clinical Practice.* Washington DC: National Association for Music Therapy

Groce, N. (1988) *Everyone Here Spoke Sign Language* (2nd edition). Harvard: Harvard University Press

Knorr-Cetina, K. & Mulkay, M. (1983) *Science Observed: Perspectives on the Social Study of Science.* London: Sage Publications

Larkin, P. (1964) *The Whitsun Weddings.* London: Faber and Faber

Latour, B. (2005) *Assembling the Social.* Oxford: Oxford University Press

Loewy, J.; Hallan, C.; Friedman, E. & Martinez, C. (2005) 'Sleep/sedation in children undergoing EEG testing: a comparison of chloral hydrate and music therapy'. *Journal of PeriAnesthesia Nursing* 20(5): 323-32

Magee, W. (2001) 'Disability and identity in music therapy'. In Macdonald, R.; Hargreaves, D. & Miell, D. (eds) *Musical Identities.* Oxford: Oxford University Press

Procter, S. 2002. 'Empowering and enabling – music therapy in non-medical mental health provision' In C. Kenny & B. Stige (eds) *Contemporary Voices in Music Therapy.* Oslo: Unipub forlag

Procter, S. (2004a) 'Playing politics: *Community Music Therapy* and the therapeutic redistribution of musical capital for mental health'. In M. Pavlicevic & G. Ansdell (eds) Community Music Therapy. London: Jessica Kingsley Publishers

Procter, S. (2004b) *Music therapy: what is it for whom? Reconsidering the role of music therapy in public provision for mental health.* PhD Proposal/document, Nordoff-Robbins Music Theapy Centre, London

Ridder, H.M. (2002) *Singing in individual music therapy with elderly persons suffering from dementia..* Available online at http://www.musictherapyworld.net

Ridder, H.M. (2004) 'When dialogue fails. Music therapy with elderly with neurological degenerative diseases'. *Music Therapy Today* 5(4). Available online at http://www.musictherapyworld.net

Rogers, P. (2000) 'Truth or illusion: evidence-based practice in the real world'. In J. Robarts (ed.) *Music Therapy Research: Growing Perspectives in Theory and Practice Vol.1.* East Barnet: British Society for Music Therapy

Rolvsjord, R. (2004) 'Therapy as empowerment: clinical and political implications of empowerment philosophy in mental health practices of music therapy'. *Nordic Journal of Music Therapy* 13(2): 98-111

Rolvsjord, R.; Gold, C. & Stige, B. (2005) 'Research rigour and therapeutic flexibility: rationale for a therapy manual developed for a randomized controlled trial'. *Nordic Journal of Music Therapy* 14(1): 15-32

Starr P. (1982) *The Social Transformation of American Medicine.* New York: Basic Books

Talwar, N.; Crawford, M.J.; Maratos, A.; Nur, U.; McDermott, O. & Procter, S. (2006) 'Music therapy for in-patients with schizophrenia. Exploratory randomised controlled trial'. *British Journal of Psychiatry* 189: 405-409

Trythall, S. (2006) 'Live music in hospitals: a new 'alternative' therapy'. *Journal of the Royal Society for the Promotion of Health* 126(4): 113

Wigram, T. (1999) 'Assessment methods in music therapy: a humanistic or natural science framework?' *Nordic Journal of Music Therapy* 8(1): 6-24

Wigram, T. (2002) 'Indications in music therapy: evidence from assessment that can identify the expectations of music therapy as a treatment for Autistic Spectrum Disorder (ASD); meeting the challenge of Evidence Based Practice'. *British Journal of Music Therapy* 16(1): 11-24

Witz, A. (1992) *Professions and Patriarchy.* London: Routledge

CHAPTER 12

POSTLUDE

TWO OR MORE FORMS OF MUSIC

Musicking as "Silent" Practice

In my home field of Sociology, there has been some discussion lately of so-called "silent practices". These practices, which may be material, aesthetic, or embodied, provide, "the unspoken realities upon which more directly symbolic or linguistically mediated activities are based" (Swidler, 2001, p. 85).

Initially, thinking of music as "silent" seems deeply ironic, since music, by definition, sounds. Thinking again, however, the concept that music may be "silent" resonates with John Cage's notion that there is no silence as long as there are ears with which to hear and subjects who respond. The idea, in other words, that music may work in ways that go unnoticed provides a rich metaphor for thinking about music as it enters and organizes social life.

In his magisterial study of the textile industries in England and Germany during the nineteenth century, Richard Biernacki has described how, "the hallowed form of unobtrusive practices" (1995, p. 36) underwrote the schemas through which labor was conceptualized and discussed. Biernacki's study explored the routine, not necessarily conscious, employment of objects because, he argued, the practices of manipulating, making and transforming objects provided a mostly unacknowledged matrix within which discourses of economics and labor policy were constructed as categories of and for conscious reflection.

Musicking also provides a matrix for thought and action, in a variety of settings (Batt-Rawden & DeNora, 2005). What, then, are we doing when we musick? How do we learn how to appropriate musical affordances? And how, conversely, do we learn, via music, what to do or to be in particular circumstances? To ask these questions is to ask about music's "silence." And to address this topic it is helpful to take a step back and ask, without too many preconceptions, just what is music? To ask this question is to ask about music's power.

Sound in Time and Space

Music's aural features occupy only time but they are heard and come to constitute material and social space. Unlike visually locatable materials, such as instruments, furnishings, or people, all of which occupy particular spatial dimensions, albeit sometimes moveable from one to another place, music, like scent or aroma, may be diffused across an entire space at once. In this sense, music is a *global* condition of a social space for all who can hear it (even if heard only by one, as with the personal stereo or MP3 player). Moreover, music may *define* the parameters of particular spaces (inside/outside or core/periphery) through its audible range.

Across a wide range of cultures and histories, music is and has been understood as pattern, movement and tonal interrelation in and/or over time. In its broadest sense, these things define music as (1) *sound* (pitch, volume, vibration, timbre) and *pattern* (rhythm, pace, combination), and over *time*, that is, (2) produced and/or perceived as materials to be *performed* and/*or heard* (or heard imaginatively) by real (or imagined) actors and (3) associated with (depending upon the circumstances of its production and hearing). *responses and or uses* which (4) may evince *social patterns*.

Thinking of music in terms of these basic features strips much of the clutter from our understanding of music. For example, it dispenses with the conventional and outmoded distinction between music and sound and makes it easier to distinguish between (without invoking particular tastes) music and noise (i.e., Does the latter meet the four criteria?). It also absolves sociomusical studies from the obligation to adjudicate between what is/is not "music."

More importantly, this simpler definition of music brings music's empirical features to the fore, highlighting music's overlap with the musical or sonic properties found in things normally classed as extramusical. In doing so, it facilitates empirical consideration of the sonic and rhythmic features of social life. For example, objects vibrate and resonate, though not necessarily always audibly, as with infra- and ultrasound. So too, objects often emit sounds, whether of their own accord (the hum of an operating refrigerator) or when handled (the clicking of keys on a computer keyboard). And, as with objects, so too human beings.

The First Musical Instrument?

There are a number of ways in which the human body (in common, it should be noted with other animal bodies) can be understood to possess sonic features. These features operate at several interconnected levels. It is worth considering these briefly (I will deal with five) before moving on to consider music and its interaction with the (socially, culturally, and biographically situated) human body.

First, and linked to metabolic features such as temperature and digestion, liver and kidney function we exhibit rhythm at a basic physiological level. Even when completely still and in short time frames (e.g., within the space of a minute), our being is *rhythmic* – think of such things as breathing, heart rate and pulse, blood pressure. Our viability, even in a time frame of mere seconds, is dependent upon our bodily ability to sustain and modify rhythm. It is also dependent upon the pace of these rhythms. Over longer time frames (hours, days, weeks, months) our bodies produce other rhythms – blood sugar levels, the evacuation of faeces and urine, sleep patterns, menstruation, hair growth, the reproduction of cells. In relation to these rhythms, some of which are inaudible and some audible only through prosthetic devices such as stethoscopes or blood pressure cuffs, we may also produce audible sounds. Our stomachs growl, we vocalize involuntarily, our joints click, we pass wind, snore, cough and sneeze, our sinuses whistle.

Second, we produce sonic variation when we act in relation to, or otherwise come into contact with, objects and/or others. Our bodies afford certain sounds. This may include the ways in which we sound in relation to material objects and practices. Hair may crackle when brushed or be literally squeaky-clean when wet, our footfalls may possess not only pace and rhythm but also pitch, depending upon the shoes we wear. We may tap a surface (table, door) to command attention, carry a point, or gain access to a building or room. The smack of a slap or kiss sound also in characteristic ways.

Third, we perform and edit bodily sound. In Western societies (but not Eastern) we suppress the sound of soup slurping. We used to suppress our grunting noises in games of tennis, whereas in recent years this has become, apparently, a strategy of play. When we speak, we employ, and may be coached in, musical qualities such as rhythm, pace, pitch, volume, and the variation of these parameters.

Fourth, and related to this, we possess, in common but also to varying degrees, specific capacities for sound production. Attempting some sounds may strain those capacities, such as reaching for a note outside a comfortable vocal range, or shouting over prolonged periods of time. Other sounds we make may elicit (in ourselves and others) psychovisceral reactions (fingernails scraping a chalkboard). The point is that sound production may reward or tax, and even damage, the body. And these effects upon the sound-producing body may in turn both require and bring about through the act of sound production certain tension levels and uses of physical, social, and psychic energy. As Shepherd and Wicke have suggested, "[t]o hear a voice, a musical sound, is to 'have knowledge' of the corporeal and somatic state which produced it. The reaction is both sympathetic and empathetic" (1997, p. 180).

Finally, fifth, the body may move in ways that simulate or partake of musical pace, rhythm or pattern and these processes may lead to iconic associations between music and motion: climbing or falling; strenuous or light, gentle or frenetic. Listeners may, in entirely embodied ways, map arousal levels on to these iconic features in ways that recalibrate their bodily states – as when, in studies of listening practice (Batt-Rawden & DeNora, 2005; Gomart & Hennion, 1999) respondents described how they used particular music to achieve emotional and embodied states.

Beyond the Symbolic: Music, Embodiment, and Informal Learning

To speak of music and its link to the body is to speak of something distinct from music's interpretive processing. At the same time it is by no means to regress to a non-dialectical understanding of music-as-stimulus. What music may achieve, silently, is, by contrast, perhaps more usefully conceptualized in terms of how bodies orient to music and in that orientation locate music's affordances (in the words of the poet Philip Larkin, "knowing what they need").

To the extent that music and body are linked, music's properties may come to anchor situations of action. It may do this by *anchoring embodied* (and by no means necessarily conscious) *practice*, including physiological features such as pace, energy, comportment, skin tone, and arousal levels (muscle tone, heart rate, breathing, perspiration, endocrine function). And these physiological manifestations, perceived by particular actors and within particular action scenarios, may come to serve as markers of status (bodily capital, positive *and* negative) and/or occasion (such as when we consider a situation to be fraught with tension or social discomfort).

Moreover, embodied features of action (including those musically anchored) are important as anchoring practices in their own right: for example, it may be difficult to perform in a tender manner while clenching one's muscles, jaw or fists, or, conversely, to express hostility while smiling gently, or when one's heart rate or blood pressure are low, or one's hands shaking. It may also be difficult to conduct a socially satisfactory conversation when participants are not mutually orienting to background stylistic and paralinguistic parameters of talk, such as volume, pace of speech, and the melodic structure of speech. Physical stances and practices may, in other words, enhance or detract from an actor's ability to perform social acts.

To speak of these matters is to recognize that action and the modes of agency that characterize situations of action may be expressed through and constituted from temporally achieved bodily conditions – embodied music. These modes of agency are put together, and not necessarily with conscious awareness, in particular environments. It is here, then, that we can arrive at anti-reductionist conceptions of both music (its meanings, affordances and anchoring potential) and the body. By contrast, bodily properties may be configured and modified in relation to music, learned as a craft of mundane experience over the life course and perhaps these oblique and informal learning processes constitute the first and deepest levels of our musical education. Thinking about the ways that we attend to and make connections between cultural and bodily music may open new avenues for thinking about music's role as a social medium in senses that also include its role as a medium of physiological ordering in daily life. As such, music studies encompass the musical not only cross-culturally, but also biologically, albeit a biology that is understood to interact with culture, custom, and convention.

References

Batt-Rawden, K., & DeNora, T. (2005). Music and informal learning in everyday life. *Music Education Research, 7*(3), November, 289–304.

Biernacki, R. (1995). *The fabrication of labour.* Berkeley, LA and London: University of California Press.

Gomart, E., & Hennion, A. (1999). A sociology of attachment: Music amateurs, drug users." In J. Law & J. Hazzart (Eds.), *Actor network theory and after* (pp. 220–247). Oxford: Blackwell.

Shepherd, J., & Wicke, P. (1997). *Music and cultural theory.* Cambridge: Polity.

Swidler, A. (2001). What anchors cultural practices? In T. Schatzki, K. K. Cetina, & E. von Savigny (Eds.), *The practice turn in social theory* (pp. 74–92). London: Routledge.

Name Index

Aasgaard, Trygve 150–1, 162, 166, 169, 183
Acord, Sophia K. xvii
Abbott, Andrew 48
Adam, Barbara 100
Adorno, Theodore W. xi, xii, xiii, xiv, xviii, 1–11
    passim, 12, 14, 15–16, 27, 100, 153
Aesop 175, 176, 179, 182
Aldridge, David 154, 182, 185
Allanbrook, Wye 78, 82
Amir, Dorit 149, 152
Anderson, Leroy 125
Ansdell, Gary xvii, 130, 148, 149, 167, 176, 177,
    180, 182, 183
Antonovsky, Aron 150
Appollinaire, Guillaume 6
Aristotle 28
Atkinson, Paul 149, 176
Auden, W.H. 28, 100
Auernhammer, Josepha 122, 139
Austin, J. 23, 24

Bach, Johann Sebastian 11, 102, 103, 113, 114,
    115–17, 119
Baker, Mark 99
Ballentine, Christopher 1, 6
Barnes, Barry 92, 147
Barthes, Roland 104
Bartky, Sandra 90
Barzun, Jacques 22, 26
Battersby, Christine 123
Batt-Rawden, K.B. xvii, 157, 162, 164, 166, 167,
    168, 169, 170, 183, 184, 189, 191
Baudrillard, Jean 93
Beaumarchais, Pierre 82
Becker, Howard S. 48, 49, 53, 106
Beethoven, Ludwig van xiv, xv, xvi, 7, 11, 20, 26,
    33, 34–45 *passim,* 94, 101, 104, 105, 113,
    119, 121–3, 124, 129, 130–32, 134–43
    passim, 147
Benjamin, Walter 9
Berg, Alban 7, 103
Berger, Bennett xiv, xv, 48
Berger, P. 21, 25

Bergh, A. xviii, 167, 184
Bernhard, Frau von 40, 139, 140
Betterton, Rosemary 90
Beynon-Davies P. 149
Biernacki, Richard 189
Birke, Lynda 90, 106, 185
Bittner, E. 21, 23, 24
Bizet, Georges 54, 59–60
Blacking, J. 20
Blau, Judith 48
Blomster, W.V. 7
Bonde, L.O. 166, 184
Borge, Victor 125
Boulez, Pierre 1, 6, 7–11, 13
Bourdieu, Pierre 28, 48, 92
Bowker, Gordon 33
Boyd, Malcolm 116
Brown, A. Peter 35
Brown, S. 157
Buck-Morss, S. xii, 2
Bull, Michael 151
Bunt, Leslie 149, 180
Burnham, Scott 131, 136

Cage, John xi, xii, xiii, xviii, 1, 6, 7–8, 10, 11–16,
    189
Carroll, Lewis 28
Chambliss, D. 159
Char, Rene 9
Charmiz, Kathy 151
Chavira, Juan 106
Chopin, Frédéric 122, 124
Cicourel, A. xiii, 25
Clark, Adele E. 49, 95
Clarke, E. 130, 161
Clayton, M. 130
Clementi, Muzio 119
Clifton, T. 20
Coomaraswamy, Ananda 13
Coker W. 20, 21
Cook, Nicholas xvi, 130
Cooke, Deryck 20–21, 28
Cope, D. 13